New York University School of Law
Series in Legal History: 3

LAW IN THE
AMERICAN REVOLUTION
AND THE
REVOLUTION
IN THE LAW

⌐⌐ ⌐⌐

A Collection of Review Essays
on American Legal History

⌐⌐ ⌐⌐

EDITED BY
HENDRIK HARTOG

Linden Studies in the Historiography of American Law

New York University Press · New York *and* London · 1981

Library of Congress Cataloging in Publication Data
Main entry under title:

Law in the American Revolution and the revolution
   in the law.

   (Series in legal history / New York University School of Law)
   Bibliography: p.
   Includes index.
   Contents: A great case makes law not revolution
/ Bruce H. Mann—The ordeal by law of Thomas
Hutchinson / John Phillip Reid—The irrelevance
of the declaration / John Phillip Reid—[etc.]
   1. Law—United States—History and criticism—
Addresses, essays, lectures.   I. Hartog, Hendrik,
1948–   . II. Series: Series in legal history.
KF352.A2L38   349.73   81-38336
ISBN 0-8147-3413-8   347.3   AACR2

Manufactured in the United States of America

For RUSSELL D. NILES of New York University

Professor of Law	1929–1973
Dean	1948–1964
Chancellor	1964–1966
President Bar Association	
City of New York	1966–1968

Contents

Introduction

⌐ Hendrik Hartog ¬

IT MAY BE too soon to publish a collection of review essays in American legal history. It is only 15 years since Daniel Boorstin labelled the history of American law an unexplored "Dark Continent." Until very recently, historiographical work in American law inevitably resolved into an analysis of why the history of American law had not been written. Now that exploration is well begun, now that substantive historical work is proceeding in law schools and in history faculties, it may be that one should sit back and await results. Silently.

This book, however, is not intended to provide a mature and considered reflection on a completed corpus of scholarship. Its purpose is to introduce historians and other nonlegal scholars to the kind of historiographical writing that is going on in American law journals. Not all historians have access to a law library; of those who do, not all, one might suspect, realize that there is anything in those endless stacks of journals worth reading. The eight essays in this volume, six of which were previously published in law reviews, indicate some of the ways law-trained legal historians, writing for an audience of lawyers, have defined the central issues in recent American legal history. The six authors of these essays are all teachers in American law schools. Some of them have had graduate training in American history. They write as historians, but they also write as legal academics. In their work they suggest some of the tensions faced by scholars who attempt to straddle two academic communities.

Legal history has always had a place in American legal education, but it has usually been a peripheral place: on the one hand devoted to offering a "perspective" (primarily in casebook introductions) for those who would demonstrate the learned and ancient stature of the legal profession, on the other hand relegated to small upper-level elective courses taught and taken by those hoping for a little antiquarian relief from the rigors of legal education. Typically, the focus of scholarship was on establishing the origins of modern law in a distant—usually medieval—past and on demonstrating the continuity of law thereafter. What was thought of as legal history in American law schools was only tangentially related to the mainstream of professional American historical writing.

It would be too much to say that all that is a thing of the past. But much has changed. The focus on origins and on continuity has faded, to be replaced by a more sociological, structural emphasis on the place of law in an American society. The relative constancy of law through time and space has become an empirical problem for investigation, rather than an assertion of faith. Legal historians now consider the concept of law itself as an artifact. They are learning to take an "external" perspective on the subject, learning to write "books about law" rather than "law books."

Today, a historian interested in the machinery of governance and in the creation, legitimation, and maintenance of social norms cannot afford to ignore the writings of legal historians. Willard Hurst, Lawrence Friedman, and Morton Horwitz, to mention just three names, have become figures of some currency within general historical circles. For all that, the concerns and interests of legal historians who are law trained members of law faculties can still be distinguished in some ways from the concerns and interests of their arts and science colleagues. In part their distinctiveness rests on their willingness and ability to reclaim an "insiders" perspective whenever it suits their purposes. John Reid, for example, in the essay on the historiography of the Declaration of Independence printed in this volume, offers a new context for understanding the Declaration by describing it from the viewpoint of an eighteenth-century lawyer. But more importantly, the differences between legal historians trained as lawyers and other legal historians may rest on the fact that a historian in a law school will be forced relatively frequently to justify the enterprise of history to an audience of lawyers and law students. The analyses of Morton Horwitz's *The Transformation of American Law* conducted by Stephen Presser and Peter Teachout in this volume are less about the historical accuracy of the argument than about the utility of the picture of the legal past Horwitz presents for contemporary legal education and contemporary legal theory. In so doing, Presser and Teachout bring home to historians who have not been trained in the law the ways Horwitz's own work has been critically shaped by his experience of being a law professor. Their understanding of the tangled intellectual history of modern legal thought makes it possible for them to unravel themes in Horwitz's book which might remain inaccessible to the untrained reader. In a very different way, Robert Gordon's review of William Nelson's *The Americanization of the Common Law* also illustrates the particular perspective of a historian located within a law school community. Gordon's argument might be resolved into a plea that legal historians learn to resist the demand for relevance of their colleagues. For him it is a proper role of the legal historian to protect the complexity and the integrity of the past from any easy appropriation by authority hungry modern lawyers.

This volume is divided into three parts. In the first part John Reid and Bruce Mann explore the place of legal events and legal discourse in the American Revolution. Their essays are examinations of the boundary between political history and legal history, and they constitute critiques of two complementary historical assumptions: that legal events necessarily have political significance and that political events can be understood without sensitivity toward legal context. In the second part Robert Gordon, Stephen Presser, Peter Teachout, and I examine from a variety of perspectives the pictures of legal change in early American history presented in the recently published works of William Nelson, Morton Horwitz, and John Reid. Gordon's essay analyzes the kinds of inferences about a legal system and culture that may legitimately be drawn from a historical record. Presser and Teachout, as I mentioned above, concentrate their attention on the significance for the modern lawyer of a "transformed" historical understanding of the past. And in my review I attempt to elucidate the relationship between the "conditions of law" in Massachusetts Bay described by Reid and the pictures of late colonial society that have emerged from recent social historical writing. Finally, in a concluding essay I outline a model description of the course of the whole of American legal history that I believe underlies a number of recently published works.

Historians accustomed to strict page limits may find the length of these review essays surprising. A word or two of explanation may be in order. There are approximately 165 accredited law schools in this country, every one of which has at least one law review maintained as much for the education of its student editors and note writers as because of the market for legal scholarship. There is no shortage of space in the world of the American law review. Young law professors usually come to teaching directly from three to five years of practice. Unlike historians and other academics most of them do not have a dissertation or other major piece of scholarship around which to organize their scholarly productivity. A long book review thus becomes a plausible and available way for a young law teacher to organize his or her thinking about a subject and to prepare for the substantive scholarship which surely must follow.

It is too soon for a balanced and considered study of the

writing of American legal history. The review essays in this volume do not pretend to provide that. They use the works under examination as tools to identify the central theoretical issues with which any history of American law must deal. At times, notably in Teachout's essay on Reid and Horwitz and in Reid's essay on the recent historiography of the Declaration of Independence, the books under review are little more than an organizing excuse for the development of the review writer's views. The coverage of this book is selective and partial. The concerns of its authors are disparate and discordant. What they do share is an insistence on the need to develop a legal theory—a concept of the place (or places) of law in society—which is historically based and which will provide an adequate basis for future historical research. And what this book offers to the interested reader is a description and a demonstration of several ways of meeting that need.

PART I

Law in the American Revolution

A Great Case Makes Law
Not Revolution*

⌁ Bruce H. Mann ⌁

T HE HISTORIAN-as-detective looms large in historians'
perceptions of themselves. By day, mild-mannered,
tweedy academicians; by night, or at least by the darkness
of the archives or the microfilm room, sleuths decked out
in capes, deerstalker hats, and meerschaum pipes, sifting
the remains of time for clues. It is a persona that has been
accorded recognition in historiographic literature[1] and
mystery novels[2] alike. Many historians do, in fact, have an
abiding weakness for good mystery novels. They are constantly on the search for unfamiliar authors, their mystery
collections often rival their professional libraries, and they
pass hard-to-find classics of the genre from hand to hand
with a care and reverence usually reserved for illuminated
manuscripts. The identity is a congenial one for many historians. The search for evidence, the sensation of assembling a puzzle with many of the pieces missing and with no

*A review of M. H. Smith, The Writs of Assistance Case (Berkeley, 1978).
This essay originally appeared in 11 U. Conn. L. Rev. 353 (1979). It is reprinted
by permission of the University of Connecticut Law Review.
[1] R. Winks, The Historian as Detective: Essays on Evidence (1970).
[2] J. Tey, The Daughter of Time (1951).

notion of what it is supposed to look like, proceeding on hunches, following leads down blind alleys, trying to reconstruct a personality from stray hairs and footprints—all describe the work of the historian as well as of the detective.[3] The similarity is close, but is not something that historians— nor, I suspect, detectives—take with more seriousness than it merits. I mention it only because it seems a particularly apt characterization of M. H. Smith's *The Writs of Assistance Case*.[4]

Though not a professional historian or an academician, Smith fits the historian-as-detective mold rather well. The Boston writs of assistance case of 1761 has traditionally received prominent mention in the annals of American revolutionary opposition to Britain. However, scholars have rarely bothered to explain why it should. Historians usually head straight for the stormy response to the Stamp Act four years later, which was bigger and, in terms of sharpening the constitutional issues, far more decisive.[5] But John Adams, eager to secure pride of place in the Revolution for Massachusetts, was obsessed with the case. As he recalled it nearly 60 years later, "Then and there was the first scene of the first Act of Opposition to the arbitrary Claims of Great Britain. Then and there the child Independence was born."[6] Thoroughly persuaded by Adams, the United

[3] One might carry the parallels still further. After one meets the historians and reads their work, it is easy to imagine that historians of different schools might feel particular affinity for certain detectives. For example, intellectual historians have a touch of Hercule Poirot about them, while many of the scrappier social historians project a Philip Marlowe style.

[4] M. H. SMITH, THE WRITS OF ASSISTANCE CASE (1978).

[5] *See* E. MORGAN AND H. MORGAN, THE STAMP ACT CRISIS: PROLOGUE TO REVOLUTION (2d ed. 1962).

[6] Letter from John Adams to William Tudor (March 29, 1817), *reprinted in* 10 C. ADAMS, THE WORKS OF JOHN ADAMS, SECOND PRESIDENT OF THE UNITED STATES 248 (Boston 1850). Adams resented the hagiographic tone of a biography of Patrick Henry, W. WIRT, SKETCHES OF THE LIFE AND CHARACTER OF PATRICK HENRY (Philadelphia 1817), which would have the reader believe that Henry had set the wheels of independence moving single-handedly. M. H. SMITH, *supra* note 4, at 250–53 (1978). Adams would doubtless have been tickled by the discovery, which was not made until this century, that Wirt fabricated Henry's most famous revolutionary declamation. E. MORGAN, PROLOGUE TO REVOLUTION: SOURCES AND DOCUMENTS ON THE STAMP ACT CRISIS, 1764–1766, at 44, 46–47 (1959).

States Supreme Court declared, albeit in dictum, that the case "was perhaps the most prominent event which inaugurated the resistance of the colonies to the oppressions of the mother country."[7] John Adams did not always remember things as they occurred, and judicial use of history is often more convenient than judicious. But the writs of assistance case was significant, even if not as central to the development of a revolutionary ideology as Adams or the Supreme Court contended. It was the first articulate expression of what became an American tradition of constitutional hostility to general powers of search. In it lay the antecedents of the fourth amendment. Nevertheless, it has not received more than passing scholarly attention.[8] Hence the occasion for Smith's sleuthing.

And an impressive accomplishment it is. Smith, a British public service administration official whose academic training was in jurisprudence, has scoured the archives on both sides of the Atlantic and pieced together a truly exhaustive study. His understanding of the legal issues involved rivals and often surpasses that of the participants. And he has presented what under a less-skilled pen might barely rise to the turgid with extraordinary vigor and literateness. Statutes and cases do not make the liveliest reading, nor do they readily volunteer the information historians usually seek. But eighteenth-century Massachusetts bred a colorful array of public figures, and with their help Smith recounts his story with far more wit than one has any right to expect. In the face of such good-natured industry it seems churlish to cavil, but even a book as good as this has its blemishes. First, however, the story.

---

[7] Boyd v. United States, 116 U.S. 616, 625 (1886).

[8] The attention it has received includes a doctoral dissertation, J. Frese, Writs of Assistance in the American Colonies, 1660–1776 (1951) (unpublished Ph.D. dissertation in Harvard University Library) and assorted articles. Dickerson, *Writs of Assistance as a Cause of Revolution,* in THE ERA OF THE AMERICAN REVOLUTION 40 (R. Morris ed. 1939); Frese, *James Otis and Writs of Assistance,* 30 NEW ENG. Q. 496 (1957); Waters & Schutz, *Patterns of Massachusetts Colonial Politics: The Writs of Assistance and the Rivalry between the Otis and Hutchinson Families,* 24 WM. & MARY Q. (3d ser.) 543 (1967). None presume to be definitive.

According to most interpretations, the immediate occasion for the Boston writs of assistance case of 1761 was the death of George II in 1760.[9] "The King is dead. Long live the King." So runs the constitutional maxim. But his writs died with him, or, to be more precise, six months later.[10] Customs officers had to apply for new writs to assist them in their search for goods that violated the navigation and trade acts.[11] Sometime after news of the king's death reached Boston in late December, 63 Boston merchants and traders petitioned the Massachusetts superior court for a hearing at its February session on the subject of writs of assistance. The surveyor general of the customs, Thomas Lechmere, also petitioned to be heard on the general issue of the writs and requested "that Writs of Assistance may be granted to him and his Officers, as usual."[12] The fact that a normally ministerial act was to be the subject of a judicial hearing indicated that issuance of the writs was not proceeding "as usual." The question lay in the nature of the customs writ of assistance.

The customs writ of assistance was an odd creature. Although used in searches, it was not a search warrant. Both the writ and the warrant pronounced a generalized command to assist and had the effect of warning the person whose premises were to be searched that the entry was by legal authority and the bearer should therefore be admitted. But in origin and operation they were quite different. The search warrant embodied a grant by the royal prerogative of a power of entry and search. Its issuance was an exercise of jurisdiction in which a justice, upon a showing of cause, went through at least a minimally judicial process

[9] Smith, however, begins his account earlier. *See* text accompanying notes 32–33, 40 *infra*.

[10] By the statute of 1702, 1 Ann., stat. 1, c. 8, § 5, writs remained valid for six months after the death of the monarch in whose name they had been issued.

[11] For a description of the British mercantile system, see 4 C. ANDREWS, THE COLONIAL PERIOD OF AMERICAN HISTORY (1938); O. DICKERSON, THE NAVIGATION ACTS AND THE AMERICAN REVOLUTION (1951); L. HARPER, THE ENGLISH NAVIGATION LAWS: A SEVENTEENTH-CENTURY EXPERIMENT IN SOCIAL ENGINEERING (1939).

[12] Petition of Lechmere, Suffolk Files 100515, *quoted in* M. H. SMITH, *supra* note 4, at 130.

of deliberation. The customs writ of assistance, on the other hand, was issued by a functionary in the court of exchequer as an administrative act. It was entirely ministerial and by itself conferred no authority on the bearer. For the power of entry and search, a customs officer had to look to section 5(2) of "An Act for preventing Frauds, and regulating Abuses in His Majesty's Customs" of 1662,[13] which made the power of entry conditional upon the presence of a constable or other local public officer. The writ of assistance merely ordered the constable to assist the customs officer in his search—a search that rested on statutory authority.[14] In practical effect, the distinction may have seemed a niggling one—after all, the net result in either case was that private property would be searched against the owner's will by officers of the crown. Historians, and, for that matter, lawyers, may be forgiven for regarding the writ as a species of general warrant.[15] Nonetheless, the difference between the writ and the warrant was quite real, and it assumed critical importance precisely because the writ was a *customs* writ of assistance.

The commercial life of the American colonies, particularly the northern ones, rested heavily on overseas trade. For Massachusetts, this reliance began shortly after the first settlement and grew steadily until, by the end of the seventeenth century, its merchants had been drawn into a larger

[13] 1662, 13 & 14 Car. 2, c. 11.

[14] The Act of Frauds of 1662 referred to the writ of assistance but was not the source of its legal status—a point of confusion that greatly facilitated later controversy over the nature of the writ. As Smith notes, the doctrinal origin of the customs writ of assistance was a passage in Coke's *Third Institute:* "And here is a secret in law, that upon any statute made for the common peace, or good of the realm, a writ may be devised for the better execution of the same, according to the force and effect of the act." E. COKE, THIRD PART OF THE INSTITUTES OF THE LAWS OF ENGLAND; CONCERNING HIGH TREASON AND OTHER PLEAS OF THE CROWN, AND CRIMINALL CAUSES 162 (London 1644), *quoted in* M. H. SMITH, *supra* note 4, at 32. The customs writ of assistance thus sprang from necessity. The Act of Frauds of 1662 met Coke's requirement of a statute made for the "good of the realm," and the writ was necessary "for the better execution" of the act. M. H. SMITH, *supra* note 4, at 31–34. None of the participants in the writs of assistance case traced the origin of the writ accurately.

[15] *See, e.g.,* E. MORGAN AND H. MORGAN, *supra* note 5, at 267–68.

Atlantic community.[16] At the head of that community stood England, but it faced strong competition from ever-enterprising Dutch traders.[17] To consolidate England's position and to exclude the Dutch, parliament passed the first of the navigation acts in 1660.[18] This and subsequent statutes laid the foundation for what became an increasingly elaborate imperial system of trade.[19] In basic outline, the system operated by limiting all trade to English bottoms ("English" included "colonial") and by establishing categories of enumerated goods that could not be shipped directly to foreign ports but instead had to be routed through England. Insofar as it affected the American colonies, the object of the navigation system—at least until 1764—was to regulate trade rather than to produce revenue, and its impact was, on the whole, beneficial.[20] The rub came in the enforcement.

After a brief attempt to place the burden of enforcement on the governors of the various colonies, the privy council vested responsibility with a board of customs commissioners in London.[21] The commissioners operated through a customs service of surveyors-general, collectors, comptrollers, and surveyors and searchers.[22] Like most public officials at the time, they depended for their income primarily on the fees they collected. In this instance, the fees were attached to the procedures required to clear a ship and her cargo into or out of port. As one might expect, fees and duties

---

[16] B. BAILYN, THE NEW ENGLAND MERCHANTS IN THE SEVENTEENTH CENTURY (1955).

[17] For a discussion of trade rivalry between the Dutch and English during this period, see 4 C. ANDREWS, *supra* note 11, at 22–49.

[18] 1660, 12 Car. 2, c. 18. The 1660 act substantially reenacted an earlier navigation act passed in 1651 under the commonwealth. All statutes of the commonwealth were, however, voided by the Restoration.

[19] The best description of the system in its basic form is still 4 C. ANDREWS, *supra* note 11, at 50–143.

[20] O. DICKERSON, *supra* note 11, at 31–62, 147–58.

[21] Andrews discusses enforcement of the navigation system. 4 C. ANDREWS, *supra* note 11, at 144–77.

[22] *See generally* T. BARROWS, TRADE AND EMPIRE: THE BRITISH CUSTOMS SERVICE IN COLONIAL AMERICA, 1660–1775 (1967).

fostered their evasion, and smuggling was rife. The principal sanction for trade violations was seizure of the offending goods or vessel and forfeiture after a condemnation
proceeding. However, the process was a risky one for the
customs official who pursued it. If he lost the condemnation
case, he not only faced a bill of legal costs, but at common
law the unjustified seizure constituted a trespass for which
he was liable in damages.[23] If he succeeded, however, the
customs official shared the proceeds of the forfeiture
equally with the king and the governor of the colony. As a
practical matter, the greatest obstacle to enforcement was
that condemnations were tried in local courts to local
juries—men of the neighborhood who, if not smugglers
themselves, were loathe to return verdicts against friends
and neighbors. So customs officials understandably hesi-
tated to prosecute seizures that they thought might be defended and concentrated instead on the safer, if less lucrative, processing of legitimate traffic into or out of ports.

The prevalence of illegal trading, together with the drain
of war with France and a threat by Scotland to break into
England's colonial monopoly, spurred parliament to tighten
the system. The "Act for preventing Frauds, and regulating
Abuses in the Plantation Trade" of 1696[24] owed much to
the recommendations of one man, Edward Randolph.[25]
Randolph, an Englishman, was a familiar figure in the colonies. Familiarity in his case did indeed breed contempt.[26]

---

[23] A statute of George II mitigated the rigors of this result by barring an action
for damages if the court certified that there had been probable cause for the seizure. 1746, 19 Geo. 2, c. 34, § 16. The Sugar Act extended this protection to
customs officials in the colonies, thereby fostering opposition to Parliament. 1764,
4 Geo. 3, c. 15.

[24] 1696, 7 & 8 Will. 3, c. 22.

[25] For an analysis of the bill's passage, see Hall, *The House of Lords, Edward Randolph, and the Navigation Act of 1696*, 14 WM. & MARY Q. (3d ser.) 494 (1957).

[26] Smith appropriately quotes Cotton Mather's assessment of Randolph: "*a
Blasted Wretch*, followed with a sensible Curse of GOD wherever he came; Despised,
Abhored, Unprosperous." C. MATHER, PARENTATOR (Boston 1727), *quoted in* M. H.
SMITH, *supra* note 4, at 53. A less vituperative, but nonetheless damning, account
of Randolph and his career is presented in M. HALL, EDWARD RANDOLPH AND THE
AMERICAN COLONIES, 1676–1703 (1960).

The remedy chosen to enforce the customs laws was to establish courts of vice-admiralty in America that, like admiralty courts in England, would operate in civil law fashion without juries. Moreover, the vice-admiralty judge would be supported by court fees rather than by grants from colonial assemblies. The points of pressure that had hindered zealous pursuit of customs violators would thus, it was hoped, be removed.[27] The act also incorporated, albeit in imperfect fashion, the search provisions of the Act of Frauds of 1662,[28] thereby opening the door for use of the customs writ of assistance in America.[29]

The promise of a perfectly enforced system faded quickly. The vice-admiralty judges, though appointed from London, were usually local men who, if lawyers, were not eager to jeopardize their private practices by inconveniencing the merchants on whom they depended. In cases where such scruples might not apply, the superior court of the province stood ready to challenge the jurisdiction of the vice-admiralty court with the time-honored writ of prohibition.[30] There were numerous ways to cow the vice-admiralty court and, through it, the customs service. But the customs service needed little help in rendering itself impotent. Particularly after the Molasses Act of 1733,[31] dutiable goods sailed directly into American ports without paying duty. The Molasses Act imposed an import duty of six pence per gallon upon molasses and related sugar products. But the going rate for bribing customs officers to allow continued importation of the cheaper French product was only one-and-one-half pence per gallon, making it cheaper to bribe

[27] For general information on colonial vice-admiralty courts, see H. Crump, Colonial Admiralty Jurisdiction in the Seventeenth Century (1931); Andrews, *Vice-Admiralty Courts in the Colonies*, in Records of the Vice-Admiralty Court of Rhode Island, 1716–1752 (D. Towle ed. 1936).

[28] 1662, 13 & 14 Car. 2, c. 11, § 4.

[29] *See* note 14 *supra* and accompanying text.

[30] Common law judges in England had used writs of prohibition to great effect in their jurisdictional battles against admiralty courts and other civil law courts in the late sixteenth and early seventeenth centuries. B. Levack, The Civil Lawyers in England, 1603–1641: A Political Study 72–81 (1973).

[31] 1733, 6 Geo. 2, c. 13.

than to pay the duty. The openness and pervasiveness of official collusion had a debilitating effect on the customs service and deepened colonial contempt for its minions. Amid the climate of official despair, customs enforcement in Massachusetts underwent a resurgence in the 1750's that other colonies did not share. The architect of the transformation was the royal governor, William Shirley, who as advocate general of the vice-admiralty court had lobbied Whitehall unsuccessfully for strengthened vice-admiralty jurisdiction. Shirley appointed Chambers Russell as vice-admiralty judge in 1747. Wealthy and not a lawyer, Russell was not susceptible to the pressures that had swayed his predecessors. Five years later, Shirley capped his strategy by naming Russell to the superior court of the province, where he served while continuing as vice-admiralty judge. Perhaps out of respect for their new colleague, the judges of the superior court now granted few writs of prohibition to halt proceedings in the vice-admiralty court. The resulting increase in condemnations spurred customs enforcement activity and sharpened the need for a legal mechanism that would enable customs officers to search for offending goods. That mechanism was the writ of assistance.

The superior court issued the colony's first customs writ of assistance to Charles Paxton, surveyor and searcher of customs for Boston, in late 1755 or early 1756. The writ drafted was oddly inappropriate and was adapted from a rather idiosyncratic writ found in a form book.[32] More importantly, it was open-ended, with no limit as to time or place. In the ensuing five years, the superior court issued seven more such writs to customs officers, who saw in the

---

[32] The English model for the Massachusetts writ of assistance was the *Breve Assisten' pro Officiar' Custum'*. Its inclusion in WILLIAM BROWN, COMPENDIUM OF THE SEVERAL BRANCHES OF PRACTICE IN THE COURT OF EXCHEQUER AT WESTMINISTER (London 1688) was the only publication of a writ of assistance until the nineteenth century. The *breve* was designed for the entropoï trade of Dover, not the simple smuggling of Boston, and it made no mention of the holder seizing the goods searched, which in Massachusetts was the object of the entry and search. M. H. SMITH, *supra* note 4, at 105–108. Smith reproduces the Massachusetts writ of assistance and its English model in Appendix E.

new forfeiture decrees a source of income. To help maximize their profit, customs officials cultivated informants who spied out the location of illegal goods. Despite the unpopularity of the process, there was no discernible objection to the writ until 1760, when an article in the *London Magazine* advanced the troubling proposition that in England the writ was granted only upon oath that the applying customs official had reason to believe that offending goods were present at a particular place—in other words, that it was "special" not "general." Fate then took over.

Chief Justice Stephen Sewall of the superior court died in September 1760. The following month James Cockle, collector of Salem and Marblehead, applied to the superior court for a writ of assistance. The surviving judges put the matter over to give themselves time to ponder the implications of the magazine article in the hope that a new chief justice would be appointed who would know what to do. The death of George II made the question even more serious—any new writs granted would be good for the life of the new king, who was only 20. Before the court reconvened, Governor Francis Bernard appointed his lieutenant governor, Thomas Hutchinson, to succeed Sewall as chief justice, a step that injected a personal edge into the controversy.

Hutchinson by 1761 was well on his way to becoming the most hated man in Massachusetts. He was, as one historian has observed with characteristic understatement, "not the kind of man who made friends easily."[33] "Virtuous but not stylish, intelligent but didactic, heavy-spirited and self-absorbed, he judged people, and often found them wanting."[34] Thirteen years before he had earned the enmity of a large segment of the population by engineering the retirement of the colony's severely depreciated paper

---

[33] E. MORGAN AND H. MORGAN, *supra* note 5, at 266. The most complete personal evaluation of Hutchinson is in B. BAILYN, THE ORDEAL OF THOMAS HUTCHINSON 15–32 (1974), in a chapter appropriately entitled "Success of the Acquisitive Man: Portrait of the Provincial Bourgeois."

[34] B. BAILYN, *supra* note 33, at 24. Bailyn aptly characterizes Hutchinson as, in essence, "the Puritan *manqué.*" *Id.* at 26.

currency. The colony gained a sound currency, but Hutchinson acquired the hatred of every debtor in the province. His elevation to chief justice drew opposition on several levels. For one thing, he was not a lawyer. This in itself was not unusual. Lay judges were commonplace, and three of the four judges remaining on the court after Sewall's death had no legal training. Hutchinson at least had long experience as judge of common pleas and judge of probate for Suffolk County.[35] But the chief justice was traditionally a lawyer, and Sewall had been a legal scholar of some distinction. In addition, professionalization of the bar had reached a high level in Massachusetts by 1760.[36]

More importantly, Hutchinson's appointment drew the everlasting ire of James Otis, Jr., a mercurial lawyer and politician of the first rank. Two previous governors had vaguely promised the next vacant seat on the court to Otis' father, doubtless to get the old colonel off their backs. Provincial politics had passed the senior Otis by—a fact that neither father nor son seemed able to accept.[37] But time

[35] Hutchinson continued to sit as judge of probate while lieutenant governor and chief justice—an aggrandizement of offices that engendered much resentment, some doubtless motivated by jealousy. The *Boston Gazette* lampooned him as "Sir Thomas Graspall," M. H. SMITH, *supra* 4, at 227. *See generally* E. BRENNAN, PLURAL OFFICE-HOLDING IN MASSACHUSETTS 1760–1780 (1945).

[36] Murrin, *The Legal Transformation: The Bench and Bar of Eighteenth-Century Massachusetts,* in COLONIAL AMERICA: ESSAYS IN POLITICS AND SOCIAL DEVELOPMENT 415 (S. Katz ed. 1971); Morris, *Legalism Versus Revolutionary Doctrine in New England,* 4 NEW ENG. Q. 195 (1931).

[37] Smith discusses in great detail the grounds for Otis' expectations and the maneuvering leading to Hutchinson's appointment. M. H. SMITH, *supra* note 4, 202–30. A good general study of the position occupied by the Otises in Massachusetts politics and society is J. WATERS, JR., THE OTIS FAMILY IN PROVINCIAL AND REVOLUTIONARY MASSACHUSETTS (1968).

Peter Oliver, who wrote a vituperatively loyalist history of the Revolution in 1781, had this to say of the senior Otis:

Mr. *Otis* was one, who in the early Part of his Life, was by Trade a Cordwainer. But as the People of the Province seem to be born with litigious Constitutions, so he had Shrewdness enough to take Advantage of the general Foible, & work'd himself into a Pettifogger; which Profession he practised in, to the End of his Life. He had a certain Adroitness to captivate the Ear of Country Jurors, who were too commonly Drovers, Horse Jockies, & of the other lower Classes in Life. He also, for many Years, had been a Member of the lower House of Assembly, too great an Ingredient of which Composition

had not yet forsaken the younger Otis. Brilliant and complex, and beset by mental instability that later declined into
insanity, he plagued Bernard and Hutchinson for the next
decade. Otis' position at the time of the writs of assistance
case was unique. Only two months before he argued against
issuance of the writs, he had been acting advocate general
of the vice-admiralty court. Had he not resigned he would
have represented the customs service in the case; in fact, he
was asked to do so. Instead, he led the most massive assault
against the vice-admiralty jurisdiction theretofore staged in
Massachusetts. Hutchinson's presence on the bench added
a nicely personal dimension to Otis' attack.

The stage was thus set for the hearing in February 1761.
It may seem a somewhat circuitous route simply to arrive at
a starting place, but it is the route Smith takes and, I think,
a necessary one. Along the way Smith has contributed
much, even if not on earth-shaking points. His construction
of the act for customs search warrants of 1660[38] and the
acts of frauds of 1662 and 1696 is talmudic in its precision
and intensity.[39] His excursus on the origin of the writs of
assistance case itself is an admirable piece of detective work
and demonstrates for the first time that the case was afoot
before the death of George II necessitated new application
for the writs.[40] And his account of the maneuvering and
politicking that surrounded Hutchinson's appointment,
while not entirely revelatory, is far richer than anyone else
has attempted or, perhaps, thought necessary to attempt.[41]

consisted of Innkeepers, Retailers, & yet more inferior Orders of Men. These
he had a great Command of, & he ever took Care to mix the Chicane of the
Lawyer with the busy Importance of the Assembly Man; by which Methods he
acquired a considerable Fortune. Thus circumstanced, he put in his Claim to
a Seat upon the Bench. . . .
    PETER OLIVER'S ORIGIN AND PROGRESS OF THE AMERICAN REBELLION 27 (D.
    Adair and J. Schutz eds. 1961) (footnote omitted).
    [38] 1660, 12 Car. 2, c. 19.
    [39] M. H. SMITH, *supra* note 4, at 25–28, 41–50, 108–11.
    [40] *Id.* at 125–48. The traditional supposition that the king's death had occasioned
the case had survived even the close scrutiny of the editors of the Adams legal
papers. 2 L. WROTH and H. ZOBEL, LEGAL PAPERS OF JOHN ADAMS 112–13, n.20
(1965).
    [41] M. H. SMITH, *supra* note 4, at 202–30. Compare the brief treatment by Hutch-
inson's most recent biographer. B. BAILYN, *supra* note 33, at 48–50.

But the detail of his groundwork pales in comparison to what follows.

In a tour de force of logical analysis, Smith reconstructs the arguments of Jeremiah Gridley, Oxenbridge Thacher, and Otis from notes taken at the hearing by John Adams, then a fledgling lawyer of twenty-five, and from a lengthier "Abstract" Adams wrote a few months afterward, supplemented by a few stray snippets from other sources. Adams' notes filled nine small manuscript pages. The Abstract, when printed today, covers seven pages.[42] Smith's parsing of the arguments extends to 118 pages.[43] Gridley was the doyen of the Boston bar. Although arguing the customs house brief, he had little belief in it and may even have pulled his punches to avoid tarnishing his hard-earned Whig credentials. Thacher appears to have been recruited in an *amicus* capacity, but his brief argument turned out to be a far more sweeping objection to writs of assistance than Otis'. Thacher altogether denied the jurisdiction of the superior court to grant the writ.

And then there was Otis. Smith saves his greatest attention for Otis, which is only just, for without Otis the case would hardly be worth remembering. Peter Oliver, never charitable, remembered him as "the first who broke down the Barriers of Government to let in the *Hydra* of Rebellion."[44] The case was Otis' first big splash into opposition politics. He chose his vehicle well. Two months earlier he had blown the whistle on excessive fees in the vice-admiralty

---

[42] Smith reproduces them in Appendices I and J, respectively. They also appear in 2 L. WROTH AND H. ZOBEL, *supra* note 40, at 123–44.

[43] M. H. SMITH, *supra* note 4, at 269–386. Smith seems somewhat bemused at the feat himself. Shortly after embarking on his disquisition he concedes the doubts one might harbor at subjecting such sources "to exegesis of almost scriptural refinement." *Id.* at 285.

[44] OLIVER'S ORIGIN AND PROGRESS, *supra* note 37, at 35. Oliver's assessment of Otis complements Adams' impression of the writs of assistance case. *See* note 6 *supra* and accompanying text. His personal ties with Hutchinson probably explain the intensity of his distaste for Otis. Oliver was an associate judge of the superior court at the time of Hutchinson's appointment, and he became chief justice in 1771 after Hutchinson resigned to become governor. His brother married Hutchinson's wife's sister, his son married Hutchinson's eldest daughter, and his granddaughter married Hutchinson's second son. B. BAILYN, *supra* note 33, at 30–31.

court and pressed a suit for restitution. But, as Smith wryly observes, "what tribune of the people ever made his name by arguing an *indebitatus assumpsit?*"[45] Otis had been well-tutored by Gridley, his mentor. The verbal pyrotechnics of his argument to the court,[46] despite the appeals to natural law on which its notoriety rests, masked a surprisingly moderate line. Otis based his entire argument on the proposition suggested by the *London Magazine* article: that the writ of assistance in England was special rather than general. Otis, of course, fashioned an elaborate, ingenious argument that fairly brimmed with erudition—reading the magazine article to the court would hardly have done—but that is what his argument reduces to. He really did not know what the customs writ of assistance was—nor, for that matter, did anyone else—but his willingness to settle for a special writ was tactically astute. He knew that as many as four of the five judges facing him harbored reservations about the general writ of assistance. A compromise special writ, one that required a sworn application each time it was needed and was good only for the time and place sworn to, was in practice as good as no writ at all. But for Hutchinson, Otis might have carried the day.

Hutchinson gained a delay until November. In the interval he secured from William Bollan, the colony's agent in London, a copy of the English customs writ of assistance that issued from the court of exchequer. It was indeed gen-

---

[45] M. H. SMITH, *supra* note 4, at 330.

[46] Adams undoubtedly embellished Otis' rhetoric in the Abstract with Otis' acquiescence and, perhaps, connivance. M. H. SMITH, *supra* note 4, at 317–20, 377–79.

Otis' reputation for impassioned oratory rests on passages such as the following, which is taken from the exordium to his argument as reported in Adams' Abstract (and reprinted by Smith in Appendix J):

> I will to my dying day oppose, with all the powers and faculties God has given me, all such instruments of slavery on the one hand, and villainy on the other, as this writ of assistance is. It appears to me (may it please your honours) the worst instrument of arbitrary power, the most destructive of English liberty, and the fundamental principles of the constitution, that ever was found in an English law-book.

Id. at 552.

eral and bore a reasonable resemblance to the form that
had served as the model for the Massachusetts variant.[47]
Thus, when the superior court reconvened in November,
Otis' rhetorical flourish was gone. Defeated, though hardly
humbled, he shifted the forum for his opposition to the
press. He wrote a series of anonymous polemics that ranted
at Hutchinson and decried the infringement of natural liberties posed by extending general writs of assistance to Massachusetts.[48] Otis continued his tirade, but it diffused into
the hatred everyone held for Hutchinson rather than becoming a focus of opposition to empire. That loftier purpose had to wait upon the protest that greeted the Stamp
Act in 1765.[49] Otis' ultimate ineffectiveness was doubtless
inevitable, given the contradictions of his position. As one
historian has observed, "Otis was the great exponent of
colonial rights, while he loved the power, the majesty, and
the order of the British empire."[50] In that respect, Otis
stood far closer to Hutchinson than he realized.[51]

New protests against writs of assistance erupted in America in 1767. Massachusetts abstained. The joke, if one may
call it that, is that in 1766 William De Grey, the British attorney general, informed the customs commissioners that a
writ of assistance requested by the customs service in Connecticut, which closely resembled the one used in Massachusetts, was illegal. The power of entry and search mentioned
in the 1696 act derived from the corresponding power that
existed in England under the 1662 act, which power was in
turn conditional upon a writ of assistance under the seal of
the court of exchequer. But exchequer process did not run
into the colonies. Hence the 1696 power of entry and
search depended on an impossible condition.[52] The Revenue Act of 1766[53] attempted to fill this new-found lacuna.

[47] *See* note 32 *supra* and accompanying text.
[48] M. H. SMITH, *supra* note 4, at 415–25.
[49] *See generally* E. MORGAN AND H. MORGAN, *supra* note 5.
[50] J. WATERS, *supra* note 37, at 173.
[51] *See* E. MORGAN AND H. MORGAN, *supra* note 5, at 269–74.
[52] M. H. SMITH, *supra* note 4, at 442.
[53] 1766, 7 Geo. 3, c. 46.

Part of the program of Charles Townshend, chancellor of the exchequer, to impose new import duties and strengthen customs enforcement, the act included provision for a customs writ of assistance. Every colony but Massachusetts, which had been issuing its own writ of assistance for twelve years, and South Carolina balked at the Townshend writ. In the six years since challenge to the writ had failed in Massachusetts, the ideological stakes in the dispute over parliamentary sovereignty had risen. Massachusetts met those stakes—and raised them—in every area but that of the customs writ of assistance. Small wonder that John Adams sought to memorialize the earlier case.

As an ideological issue, writs of assistance played only a small role in the opposition to parliamentary sovereignty.[54] The depredations that occurred during the era of customs racketeering from 1768 to 1772,[55] although important in galvanizing colonial resistance, did not rest on the writ. Consequently, Smith's efforts to place the case in the larger context of an emerging revolutionary ideology[56] are fated to be unsatisfactory. For all his erudition and industry, Smith's discussion of the main strands of colonial opposition is rather cursory and imprecise. On the other hand, if the writs of assistance case was not particularly influential in rallying popular sentiment against Parliament, a fuller attempt to develop the relationship would have been just as unavailing. In any event, the discussion is tangential to his main purpose.[57] What Smith has given us is a remarkably thorough and intricate study of a particularly recondite phenomenon that bears more on the Constitution than it does on the Revolution. Here we have the definitive account of an incident that lay deep in the collective consciousness of

---

[54] B. BAILYN, THE IDEOLOGICAL ORIGINS OF THE AMERICAN REVOLUTION 176–77 (1967).

[55] *See* O. DICKERSON, *supra* note 11, at 208–65.

[56] *E.g.*, M. H. SMITH, *supra* note 4, at 465–97.

[57] As an aside, I must admit that his remark that "[t]he governing mind of empire . . . stupefied on its own hokum" is one of the most delightfully pithy assessments of the British response to American opposition I have read. M. H. SMITH, *supra* note 4, at 491.

the men who drafted the fourth amendment. If Smith has occasionally told us more than we care or need to know, and if he has perhaps answered some questions that he might not have bothered asking, he can be forgiven. The criticism is merely one of balance, not of substance. The scholar who stands on Smith's shoulders to study the fourth amendment will have a remarkable view.

The Ordeal by Law of Thomas Hutchinson*

⌒ John Phillip Reid ⌒

THOMAS Hutchinson is an American contradiction. To Chief Justice Peter Oliver he was the best of men. To lawyer John Adams he was the worst of men (p. 375).[1] Seen by historians as the unselfish public servant,[2] he was known to contemporaries as "dark, intriguing, insinuating, haughty and ambitious."[3] High honors brought him slight credit in his native land. He was the "usurper" hired "to TYRANNIZE

---

*A review of BERNARD BAILYN, THE ORDEAL OF THOMAS HUTCHINSON (Cambridge, Mass., 1974). This essay originally appeared in 49 N.Y.U.L. REV. 593 (1974). It is reprinted by permission of the New York University Law Review.

[1] Adams called Hutchinson "that Arch Corruptor and Deceiver." Letter from John Adams to Abigail Adams, June 30, 1774, in 1 ADAMS FAMILY CORRESPONDENCE 116 (L. Butterfield ed. 1963). See also 2 DIARY AND AUTOBIOGRAPHY OF JOHN ADAMS 55, 84–85 (L. Butterfield ed. 1961); G. WOOD, THE CREATION OF THE AMERICAN REPUBLIC 1776–1787, at 146 (1969); Shipton, Thomas Hutchinson, in 8 SIBLEY'S HARVARD GRADUATES 149, 165–66 (1951).

[2] See generally J. HOSMER, THE LIFE OF THOMAS HUTCHINSON, ROYAL GOVERNOR OF THE PROVINCE OF MASSACHUSETTS BAY (1896) [hereinafter HOSMER, THOMAS HUTCHINSON].

[3] 1 M. WARREN, HISTORY OF THE RISE, PROGRESS AND TERMINATION OF THE AMERICAN REVOLUTION 79 (1805).

over us,"[4] the "damn'd *arch traitor*."[5] In an age of personal bitterness, he was gentle in his judgments,[6] yet he, too, could show maleficence.[7] Tolerant in a sea of intolerance,[8] he is remembered as the most tory of Americans.[9] Even his family was not what we would expect. The scion of "four generations of enterprising New England leaders,"[10] he did not have politically useful kinfolk scattered throughout the province. An incredible series of endogamous marriages had reduced his circle of relatives to a small, inbred group of fellow tories (pp. 30–31).[11] He loved his place of birth as few in the opposition loved it, yet he was steadfastly loyal to a distant, decadent empire. A puritan Yankee to the end of his life, he could not feel at home in the London for which he lost all that he treasured, and today his spirit is not at

[4] Letter from "Mucius Scaevola," in Massachusetts Spy, Nov. 14, 1771, at 1, col. 3.

[5] Letter from John Andrews to William Barrell, May 18, 1774, in Sargent, *Letters of John Andrews, Esq., of Boston*, [1864–1865] PROC. MASS. HIST. SOC'Y 316, 328 (1866). *See also* Letter from William Palfrey to John Wilkes, Oct. 23–30, 1770, in Elsey, *John Wilkes and William Palfrey*, 34 PUB. COLONIAL SOC'Y MASS. 411, 419 (1941) [hereinafter Palfrey Letter].

[6] A reviewer wrote of the second volume of Hutchinson's *History:*
   If he commends, 'tis without flattery and fawning: And when he blames, it is without anger or acrimony. If he makes mention of measures that he is obliged to condemn, he says so much in mitigation of them, as must make every one see that he loved his country. He has touched his characters very tenderly: But I cannot find he has been niggardly in bestowing praise where he could do it with justice. . . .
                    Boston Evening-Post, Mar. 10, 1766, at 1, col. 2.

[7] *See* the valuable discussion of Hutchinson's treatment of contemporaries in volume three of his *History* in Knollenberg, Book Review, 10 WM. & MARY Q. (3d ser.) 117, 119 (1953).

[8] Shipton, *supra* note 1, at 163–64. Hutchinson's tolerance as well as his politics permitted him to show sympathy for the Church of England, *id.* at 197, a step the whigs made certain was publicized. *See* Boston Gazette, Apr. 1, 1771, at 1, col. 3.

[9] It may be, however, that "Loyalist" is a better label for Hutchinson than "Tory." *See* LETTERS OF JAMES MURRAY LOYALIST 152 (N. Tiffany ed. 1901).

[10] Bailyn, *The Central Themes of the American Revolution*, in ESSAYS ON THE AMERICAN REVOLUTION 3, 13 (S. Kurtz and J. Hutson eds. 1973) [hereinafter Bailyn, *Central Themes*].

[11] And especially, as the political controversy intensified, Hutchinson children married children of the Oliver brothers, his closet Tory allies. Boston Gazette, Feb. 5, 1770, at 3, col. 1; Massachusetts Spy, Oct. 12, 1770, at 1, col. 2.

rest in our history books, not even those written from the heart of old "Tory Row." A Cantabrigian can still reveal a tinge of embarrassment when rediscovering those personal qualities blotted out by Mercy Otis Warren and obscured to the generations of Bancroft and Trevelyn: Thomas Hutchinson had honor and Thomas Hutchinson had strength.

It does not do to overemphasize our field of interest, yet even if we are cautious we can claim much. Hutchinson's honor was the honor of a law-minded man. His strength was proven by his adherence to the rule of law. It was also his ordeal, his dilemma and his undoing.

It should not be difficult to recapture Thomas Hutchinson. He has left us a vast correspondence and we have all his state papers. The subject is not elusive. It is the observer who feels inadequate. There is an inner doubt when dealing with one we know a loser; it is an inescapable fact that Hutchinson's career ended in exile and failure. He was a better man than John Adams thought, we can concede that much. But is it possible even to wonder if he was great?

Harvard's Bernard Bailyn has performed a remarkable feat in this long-awaited and splendidly constructed biography: he understands Thomas Hutchinson, perhaps better than Hutchinson understood himself. The task was not easy, a point that must be emphasized. The struggles may have been political, the debates may have been legally technical, yet no historian who approaches Massachusetts's penultimate royal governor can remain detached from the subject. The ordeal was too personal, the decisions and motivations too individual, to be examined from an objective distance. Only a lawyer, by resolving the choices that existed during the prerevolutionary era in terms of a cold legal logic, can avoid sharing the ordeal of Thomas Hutchinson. And even then, the writer might realize that for a law-minded man to be trapped by law was the cruelest ordeal of all.

The ordeal of Thomas Hutchinson portrayed by Bernard Bailyn is the ordeal of a patriot politician overwhelmed by a movement he comprehends but cannot control, not of a law-minded man crushed by a law the existence of which his instincts will not permit him to acknowledge. This is Bailyn's choice, for we may be certain he saw the dilemma of law. Earlier he gave us the best discussion of prerevolutionary constitutional history yet available.[12] Since then he has found "eighteenth-century radical libertarianism" a more compelling theme.[13] The British constitution remains a central consideration in this outstanding biography, but it is a constitutionalism of words and attitudes rather than law and legal argument. While more than an exercise in polemics, the constitutional debates as Bailyn represents them are a jockeying for position, a fight to obtain an advantage in argumentation, rather than a critique of institutional realities or a formulation of theories which an impartial judiciary would take into consideration. He traces the evolution of an idea through chronological steps as one assertion is used by the Whig opposition to justify the next, but his purpose is to illustrate political consequences, not constitutional changes. His story focuses on the rise of whig politicians and the decline of imperial influence, while a lawyer might concentrate on the usurpations of the town meeting (where people voted on constitutional questions), the veto of the council, the rejection of imperial law by local jurors, and the emergence of a Whig theory of law.

The Ordeal of Thomas Hutchinson is indeed a splendid biography on its own essentially political terms. This reviewer would argue, however, that the legal focus which Bailyn has chosen to treat as a secondary factor may yield additional insight into Thomas Hutchinson's political dilemma and his demise resulting in large part from the conditions of law in prerevolutionary Massachusetts.

True it is that law and politics were often one during those years when the Whig opposition was feeling its way

---

[12] 1 B. BAILYN, PAMPHLETS OF THE AMERICAN REVOLUTION, 1750–1776 (1965) [hereinafter BAILYN, PAMPHLETS].

[13] Bailyn, *Central Themes, supra* note 10, at 26–27; Greene, *Political Mimesis: A Consideration of the Historical and Cultural Roots of Legislative Behavior in the British Colonies in the Eighteenth Century,* 75 AM. HIST. REV. 337, 338–39 (1969).

through uncharted waters to legal and political power.[14]
Hutchinson understood that fact of life, though insensitivity
led him to blunder, as when the timing of his early appointment as acting governor, of a brother to be judge of probate of Suffolk County, permitted the Whig press immediately to color his administration with the appearance of
nepotism.[15] To him it was a minor legal post, politically
neutral. To the Whig the action reinforced claims of one-
family dominance of public positions,[16] a grievance closely
related to the constitutional issue of plural officeholding,
also largely directed against Hutchinson (pp. 52–53), who
"was for years together Lieutenant Governor, Councellor,
Chief Justice of the province, & a Judge of the probate."[17]
That complaint led in turn to the Whigs formulating a sep-
aration-of-powers doctrine,[18] and to the humiliation of
Hutchinson's removal from the executive council, not for
political reasons (which of course played a role), but on the
excuse that he all along had been violating the constitution.[19] The political theory of the natural imperfection of
all men and the temptations of power and luxury has been

[14] If any era of modern times found its political ideals incorporated in a particular national institution, it was the eighteenth century. For the Age of Enlightenment was also the classic age of the English constitution. Perhaps never
before and surely never since has any single nation's constitution so dominated Western man's theorizing about politics.

WOOD, *supra* note 1, at 10–11.

[15] *See* Boston Gazette, Aug. 7, 1769, at 2, col. 2. Even Tory newspapers gave the
same impression. *See* Boston Chronicle, Aug. 3–7, 1769, at 251, col. 3.

[16] "Is not this amazing ascendency of one Family," John Adams asked, "Foundation sufficient on which to erect a Tyranny." *Quoted in* WOOD, *supra* note 1, at
146. For Samuel Adams's comments regarding judgeships and Hutchinson's relatives, see Letter from Samuel Adams to Arthur Lee, Apr. 4, 1774, in 3 THE WRIT-
INGS OF SAMUEL ADAMS 97, 99–100 (H. Cushing ed. 1907) [hereinafter WRITINGS].

[17] Letter from the House of Representatives to Dennys De Berdt, Mar. 16, 1767,
in Boston Gazette, Apr. 6, 1767, at 1, col. 1, 2, col. 3.

[18] *See id.;* Boston Evening-Post, Dec. 1, 1767 (Supp.), at 2, col. 1; Instructions of
the Town of Boston to Its Representatives in the General Court, May 1764, in 1
WRITINGS, *supra* note 16, at 1, 3.

[19] Letter from the House of Representatives to the Earl of Shelburne, Feb. 22,
1768, in Boston Evening-Post, Apr. 11, 1768, at 2, col. 1; Letter from Samuel
Adams to Dennys De Berdt, Dec. 2, 1766, in 1 WRITINGS, *supra* note 16, at 104,
107–08. *But see* Minutes of the Council, Jan. 28, 1766, in Boston Evening-Post,
Feb. 3, 1766, at 3, col. 2.

well developed by Bailyn in other writings,[20] but it was Hutchinson's career that permitted the Whigs to articulate a constitutional rule and, once he became acting governor, to call into question the validity of judicial actions, further undermining the legitimacy of imperial government.[21] Except for his work on border commissions, all that Hutchinson did was criticized, all that he stood for challenged. Early he went on the defensive, not always, as Professor Bailyn demonstrates, comprehending the forces that opposed him.[22]

> That he was defeated in the end—trapped and destroyed— was in no way the consequence of the poverty of his mind. His failure was the result of other forces which he could not control—political forces in England entirely beyond his reach and instincts within him, bred into the marrow of his personality and nourished by decades of success. And it was the consequence too of something even more fundamental: the incapacity of sheer logic, of reason, compelling in its own terms, but operating within the limits of the received tradition, to control or even fully to comprehend an upsurge of ideological passion. Within his own terms of reference, within his own assumptions—which were ordinary assumptions of the age taken to a high degree of refinement—his arguments are irrefutable: which is why ultimately they became the revolutionaries' chief target. They mark the boundaries of traditional thought, and they therefore establish the point of departure for what became, to posterity, the innovative and creative thought of the time (p. 75).

We may well agree, yet further ask how the trap was laid and what were the creative sources of innovation.

[20] For a summary of the arguments by Bailyn and others, see Greene, *An Uneasy Connection: An Analysis of the Preconditions of the American Revolution*, in ESSAYS ON THE AMERICAN REVOLUTION 32, 54–55 (S. Kurtz & J. Hutson eds. 1973). *See also* Bailyn, *Central Themes, supra* note 10, at 12–13.

[21] Some have started a Question, whether the Commission of Chief Justice was not *ipso Facto* vacated by his Honour's taking the [governor's] Chair;—and, if so, have inquired how far the future Proceedings of this Term were irregular and erroneous:—and, therefore, reversable on a Writ of Error.

    Memoranda on the August Term, 1769, of the Massachusetts Supreme Court, by Josiah Quincy, Jr., Quincy Rep. 316.

[22] *See* Bailyn, *Central Themes, supra* note 10, at 17–18.

Perhaps we should not put the stress on law even if it is the central thrust. It may be too pedestrian for our generalist colleagues. "Coke can hardly be left out of an inquiry into the intellectual origins of the English Revolution," Christopher Hill has warned, "yet he presents difficulties. He was a lawyer, not an intellectual."[23] Hutchinson, Bailyn assures us, "was an extremely intelligent man" (p. 75), but, except for his insistence that the colonies could not survive without the protection of Great Britain,[24] all his public stands were based on law and all his arguments legal arguments. We may note the warning, but we must ignore it if we seek to know the English Coke or the American Hutchinson and the revolutions of their times.

There is an irony to the constitutional stand taken by Thomas Hutchinson. The man who started the political movement that eventually forced Hutchinson into exile was James Otis. As Bailyn has so brilliantly shown, Otis could not escape the logic of one constitutional dogma—the supremacy of parliament. It was inexpedient, unprecedented and therefore wrong for parliament to tax the colonies, but it was not unconstitutional.[25] Thomas Hutchinson agreed. Like Otis and the vast majority of Whigs, he recognized what they called the "superintending authority of his Majesty's high Court of Parliament over the whole Empire,"[26] an authority limited to imperial affairs. As much as any Whig, Hutchinson appreciated the menace posed to colonial freedom by the Sugar and Stamp Acts,[27] and felt Lon-

---

[23] C. HILL, INTELLECTUAL ORIGINS OF THE ENGLISH REVOLUTION 227 (1965).

[24] And even on this argument, Bailyn believes, constitutional considerations were used by Hutchinson to make his point:

It was all tied together: the bond with England was the guarantor of the independence of the first branch of the constitution in America; without the independence of the first branch the constitution would be overwhelmed by the democracy, and freedom would vanish into first a plebiscitarian, and then a military, dictatorship (p. 201).

[25] *See* BAILYN, PAMPHLETS, *supra* note 12, at 121–23, 414–17.

[26] Letter from the House of Representatives to Lord Camden, Jan. 29, 1768, in Boston Evening-Post, Apr. 4, 1768, at 1, col. 1.

[27] *See, e.g.,* Letter from Lieutenant Governor Thomas Hutchinson to William Bollan, Nov. 9, 1764, *quoted in* Quincy Rep. 435.

don should leave the internal government of each colony alone—taxation and legislation in general to be matters for the provincial assemblies without interference from overseas.[28] But when parliament insisted on its right to tax, both with the Declaratory Act and the Townshend Duties, Hutchinson, like James Otis, could see no alternative to the doctrine of parliamentary supremacy.

There was a story told in Massachusetts during 1770. At a dinner, Hutchinson was asked by a fellow Bostonian:

> Pray Sir do you think if the Parliament of Great Britain should pass a Law to deprive me of my Estate without my having been guilty of any crime to forfeit it that I should be bound in duty & loyalty to comply. [Mr. Hutchinson] answer'd very solemnly & seriously Without doubt Sir.[29]

James Otis would have said the same: parliament would have been morally wrong but legally right. By 1770, Otis was a voice from the past. Both time and constitutional theory had passed him by. More an embarrassment than an elder statesman, Otis was permitted to slip off to North Andover and chase bolts of lightning. Hutchinson had to remain in Boston and defend the new order.

For it was the British parliament, not the American Whigs, who were the constitutional innovators. Hutchinson acknowledged as much. What he could not accept, what parted him from conservative John Adams, was the legitimacy of opposition. The doctrine of parliamentary supremacy upon which he took his stand had been formulated as an absolute check upon royal absolutism and hence on royal irresponsibility. It was the bedrock of British liberty and the British constitution, but applied to the unrepresented colonies it created an issue constitutionally related to those of 1642 and 1688: parliamentary irresponsibility. When the Americans challenged the Stamp Act, the legal theorists of Great Britain had to react. If they diluted the sovereignty

[28] *See* Hosmer, *The Debt of Massachusetts to Thomas Hutchinson,* 12 PUB. COLONIAL SOC'Y MASS. 238, 242 (1909).

[29] Palfrey Letter, *supra* note 5, at 420.

of parliament they ran the risk of reintroducing constitutional prerogativism. Lord Mansfield has been depicted as a narrow lawyer for insisting on the word "sovereignty" and not foreseeing the British commonwealth of nations,[30] but he had valid reasons. George III was not George V or even a Victoria. If the colonies were independent of parliament, bound only by legislation regulating imperial commerce, and tied together by mutual allegiance to a common monarch, the crown would be potentially stronger. Who could predict what might happen? The patronage the king possessed in Ireland was a warning of the leverages of power. The Glorious Revolution was too fresh in people's memories to run risks.[31]

The Revolution of 1688 was also fresh in the minds of American Whigs. After all, they were refighting it. The case had been won against the royal prerogative. Now it had to be reargued against parliamentary supremacy: an American reenactment of one of England's greatest struggles. As much as any Whig, Thomas Hutchinson gloried in the rights won by past victories, but he lived in the triumph of the present; he could not rally to the call of historical precedent. He defined "law" and "government" in terms of the existing arrangement, and in his vocabulary those challenging authority were opposed to "government" and even to "morality."[32] Hutchinson was puzzled; indeed, he did not understand what was meant when the council told him "that unconstitutional acts are not obligations."[33] As John Adams observed, a major difficulty lay in the "different ideas" op-

[30] *See* C. McIlwain, The American Revolution: A Constitutional Interpretation 117–19 (1924).

[31] Like most historians, Bailyn takes the "sovereignty" debate seriously (pp. 297 & 297–98 n.33). There is work to be done here by legal historians. The question is whether the issue was not the legal abstraction called "sovereignty" but rather retaining unchanged the revolutionary arrangement settled in 1688. There could have been few doubts about the viability of divided sovereignty. It had been working in the colonies for a century and a half. What parliamentary lawyers such as Mansfield could not concede was divided sovereignty at home. For that reason, what already existed in Boston could not be acknowledged in London.

[32] Hosmer, Thomas Hutchinson, *supra* note 2, at 138.

[33] *Id.* at 169–70.

posing sides received "from the words *legally and constitutionally.*"[34]

Hutchinson equated "law" with the sovereign and with the constitution. He did not think of the constitution as fundamental law, but as the form of government that currently existed. Eventually Americans would see the form of government not as the constitution but as the creature of the constitution. For the moment, those among them who were Whigs associated legitimate power with fundamental law— not natural law or enacted law, but the "good law" of medieval legal theory.[35]

Both sides agreed on one point: the end of government was to preserve the security of person and property. From there, they parted company. Thus Thomas Hutchinson could argue:

> Now, as the End of Society is to preserve to us that Security in our Persons and Property which we could not have in a State of Nature . . . the best Constitution of Government must certainly be that, in which we part with the fewest of our natural Rights;—that is, where we part with no more than is absolutely necessary to attain the very Ends of Society and Government. . . . The Constitution of Government, under which we have the Happiness to live, is, therefore, the most happy, because we have never yielded up more of the private Rights of Individuals than was needful to invest the Government with Power sufficient to protect us as Citizens.— It is, therefore, the Duty of every good Citizen, who is bound to preserve the Laws of the State under which he lives, to apply to the Legislative Body for a Redress of all Grievances which arise from the Laws. To aim at a Redress in any other Way is to bring Everything into Confusion.[36]

The Whigs disagreed. In the *Boston Gazette* they answered:

> The *end* of all government being *common security*, . . . [i]mposition of laws or taxes on any community without their

[34]*Quoted in* WOOD, *supra* note 1, at 261 (emphasis in original).

[35]*See* F. KERN, KINGSHIP AND LAW IN THE MIDDLE AGES 149 (S. Chrimes transl. 1939).

[36]Charge of Chief Justice Thomas Hutchinson to the Suffolk Grand Jury, March Term 1769, Quincy Rep. 306, 307.

consent, being inconsistent with the faintest idea of public or private *security*, is utterly subversive of all good *government;* it is a corruption of its very principles, and therefore it is the duty of every loyal subject, of every honest man, to treat the authors, aiders and abettors of such ruinous, illegal and unconstitutional usurpations, as traitors and public enemies. . . .[37]

In a very true sense, the American Whigs were returning to early Germanic legal concepts and denying the Romanist doctrine that whatever the king enacted in parliament was lawful. At least in the constitutional area, they refused to abandon the old maxim that legality means harmony with preexistent custom. It was a legal conservatism that politically conservative Thomas Hutchinson could not recognize as even semi-legal. Colonist and provincial he may have been, but from the law's perspective he is best described as a child of the new liberalism of 1688.

Fascinating are the legal twists an old whig in America could be forced to take as he attempted to answer the constitutional defenses of the new Whigs. "I have," Thomas Hutchinson assured the Massachusetts house of representatives, "not the least doubt of the Right of the Crown to controul the Governor by Instructions or other Signification of the Royal Pleasure."[38] He meant that he would take orders from the ministry—that is, parliament—but the legal terminology he was forced by custom to employ trapped him, for it was the language of prerogativism—"his constant apology for every arbitrary step."[39] Echoing the "parliamentary lawyer" of former Whig days,[40] the new Whigs on

[37] Letter from "Mutius Scaevola," Jan. 28, 1771, in Boston Gazette, Mar. 4, 1771, at 1, col. 1.

[38] Message from Lieutenant Governor Thomas Hutchinson to the House of Representatives, June 15, 1770, in Boston Chronicle, June 14–18, 1770, at 195, col. 1.

[39] 1 WARREN, *supra* note 3, at 82.

[40] John Selden wrote: "To know what obedience is due to the prince you must look into the contract betwixt him and his people; as if you would know what rent is due from the tenant to the landlord, you must look into the lease." *Quoted in* E. WILLIAMS, 2 A DOCUMENTARY HISTORY OF ENGLAND: 1559–1931, at 84 (1965). In

the council told him that the charter was a compact between the crown and the people.

> There is no reservation in it that instructions shall be a rule of government to the Governor; no instructions therefore can be a rule to him in cases, wherein they alter those powers, or in any other way affect the charter.[41]

Another governor might have ignored the argument. In private, Hutchinson wrung his hands and said his opponents used the word "law" unfairly, but publicly he met them on the very ground they selected, and debated not his but their law:

> Your main reserve, if it could be admitted, that whensoever the prerogative shall be exercised in a manner not for the publick good, of which you are to be judges, it ceases to be a prerogative, is unanswerable. In all controversies as soon as one party is allowed to be the sole judge, the knot is cut, and there must be an end of strife. . . .[42]

Fair enough, the Whigs could reply, but if what Hutchinson claimed were true, Massachusetts Bay was now "controuled by an absolute despot, unmoveable by any influence but ministerial instructions."[43]

It is a matter of marvel how Hutchinson could contend that the Massachusetts assembly should not be "the sole judge" of its own pretensions. Did he really miss the point that the American Whigs were arguing that such was precisely one of their chief complaints against parliament? They were being taxed by the very body that had once prevented arbitrary taxation in the mother country. Members

1688, the House of Lords, debating whether James II was still king, voted that the English monarchy existed by an "original contract" rather than divine right. The next question, whether the king had broken the contract, the house resolved in the affirmative, with almost no opposition. S. Prall, The Bloodless Revolution: England, 1688, at 263 (1972).

[41] Message from the Council to Lieutenant Governor Thomas Hutchinson, June 19, 1770, in Boston Chronicle, June 18–21, 1770, at 199, col. 2.

[42] Message from Lieutenant Governor Thomas Hutchinson to the House of Representatives, Aug. 3, 1770, in Boston Gazette, Aug. 6, 1770, at 3, col. 3, 4, col. 2.

[43] Massachusetts Spy, Mar. 21, 1771, at 1, col. 1, 3.

of parliament for whom no American voted had enacted the Townshend Duties and the colonies could "appeal for relief from their final decision to no power on earth, for there is no power on earth above them."[44]

The ordeal of Thomas Hutchinson took many forms and one was the dilemma of having to carry on, at the center of the controversy and almost alone, a constitutional struggle that could not be resolved by any means he would have called constitutional. There was no supreme court to which to appeal; the only forum was parliament, the very institution which the Whigs rejected. In England, the lack of machinery to settle conflicts had led to civil war in 1642[45] and would have done the same in 1688 had James II been in a stronger political position. A politically minded governor might have lived with the dilemma and attributed the rising discontent not to the failure of institutions but to ambitious rabble-rousers bent on stirring up the people for personal gain. Thomas Hutchinson agreed that troublemakers lay behind the agitation, but as a law-minded man he found unacceptable the idea that the constitution did not furnish definitive answers. He knew what issue went to the heart of Whig restlessness: "If Parliament has a constitutional authority over the colonies, a declaration that they have not will have no force whenever another declaration is made to the contrary."[46] Faced with the reality that no tribunal could decree a constitutional solution, Thomas Hutchinson abandoned his determination not to argue law with the general court.[47] He opened a debate with the council and house

[44] Letter from the House of Representatives to the earl of Shelburne, Jan. 15, 1768, in 1 WRITINGS, *supra* note 16, at 152, 158; Letter from the House of Representatives to Dennys De Berdt, Jan. 11, 1768, in Boston Gazette, Apr. 4, 1768, at 1, col. 1, 2.

[45] PRALL, *supra* note 40, at 35.

[46] Letter from Former Governor Thomas Hutchinson to an American Whig, Aug. 8, 1774, in 1 THE DIARY AND LETTERS OF HIS EXCELLENCY THOMAS HUTCHINSON, ESQ. 217 (P. Hutchinson ed. 1883) [hereinafter DIARY].

[47] "I am sure no advantage can arise from my engaging in a controversy with you upon those points. I have industriously avoided it. I have avoided giving you any occasion for it." Message from Lieutenant Governor Thomas Hutchinson to the House of Representatives, Apr. 26, 1770, in Boston Chronicle, Apr. 26–30, 1770, at 138, col. 3, 139, col. 1.

of representatives, hoping to win a decision in the only forum available: public opinion. He sought, true enough, a political resolution, but did so on a constitutional argument. In the debate of 1773, Hutchinson was answering the Boston Declaration[48] which was steeped in natural law. Ignoring that nonsense, Hutchinson concentrated on the constitution and utilized his legal theory concerning the relevance of history in constitutional interpretation.[49] The council and house answered him in kind. If we keep in mind that the eighteenth-century British constitution was whatever could be plausibly argued and forcibly maintained, the messages that the two sides exchanged—Hutchinson's address;[50] the answers of the council[51] and the house;[52] Hutchinson's replication;[53] and the rejoinders of the council[54] and the house[55]—may be seen for what they were: legal briefs "filed" in the only constitutional "court" then available. It was the one occasion when the constitu-

---

[48] The Rights of the Colonists, A List of Violations of Rights and a Letter of Correspondence, Nov. 20, 1772, in 2 WRITINGS, *supra* note 16, at 350.

[49] I cannot agree with you that it would be of dangerous tendency to determine the design of the present Charter by anything besides the Charter itself. Where there is any ambiguity there seems to be the same reason for recurring to the particular circumstances attending the solliciting and granting it, as there is to historical facts for the construction of any uncertain ambiguous Expressions in any ancient Statutes.

Message from Lieutenant Governor Thomas Hutchinson to the Council, June 25, 1770, in Boston Gazette, July 2, 1770, at 1, col. 2, 3.

[50] Speech of Governor Thomas Hutchinson to the Two Houses, Jan. 6, 1773, in HOSMER, THOMAS HUTCHINSON, *supra* note 2, at 363.

[51] Answer of the Council to the Speech of Governor Thomas Hutchinson of January 6th, Jan. 25, 1773, in *id.* at 370.

[52] Answer of the House of Representatives to the Speech of Governor Thomas Hutchinson of January 6th, Jan. 26, 1773, in *id.* at 380.

[53] Speech of Governor Thomas Hutchinson to Both Houses, Feb. 16, 1773, in *id.* at 396.

[54] Answer of the Council to the Speech of Governor Thomas Hutchinson of February 16th, Feb. 25, 1773, in *id.* at 411.

[55] Answer of the House of Representatives to the Speech of Governor Thomas Hutchinson of February 16th, Mar. 2, 1773, in *id.* at 414. There was no surrejoinder, rebutter or surrebutter. Hutchinson acknowledged his mistake and let the house close the debate. But later he ended the session with an address which, in his *History*, he summarized as if it were a surrejoinder, and which, for students of Thomas Hutchinson, should be considered one of his "briefs." *See* T. HUTCHINSON, THE HISTORY OF THE PROVINCE OF MASSACHUSETTS BAY, FROM 1749 TO 1774, at 381–83 (1828).

tional controversy was joined and these "briefs" may well be the most important legal documents of the prerevolutionary era. They were the high point of Thomas Hutchinson's public career and, when they failed to still the controversy, may well have convinced him he would not escape the coming ordeal. We might think it strange that Bailyn dismisses them as having something to do with the question of whether British or Spanish colonies were more free (pp. 209–11), did we not know that legal historians have ignored them as well. Contemporaries knew their importance. Speaking for the Tories, Thomas Gage called them "Disputes . . . on the Supremacy of Parliament,"[56] and for the Whigs Samuel Adams said that "it must be placed to the credit of the governor, that he has quickened a spirit of enquiry into the nature and end of government, and the connexion of the colonies with Great Britain."[57]

Hutchinson lost, but he lost brilliantly. His law was sound, but so was the law of John Adams who answered him on behalf of the house. Adams's task may not have been easy but it cannot be called difficult. Hutchinson's was impossible.

Hutchinson did not try to create in the minds of Americans a respect and trust for parliament. He sought to legitimize its prerogatives; to use legal reasoning and historical analysis to inculcate in people's minds a consensus that the power of parliament to tax the colonies was as valid in principle and constitutional history as it was in contemporary law. His willingness to debate within the framework of the British constitution indicates a belief that legal problems were solvable on the premises of existing law. But there was a fatal flaw. He was too legal. Without a supreme arbiter, law could not stave off his ordeal. It was a political truth that he, clinging to law, both realized and failed to realize.

[56] Letter from Major General Thomas Gage to Lord Barrington, Apr. 7, 1773, in 2 The Correspondence of General Thomas Gage with the Secretaries of State, and with the War Office and the Treasury: 1763–1775, at 640 (C. Carter ed. 1933).

[57] Letter from Samuel Adams to Arthur Lee, May 6, 1773, in 3 Writings, *supra* note 16, at 37, 38.

"The leaders here seem to acknowledge that their cause is not to be defended on constitutional principles," Hutchinson wrote shortly after the debate ended, "and Samuel Adams now gives out that there is no need of it; they are upon better ground; all men have a natural right to change a bad constitution for a better, whenever they have it in their power."[58]

If Thomas Hutchinson was too legal, he was also too law-minded. Everywhere he turned he was confronted by legal arguments,[59] and even when he resolved them he could be troubled. Sent instructions by the ministry to place Castle William under the command of the regular army, Hutchinson noted that the charter gave command of all forts and garrisons to the governor. Could he legally, he wondered, surrender command to another officer? (pp. 173–74). There was no provision in the charter requiring him to call the general court into annual session.

> I think if the practice had been otherwise it would have been well warranted; and it would have strengthened government if the governor could have continued a house of representatives that should be well disposed, but an usage of fourscore years has rendered such continuance as impractable [*sic*] as if the charter had been expressly in favor of it (pp. 179–80 n. 43).

Even custom could render him immobilized.

We must be fair. It does not do for lawyers and legal historians to press upon general historians law as a central theme or criticize them for treating law as but one aspect of a greater story. But once a legal point is raised we may ask

[58] Letter of Apr. 7, 1773, *quoted in* J. HOSMER, SAMUEL ADAMS 233 (1899).
[59] The Whig opposition understood his respect for law and perhaps to torment him often submitted farfetched arguments that might not have been submitted to a different governor. For example, when Hutchinson contended that the charter gave him "full power to govern the Militia," the members of the council disagreed. If the words in the charter, they contended, meant "any thing further than the training, instructing and exercising the Militia," they "cannot be understood to give a greater power than may be exercised over the inhabitants in general." Message from the Council to Lieutenant Governor Thomas Hutchinson, June 25, 1770, in Boston Gazette, July 2, 1770, at 1, col. 2.

that it be explained. When discussing the Boston "massacre," for example, Professor Bailyn speaks of Thomas Hutchinson's "circumspection in using the troops" (p. 163) and elsewhere suggests that, as acting governor or governor, Hutchinson could have called out the military—to protect Tory publisher John Mein, for example (p. 134). But what is Bailyn's authority for making these assertions, and, more to the point, did Thomas Hutchinson understand that he possessed the constitutional authority to employ the army or navy against civilians?

Throughout the empire, British troops were not authorized to act against civilians unless regulated by and serving under the direction of a civil magistrate.[60] The only exception was in Ireland, partly, as Hutchinson wrote, because the Irish "were used to military force" (p. 134), but also because the law there was different than in North America. It may be (though he does not say so) that Bailyn believes that, as governor, Hutchinson was a civil magistrate within the meaning of the law authorizing the employment of military force in nonmartial matters. What must be taken into account is that Thomas Hutchinson did not believe he could call up troops without the advice and consent of the council, something he could never obtain.

Both Hutchinson and his predecessor as governor, Francis Bernard, had no doubts on the question, and each steadfastly based his official conduct on the premise that he had no constitutional power to apply force against civilians unless the council concurred. Former governor Thomas Pownall disagreed. During 1774 he made a speech in parliament declaring that he had

> as Governor, without communion of power with the Council, done every civil act of Government, which the King, actuating the powers of the Crown, does here within the Realm. And as to the military, if it had been my misfortune to have been Governor in these times [*i.e.*, the week of the Boston Tea

[60] Some authorities pertaining to North America are cited in Reid, *A Lawyer Acquitted: John Adams and the Boston Massacre Trials*, 18 AM. J. LEGAL HIST. 189, 192 n.6 (1974).

Party], and if the interposition of the military had been necessary, I would not have applied to them for their aid—I
would have sent them an order. . . .[61]

Hutchinson, who was in London and had written a history
of Pownall's administration, was astonished. He challenged
the former governor to name one occasion when he had
applied force without the advice and consent of his council.
Pownall replied that he had done so in every instance. Rec-
ollect one, Hutchinson demanded. Again, Pownall said
"All" and the discussion ended.[62]

Another former governor who believed he had had the
authority to use troops without consulting his council was
George Johnstone of West Florida. While Pownall had
found his power in both the colonial charter and his commission as governor,[63] Johnstone drew his from the instructions issued by the ministry to each new appointee. Criticiz-
ing Hutchinson for not acting to prevent the Boston Tea
Party, Johnstone asserted that

there is a volume of instructions to every Governor on this
subject, whereby he is commanded under the severest penalties, "To give all kind of protection to trade and commerce,
as well as to the officers of his Majesty's Customs, by his own
authority, without the necessity of acting through his Council." Nor can I conceive a possible excuse for the destruction
of those teas, while two men-of-war lay in the harbor, without
the least application having been made to the Admiral for
protection, during so long a transaction.[64]

Subsequent to the speeches of both Pownall and Johnstone, Thomas Hutchinson met the solicitor general of England and discussed yet another constitutional theory: that
a colonial governor was invested with the power of a justice

[61] Speech of Governor Thomas Pownall in the House of Commons, Apr. 22,
1774, *reprinted in* 1 AMERICAN ARCHIVES (4th ser.) 75 (1837) [hereinafter Pownall
Speech].
[62] Entry of July 19, 1774, 1 DIARY, *supra* note 46, at 194–95.
[63] Pownall Speech, *supra* note 61, at 75.
[64] Speech of Governor George Johnstone in the House of Commons, Mar. 25,
1774, *reprinted in* 1 AMERICAN ARCHIVES (4th ser.) 55 (1837).

of the peace to "call upon the troops to fire, in case of any riotous, violent resistance of the people."[65] Expressing his own doubts, Hutchinson requested a legal opinion. The solicitor general answered that "the king's law servants seemed generally to be of that opinion, and mentioned the Lord Chancellor in particular, but says he, I own *I am in doubt* or *not without a doubt.*"[66]

In truth, no one knew the law for it had never been formulated. In Boston, the Massachusetts house, trying to force the governor to order the troops out of the province, insisted that he possessed the same authority as the lord lieutenant of Ireland, and that "it indubitably follows, that all officers . . . are subject to the order, direction and control of your Excellency."[67] This was a partisan argument, limited to whether Hutchinson could be blamed for troops remaining in Massachusetts Bay. The Whigs, of course, were not saying that during peacetime a standing army could be used to police colonial civilians. In London, by way of contrast, the house of lords resolved that the army and navy could be used to maintain the law. Yet, while deploring the destruction of East India Company property during the tea party, the lords agreed that Hutchinson had done everything constitutionally possible to protect that property. Without the consent of the council he was powerless to call for military aid.[68]

Perhaps the question came down not to what was the law but to what man was governor. Johnstone was reckless. During his gubernatorial administration he was at odds with the military, trading public charges and countercharges with most of the army officers stationed in his province, and finally being recalled for commencing a war with the powerful Creek nation contrary to his instructions. Pownall was a bold administrator and probably would have acted as necessity required, confident that the government in London

[65] Entry of July 5, 1774, 1 DIARY, *supra* note 46, at 183.

[66] *Id.* (emphasis in original).

[67] Message from the House of Representatives to Governor Francis Bernard, June 13, 1769, in 1 WRITINGS, *supra* note 16, at 342, 343.

[68] Report of the Lords' Committee, Apr. 20, 1774, *reprinted in* 1 AMERICAN ARCHIVES (4th ser.) 12, 28 (1837).

would support him—if he was successful. Bernard was by nature cautious; constitutional ambiguities paralyzed him and may even have terrorized him. His instructions were so vague they could be cited whenever he needed an excuse not to act. It is hardly surprising that he read them differently than did Johnstone. "I am directed to have the advice of the Council whenever I call for military aid," he insisted,[69] and never getting that advice he never called for military aid. Hutchinson faced the cruelest dilemma. A man of courage and conviction, he was also a man of law. When the law was not clear he could not tread. Legality was more than his guide, it was his moral strength and his ultimate despair.

Interestingly, the one time that, by his own understanding of the law, Hutchinson might have used troops was the occasion for which he was criticized—the Boston Tea Party.[70] He did not do so for reasons satisfactory to himself, but as they were reasons that only marginally reveal his law-mindedness we must pass them by.[71] It is best to conclude

[69] Letter from Governor Francis Bernard to the earl of Halifax, Aug. 31, 1765, in 9 ENGLISH HISTORICAL DOCUMENTS: AMERICAN COLONIAL DOCUMENTS TO 1776, at 675, 678 (M. Jensen ed. 1955).

[70] Technically, the members of the armed watch assigned by the Whigs to guard the tea ship after it docked in Boston could have been proclaimed rebels and the governor, to have employed troops to quell them, would not have needed the aid of a magistrate or even the advice of the council, as he did when acting against civilian rioters. The definition of rebellion might not be precise and could have given him hesitation, but the decision of proclaiming a state of rebellion was vested in him alone by the charter. He did not have to have the consent of the councillors.

[71] Hutchinson's prime reasons were based on the conditions of imperial and Whig law then prevailing in the province:

The house of representatives openly avowed principles which implied complete independency. The council, appointed by charter to be assisting to him, declared against any advice from which might be inferred an acknowledgement of the authority of parliament in imposing taxes.

The superior judges were intimidated from acting upon their own judgments, by the censure of the house of representatives, and by the threats of impeachment of all who shall receive their salaries under the authority of an act of parliament. . . .

There was not a justice of the peace, sheriff, constable, or peace officer in the province, who would venture to take cognizance of any breach of law, against the general bent of the people.

The military authority, which, by the charter, was given to the governor,

this review by asking why Hutchinson did not give a pass to *Dartmouth* so that she could carry the tea out of Boston harbor.

Dartmouth was the ship that brought the tea-party tea to Boston. She was moored at a town wharf for over two weeks during December 1773, while the Whigs pressured Hutchinson to have her sail back to Great Britain. Relying on acts of parliament, he concluded he could not do so and refused. The Whigs said he was wrong, as did many tories, and admittedly the statutes were vague. In fact, we may ask if poor draftsmanship of imperial laws was not at least as responsible for the Boston Tea Party as were Thomas Hutchinson and Samuel Adams.

First there was the question whether the tea had been imported. Under the terms of the Townshend Act,[72] tea became liable to a duty upon importation into the colony. But the statute did not define what was meant by "importation." Did goods become imported upon arrival at the port, when entered at the customs house, when brought up to a wharf, when unladed or when bulk was broken?[73] The Townshend Act, while it did not deal specifically with this issue, incorporated by reference a section of the Molasses Act of 1733[74] implying that importation preceded entry: that goods became "imported" upon arrival. And even if "arrival" in port did not constitute "importation," entry at the customs house did.[75]

The definition of "importation" was important for two reasons. First, tea, once imported into the colonies, could

had been assumed by the body of the people, who appointed guards and officers, which appeared sometimes with fire-arms, though generally without them. And when he required the colonel of the regiment of militia in the town, to use the powers with which by law he was intrusted, he excused himself, by urging the hazard to which he should be exposed, and the inefficacy of any attempt.

HUTCHINSON, *supra* note 55, at 437–38.

[72] 7 Geo. 3, c. 46 (1766).

[73] *See* B. LABAREE, THE BOSTON TEA PARTY 126 (1968); 2 LEGAL PAPERS OF JOHN ADAMS 105 & n.27 (L. Wroth and H. Zobel eds. 1965) [hereinafter LEGAL PAPERS].

[74] 6 Geo. 2, c. 9, § 2 (1733).

[75] LABAREE, *supra* note 73, at 126.

not be returned to Great Britain on penalty of forfeiture,[76] as Bostonians well knew.[77] Second, the law required that once in harbor, tea had to be "entered" at the customs house,[78] after which duty was paid. It was this payment that the Whigs opposed. There was no room for compromise once the duty was paid. After that, it would not matter if the tea was never sold, or was stored, rotted, burnt or returned to Great Britain. Payment of the duty was what the controversy was about; the very payment itself would have represented a symbolic victory for the tories.

Hutchinson also saw no ground for compromise. Again the statutes were vague, but, as he interpreted them, a ship, once entered, had to be unladed of all cargo before a clearance could be issued by the customs house. Without a clearance the governor was not authorized to grant the captain the pass needed to sail by the guns of the harbor fort.[79] Thus, Hutchinson thought himself powerless to act, and wrote of his dilemma:

> The governor was unjustly censured by many people in the province, and much abused by the pamphlet and newspaper writers in England, for refusing his pass . . . ; but he would have been justly censured, if he had granted it. He was bound, as all the king's governors were, by oath, faithfully to observe the acts of trade, and to do his endeavour that the statute . . . be carried into execution. His granting a pass to a vessel which had not cleared at the customhouse, would have been a direct violation of his oath, by making him an accessary in the breach of those laws which he had sworn to observe. . . .[80]

Therefore, Hutchinson concluded that *Dartmouth* "can neither be cleared here [because of the Whig mob] nor entered in England."[81]

---

[76] *See id.* at 26, 119.

[77] *See* Boston Gazette, Apr. 20, 1770, at 2, col. 3.

[78] Townshend Act, 7 Geo. 3, c. 46, § 9 (1766).

[79] *See* 1 DIARY, *supra* note 46, at 104; HUTCHINSON, *supra* note 55, at 435.

[80] HUTCHINSON, *supra* note 55, at 436–37.

[81] Letter from Governor Thomas Hutchinson to Governor William Tyron, Dec. 1, 1773, *quoted in* LABAREE, *supra* note 73, at 132.

There were not only contemporaries but historians who have maintained that Hutchinson could have issued *Dartmouth* a pass. We need not detail their arguments to admit they have some validity, but they do not tell the "ordeal" story. As with many other matters relating to the interpretation of eighteenth-century British imperial law, competent lawyers could write convincing briefs for both sides of the question. As there were no courts in which the issue could be resolved, legal opinions are beside the point. The decision of history cannot be based on what a court would have decided or how individual historians interpret statutes. It is the opinion of Thomas Hutchinson alone that counts. He knew that if he granted the pass *Dartmouth* could have sailed. The guns of the castle would not have fired and the naval ships would not have taken up pursuit. In that sense, Hutchinson would have admitted, he had discretionary authority to resolve the crisis and save the tea. But to have done so would have been an act of political, not legal, discretion.

The Whigs were demanding not only that *Dartmouth* depart with the tea without paying duty, but that it return to Great Britain. The voyage would have been unlawful. True, the penalty of the law was directed not against the governor, but against the owners of the tea. That could well mean that the consignees would ultimately be liable when the tea was forfeited. We may grant that family ties to the consignees[82] would give Hutchinson personal reasons to be reluctant to exercise discretion. The fact remains, however, that he was being asked to authorize an illegal sailing. It would have been inconsistent with all his principles for Hutchinson to have done so.

"I am sure," Hutchinson wrote a friend, "if I could have preserved the property that is destroyed, or could have complied with the general desire of the people, consistent with the duty which my station requires, I would most read-

---

[82] *See* HUTCHINSON, *supra* note 55, at 425 n.*.

ily have done it."[83] If we are willing to take the man at his word, it should be concluded that he, at least, had no doubts as to the law. He did not believe he had the power to allow *Dartmouth* out of the harbor without a clearance from the customs house.[84] And Thomas Hutchinson took his lead from law, not from political expediency.

It may be thought that he was too precisian, that he could have bent the spirit of the strict interpretation just as he had during another crisis when the Whigs demanded that the military leave Boston following the "massacre." Hutchinson then had exceeded his jurisdiction (as he understood it) by ordering the troops out of town. He could have done the same in this instance. Even recalling that the governor tried to avoid the appearance of exceeding his authority— he said he did not "order" but "desired" that the troops leave Boston (p. 159)—we may wonder if he saw the two situations in a similar light. During March 1770, he was faced with the prospect of further bloodshed if the soldiers remained in Boston. During the tea crisis of December 1773, lives were not at stake, only property. There was another distinction from a legal point of view, one that may seem meaningless to historians but which commanded Hutchinson's respect. The doctrines governing military command were constitutional and hence flexible under the circumstances. The acts of trade, on the other hand, were penal and subject to the strict rules of construction that governed eighteenth-century criminal law.

If comparisons are to made—comparisons that shed light on the law-mindedness of Thomas Hutchinson—it is better that the tea affair be compared to the case of Ebenezer Richardson. Hutchinson had believed Richardson wrongly convicted of murder and unjustly imprisoned. The judges of the superior court had said the same in their instructions

---

[83] Letter from Governor Thomas Hutchinson to Samuel Swift, Jan. 4, 1774, in Frothingham, *Paper Delivered on the One Hundredth Anniversary of the Destruction of the Tea in Boston Harbor*, [1873–1875] PROC. MASS. HIST. SOC'Y 156, 175 (1875).

[84] *See* authorities cited in note 79 *supra*.

to the Whig-packed jury. Hutchinson thought Richardson not only should be pardoned but might be in danger from the whig mob which could easily break into the Boston jail. When Richardson's pardon arrived from London it was incorrect, a mere technicality due to poor draftsmanship. Justice and Hutchinson's own conscience required that Richardson be immediately released, but he was not—not until a new, proper pardon was received several months later.[85] If the governor refused to disregard technical law to free a man with whose plight he sympathized, it is difficult to accept the judgment that he was willfully obstinate[86] because he refused to disregard the same law to save property from destruction.

The praise that Thomas Hutchinson received from his superior, the earl of Dartmouth, and from his king was to be both his vindication and the undoing of the British empire. They did not criticize him; they reassured him that he had acted properly.[87] They gave no hints that the ministry believed that he had the discretion to defuse the tea crisis. He had obeyed the law. The trouble was that the law he obeyed was both too vague and too precise. Its vagueness allowed the whigs to ask more than Thomas Hutchinson could give. Its precision left him, according to his own premises, unable either to accommodate their demands or to take any other action short of bloodshed. Far from the seat of authority, he could not free Ebenezer Richardson. Left to his own devices, he was expected to resolve the tea controversy by combatting a dynamic, aggressive local law with an anemic, confining imperial law.

Another governor might have acted differently in both the Richardson case and the tea crisis. But that governor would have had a different attachment to the rule of law than did Thomas Hutchinson. His ordeal may well have arisen, as Bernard Bailyn believes, from the fact that his situ-

[85] *See* 2 LEGAL PAPERS, *supra* note 73, at 408–09.

[86] A. SCHLESINGER, THE COLONIAL MERCHANTS AND THE AMERICAN REVOLUTION, 1763–1776, at 283 (1918).

[87] Letter from the earl of Dartmouth to Governor Thomas Hutchinson, Apr. 9, 1774, in HUTCHINSON, *supra* note 55, at xvi.

ation was politically weak. No "court" against "country" division existed in Massachusetts to furnish him with the support of one group just because his enemies were their enemies. There could be no rallying of a loyal party. The political dynamics of prerevolutionary Massachusetts Bay would not have tolerated the Cavaliers who stood with Charles I, the Tories who emerged in the days of Charles II. As early as 1768, when the controversy was put to a test of strength in the house of representatives, the vote had stood 92 for the Whigs and only 17 on the side of what Hutchinson called "government" and "law."[88]

We may agree with Bernard Bailyn and grant the political peril while still insisting that there was more to Hutchinson's ordeal than politics. His situation was even more weak legally. The fault lay with the law, not with the man. Perhaps the only way in which the eighteenth-century British empire could have been preserved would have been to have entrusted its governance not to men with the legal values of Thomas Hutchinson but to those less law-minded; the type of men sent across the Irish sea to rule George III's other kingdom. But that was not the British tradition in North America. Had it been, the American Whigs would have rebelled many years earlier.

Thomas Hutchinson could never have been lord lieutenant of Ireland. He was born to the governorship of Massachusetts Bay. His ordeal arose from the fact that he was a dedicated, decent man—a good man for an impossible task. The ordeal was compounded by his law-mindedness, which made him a better man for the protection of Whig civil rights than for the service of his king.

[88] HUTCHINSON, *supra* note 55, at 197.

The Irrelevance
of the Declaration*

ᶜᵛᵒ John Phillip Reid ᶜᵛᵒ

TO ASSERT that the biographer of Thomas Hutchinson ignored certain legal issues or did not ask certain questions about law, does not suggest error. It is a matter of depth, of interest, and of different perceptions of what aspects of a story are important. To assert that historians have misunderstood the legal and constitutional history of the American Revolution, to the contrary, does more than suggest error. It says not only that the story could have been told differently, but that it was told incorrectly.

The Declaration of Independence is the prime exhibit in any array of evidence revealing how writers of revolutionary history substitute philosophy or political theory for law when explaining events. Occasionally—indeed, it should be said very rarely—an historian will point out that the Declaration was not a revolutionary manifesto, but "a legal brief wherein the plaintiff epitomizes the reasons for a contemplated separation".[1] It is far more common to encounter writers, including lawyers, saying that the Declaration of In-

---

*A review of GARRY WILLS, INVENTING AMERICA (New York, 1978) and MORTON WHITE, THE PHILOSOPHY OF THE AMERICAN REVOLUTION (New York, 1978). This essay is first published in this volume.

[1] S. ELKINS, SLAVERY: A PROBLEM IN AMERICAN INSTITUTIONAL AND INTELLECTUAL LIFE 146n8 (1959).

dependence contained no legal arguments,[2] that it was a "political, non-constitutional appeal to natural law, no longer as a part of the British constitution, but as the rights of man in general."[3] Put another way, historians studying the Declaration, eschew law to look for its meaning in roots more intellectually fashionable. Generations of scholars have found it disarmingly easy to interpret the document not as a statement of grievances or an evulgation of rights, but as "a literary masterpiece, one of the great products of the American Enlightenment."[4] After all, as Gary Wills points out, "it is written in the lost language of the Enlightenment".[5]

Wills is the author of one of two books published in 1978 dealing with the Declaration of Independence. The other, *The Philosophy of the American Revolution,* was written by Morton White. They are works of remarkable contrasts. Wills has furnished us with a fresh study of the Declaration, important in its originality although iconoclastic toward some pet beliefs cherished by American historians. White perpetuates those beliefs, repeating the familiar platitudes about natural law, and asserting by implication that the Declaration of Independence had nothing to do with law and that America's controversy with Great Britain was unrelated to constitutional issues.

I. The Irrelevance of Natural Law

We must first give attention to the broader theme. Disdain for the mundane topics of law and constitutionalism has led scholars to omit a vital dimension from their tale of the American Revolution. More seriously, the story they tell

[2] Grey, *Origins of the Unwritten Constitution: Fundamental Law in American Revolutionary Thought,* 30 STAN. L. REV. 843, 891 (1978) [hereinafter cited as Grey, *Unwritten Constitution*].

[3] C. MCILWAIN, THE AMERICAN REVOLUTION: A CONSTITUTIONAL INTERPRETATION 152 (1923) [hereinafter cited as MCILWAIN, REVOLUTION].

[4] Jones, *The Declaration of Independence: A Critique,* in THE DECLARATION OF INDEPENDENCE: TWO ESSAYS OF HOWARD MUMFORD JONES AND HOWARD H. PECKHAM 1, 18–19 (1976).

[5] G. WILLS, INVENTING AMERICA: JEFFERSON'S DECLARATION OF INDEPENDENCE xiv (1978) [hereinafter cited as WILLS, INVENTING AMERICA].

has been wrong. In no other respect is this fact so glaring than the emphasis many place on what they call "natural law," when misreading the Declaration of Independence.

The Declaration, Charles Howard McIlwain argued in a book purportedly concerned with constitutional history, was "based on the law of nature instead of the constitution of the British Empire."[6] And Carl Becker, in a very influential but remarkably inaccurate and simplistic study of the Declaration, asserted that it denounced "George III to a 'candid world' for his violation of the natural rights of man."[7] That assertion has become one of the most widely accepted myths of American history. It is also one of the most unsubstantiated. Although the Declaration accused King George of violating legal, constitutional, and fundamental rights of American colonists, the truth is the direct opposite of what Becker claimed: He was not accused of violating a single natural right.[8] Natural law simply was not as important during the prerevolutionary controversy as many historians have assumed.[9] Indeed, more likely than not, when a tabulation is made it will be found that natural-law principles played a relatively minor role in either the debates with the mother country or in motivating Americans to support the Whig cause.

This is not the place to measure the irrelevance of natural law during the American Revolution. As a preliminary study however, it should be useful to consider reasons why

[6] McILWAIN, REVOLUTION, *supra* note 3, at 192.

[7] C. BECKER, THE DECLARATION OF INDEPENDENCE: A STUDY IN THE HISTORY OF POLITICAL IDEAS xiv (1958) [hereinafter cited as BECKER, THE DECLARATION].

[8] The only exceptions that may be interpreted as violations of natural rights are:
[First] He has refused his assent to laws, the most wholesome and necessary for the public good.
[Second] He has erected a multitude of new offices, and sent hither swarms of officers to harass our people, and eat out their substance.
[Third] He has constrained our fellow citizens, taken captive on the high sea, to bear arms against their country, to become the executioners of their friends and brethren, or to fall themselves by their hands.

[9] The correct word is "assumed." Few scholars have attempted to separate natural-law arguments from legal or constitutional arguments. For an exception that seeks to isolate natural law see B. WRIGHT, JR., AMERICAN INTERPRETATIONS OF NATURAL LAW: A STUDY IN THE HISTORY OF POLITICAL THOUGHT 62–99 (1931).

historians have been so mistaken—why there has been such an emphasis on a topic that was of little concern to people during the prerevolutionary era.

First: There were, admittedly, some official documents that defended American rights against parliament on grounds of natural law, but they are few and far between.[10] Generally, those relying on arguments based on natural law were clergymen[11] and, occasionally, other nonlawyers.[12] Although clergymen sometimes adopted the more common technique of blending natural law with arguments drawn from the constitution and statutes,[13] their tendency to appeal to divine rather than human law has helped lead us astray.[14] It would be well for historians to heed Edmund Morgan's warning that sermons and pamphlets do not deserve the weight they are accorded. Official documents are the primary sources of revolutionary thought. "These statements, in the form of resolutions, petitions, memorials, and remonstrances, are the safest index of colonial opinion about parliamentary power. They were carefully phrased by the regularly elected representatives of the voting population and adopted, in many cases unanimously, after delib-

[10] For example, the Massachusetts Resolves of 29 October 1765, The Massachusetts Gazette and Boston Post-Boy and the Advertiser, August 22, 1774, at 1, col. 2.

[11] [J. ALLEN,] THE AMERICAN ALARM, OR THE BOSTONIAN PLEA, FOR THE RIGHTS AND LIBERTIES OF THE PEOPLE. HUMBLY ADDRESSED TO THE KING AND COUNCIL, AND TO THE CONSTITUTIONAL SONS OF LIBERTY IN AMERICA 15 (1773); S. HOWARD, A SERMON PREACHED TO THE ANCIENT AND HONORABLE ARTILLERY-COMPANY, IN BOSTON, NEW ENGLAND, JUNE 7th, 1773. BEING THE ANNIVERSARY OF THEIR ELECTION OF OFFICERS 6–12 (1773); E. FISH, A DISCOURSE DELIVERED AT WORCESTER, MARCH, 28th, 1775, AT THE DESIRE OF THE CONVENTION OF COMMITTEES FOR THE COUNTY OF WORCESTER [1775].

[12] For example, Alexander Hamilton, before studying law. A. HAMILTON, THE FARMER REFUTED: OR A MORE IMPARTIAL AND COMPREHENSIVE VIEW OF THE DISPUTE BETWEEN GREAT-BRITAIN AND THE COLONIES, INTENDED AS A FURTHER VINDICATION OF THE CONGRESS 104–05 (1775), reprinted in 1 THE PAPERS OF ALEXANDER HAMILTON 81–165 (H. Syrett ed. 1961) [hereinafter cited as HAMILTON, FARMER REFUTED].

[13] *E.g.* [M. MATHER,] AMERICA'S APPEAL TO THE IMPARTIAL WORLD (1775).

[14] It is not suggested that only lawyers understood the constitutional case for America. Indeed, a few lawyers misunderstood constitutional law as much as did any layman. An example is James Otis.

eration and debate."[15] One could even go further, and assert that in a constitutional dispute, government resolutions, petitions, and remonstrances are the prime evidence upon which we should rely. If we did for the prerevolutionary debate, arguments from natural law would be relegated to a very insignificant place.

Second: Another reason historians have overemphasized the role of natural law in the American Revolution is that some contemporaries insisted it was important. What has not been noticed is that those saying colonial arguments depended on natural law were generally imperial officials,[16] British lawyers,[17] or American Tories[18] seeking to disparage what was being said. There was no more effective means of neutralizing an otherwise unanswerable constitutional argument than to demean it as natural law.[19]

Third: Another factor seldom noticed is that appeals to natural law were almost always coupled to reliance upon some other authority such as constitutional rights in general,[20] the British constitution,[21] the English constitu-

[15] Morgan, *Colonial Ideas of Parliamentary Power 1764–1766,* 5 WM. & MARY Q. 311, 314 (1948) [hereinafter cited as Morgan, *Colonial Ideas*].

[16] *E.g.,* Letter from General Thomas Gage to Lord Barrington, May 4, 1772, in THE CORRESPONDENCE OF GENERAL THOMAS GAGE WITH THE SECRETARIES OF State, and with the War Offices and the Treasury 1763–1775, at 604 (C. Carter ed. 1933).

[17] *E.g.,* J. ABERCROMBY, DE JUNE ET GUBERNATIONE COLONIARUM, OR AN INQUIRY INTO THE NATURE, AND THE RIGHTS OF COLONIES, ANCIENT, AND MODERN 3 (ca. 1780) (ms., HM 513, Huntington Library, San Marino, California).

[18] *E.g.* [J. GALLOWAY,] A CANDID EXAMINATION OF THE MUTUAL CLAIMS OF GREAT-BRITAIN, AND THE COLONIES: WITH A PLAN OF ACCOMMODATION ON CONSTITUTIONAL PRINCIPLES 3 (1775).

[19] A few special pleaders among the Americans, such as abolitionists, also contended that the colonial case rested on natural law, arguing, for example, that by the same principles slaves were entitled to manumission. *An unfeigned Lover of genuine Liberty,* in The Massachusetts Gazette and Boston Post-Boy and the Advertiser, Aug. 22, 1774, at 1, col. 2.

[20] Statement of the Suffolk County Grand Jurors, The Massachusetts Gazette and Boston Post-Boy and Advertiser, Sept. 5, 1774, at 2, col. 2; Petition of the New York Assembly to the House of Commons, 31 December 1768, The Boston Post-Boy and Advertiser, May 8, 1769, at 2, col. 1; Grey, "Unwritten Constitution," *supra* note 2, at 881.

[21] AN APPEAL TO THE WORLD: OR, A VINDICATION OF THE TOWN OF BOSTON, FROM MANY FALSE AND MALICIOUS ASPERSIONS CONTAINED IN CERTAIN LETTERS AND MEMORIALS 25 (1769); Remonstrance of Rhode Island to the King, The Mas-

tion,[22] the American constitutions,[23] the colonial charters,[24] the original contract,[25] magna carta and the bill of rights,[26] or common law.[27] Even those saying that there were such entities as "natural rights" usually tied their existence to "constitutional rights."[28] Almost universally, historians discount the constitutional or legal references, by suggesting they were strategic window dressing[29] or ignoring them completely. In 1768, for example, James DeLancey moved in the New York assembly that the British mutiny act was a "high enfringement of the freedom of the inhabitants of this Colony and tends to deprive them of their natural and constitutional rights and privileges." Referring to this motion, an historian noted that DeLancey's party won the next election and concluded that "Captain DeLancey's bold attack on the authority of parliament and in the name of human rights had clearly not hurt his faction."[30] The appeal to constitutional rights, apparently, was immaterial.

---

sachusetts Gazette and Boston Post-Boy and the Advertiser, May 15, 1769, at 2, col. 1.

[22] The New London Resolves, January 1766, The Massachusetts Gazette and Boston News-Letter (Supplement), Jan. 23, 1766, at 2, col. 2.

[23] Resolves of the Massachusetts Provincial Congress, Dec. 5, 1774, The Massachusetts Gazette and Boston Post-Boy and the Advertiser, Dec. 12, 1774, at 1, col. 1.

[24] Resolves of the Connecticut House of Representatives, May 1774, The Massachusetts Gazette and Boston Post-Boy and the Advertiser, June 20, 1774, at 4, col. 1.

[25] Resolution of the Continental Congress, 10 October 1774, The Massachusetts Gazette and Boston Post-Boy and the Advertiser, Oct. 24, 1774, at 2, col. 3.

[26] Resolves of the Massachusetts House of Representatives, June 29, 1769, in SPEECHES OF THE GOVERNORS OF MASSACHUSETTS, FROM 1765 to 1775; AND THE ANSWERS OF THE HOUSE OF REPRESENTATIVES, TO THE SAME: WITH THEIR RESOLUTIONS AND ADDRESSES FOR THAT PERIOD 178 (1818) [hereinafter cited as SPEECHES].

[27] See, Grey, *Unwritten Constitution, supra* note 2, at 871.

[28] Statement of the Grand Jurors of Suffolk County, The Massachusetts Gazette and Boston Post-Boy and the Advertiser, Sept. 5, 1774, at 2, col. 2.

[29] "For strategic reasons, the appeal to natural rights . . . almost took second place to appeals to charter rights or to the rights under the 'British Constitution.' " P. CONKIN, SELF-EVIDENT TRUTHS: BEING A DISCOURSE ON THE ORIGINS & DEVELOPMENTS OF THE FIRST PRINCIPLES OF AMERICAN GOVERNMENT—POPULAR SOVEREIGNTY, NATURAL RIGHTS, AND BALANCE & SEPARATION OF POWERS 105–06 (1974) [hereinafter cited as CONKIN, SELF-EVIDENT TRUTHS].

[30] Varga, *The New York Restraining Act: Its Passage and Some Effects 1766–1768,* 37 N.Y. HIST. 233, 253 (1956).

Fourth: Yet another fallacious assumption sometimes made is that Americans had no choice; they had to rely upon natural law. All the relevant constitutional conventions and principles, it is said, supported the British side of the controversy, leaving colonial Whigs nothing to argue in reply but natural law. Proof is not needed. The conclusion is so intellectually appealing it can be stated without evidence or authority.

> Those who defended the position of Blackstone and Mansfield could appeal to the constitutional bases of Parliament itself for their arguments. But the defenders of the American point of view were forced to appeal, at last, to the higher law of nature which governed all men and was supreme even over sovereign parliaments. Such was the ultimate resort of the ablest of the American writers, and their appeal to natural law received its formal expression in the Declaration of Independence.[31]

Fifth: Closely related to the last explanation, and especially pertinent to misunderstanding the Declaration of Independence, is the contention that American Whigs had no choice but to fall back on natural law because there was no constitutional right to resist legitimate authority. The very act of rebellion, in itself, was a rejection of constitutional law.[32] That supposition is true only if one accepts Tory arguments, Tory political theory, and Tory constitutionalism, or if one defines law as it came to be defined in the nineteenth and twentieth centuries, not as it had been defined in the seventeen and eighteen hundreds.

The right of rebellion can, of course, be premised on nat-

---

[31] J. Boyd, Anglo-American Union: Joseph Galloway's Plans to Preserve The British Empire, 1774–1788, at 11 (1941). See also, H. Colbourn, the Lamp of Experience—Whig History and the Intellectual Origins of the American Revolution 190 (1965).

[32] Grey, *Unwritten Constitution, supra* note 2, at 890–91. A related argument was the contention that American grievances were not serious enough to justify legal rebellion. Sioussat, *The English Statutes in Maryland,* 21 Johns Hopkins U. Studies in Hist. & Pol. Sci. (#11) 67 (1903).

ural law. Many English[33] and American[34] theorists did so.[35] One technique was to analogize the constitutional right of rebellion to the private right of self-defense, a right that can easily be premised on natural law. What should not be overlooked is that the right of self-defense can just as readily be based on positive law and, in fact, the eighteenth-century constitutional doctrine of lawful resistance looks suspiciously similar to the common-law definition of self-defense.[36] By the same token, the right of rebellion could be derived as much from English precedent as from natural principles. Put more simply, historians encountering the contention that Americans rebelled by legal right have assumed that the argument was drawn from natural law, not

[33] THE WORKS OF THE LATE REVEREND MR. SAMUEL JOHNSON, SOMETIME CHAPLIN TO THE RIGHT HONOURABLE WILLIAM LORD RUSSEL 159–66 (2d ed. 1708).

[34] *RUSTICUS*, REMARKS ON A LATE PAMPHLET ENTITLED PLAIN TRUTH 7 (1776); ANON., AN ESSAY UPON GOVERNMENT, ADOPTED BY THE AMERICANS WHEREIN; THE LAWFULNESS OF REVOLUTIONS ARE DEMONSTRATED IN A CHAIN OF CONSEQUENCES FROM THE FUNDAMENTAL, PRINCIPLES OF SOCIETY 70 (1775); J. CARMICHAEL, A SELF-DEFENSIVE WAR LAWFUL, PROVED IN A SERMON, PREACHED AT LANCASTER, BEFORE CAPTAIN ROSS'S COMPANY OF MILITIA, IN THE PRESBYTERIAN CHURCH, ON SABBATH MORNING, JUNE 4th 1775, at 10–13 (n.d.); J. DUCHÉ, THE DUTY OF STANDING FAST IN OUR SPIRITUAL AND TEMPORAL LIBERTIES, A SERMON PREACHED IN CHRISTCHURCH, JULY 7th, 1775 (1775); [J. ALLEN,] AN ORATION UPON THE BEAUTIES OF LIBERTY, OR THE ESSENTIAL RIGHTS OF THE AMERICANS DELIVERED AT THE SECOND BAPTIST CHURCH IN BOSTON, UPON THE LAST ANNUAL THANKSGIVING 21 (3d ed. 1773); R. BLAND, AN INQUIRY INTO THE RIGHTS OF THE BRITISH COLONIES, INTENDED AS AN ANSWER TO THE REGULATIONS LATELY MADE CONCERNING THE COLONIES, AND THE TAXES IMPOSED UPON THEM CONSIDERED 26 (1766); A. ELIOT, A SERMON PREACHED BEFORE HIS EXCELLENCY FRANCIS BERNARD, ESQ; GOVERNOR, THE HONORABLE HIS MAJESTY'S COUNCIL, AND THE HONORABLE HOUSE OF REPRESENTATIVES . . . 42 (1765).

[35] There were also a few "official" resolutions citing natural law as authority to resist statutes such as the stamp act. For example, New London Resolves, Dec. 10, 1765, The Massachusetts Gazette and Boston News-Letter, Dec. 19, 1765, at 2, col. 1. Also quoted in E. MORGAN, THE CHALLENGE OF THE AMERICAN REVOLUTION 9 (1978); Morgan, *Colonial Ideas, supra* note 15, at 314.

[36] *E.g.*, T. BURNET, THE DIVINE AUTHORITY OF GOVERNMENT, WITH THE MEASURE OF SUBJECTION STATED, AND THE LAWFULNESS OF THE REVOLUTION DEMONSTRATED 65 (1726); [W. FLEETWOOD,] THE THIRTEENTH CHAPTER TO THE ROMANS VINDICATED FROM THE ABUSIVE SENSES PUT UPON IT 19–20 (1710); [D. DEFOE,] A SPEECH WITHOUT DOORS 3 (1710); N.S., THE DIVINE RIGHTS OF THE BRITISH NATION AND CONSTITUTION VINDICATED 20–21 (Second edition corrected, 1710); [M. TINDAL,] THE JACOBITISM, PERJURY, AND POPERY OF HIGH-CHURCH PRIESTS 6 (1710).

from its true source, British constitutional legitimacy.[37] If it was not legal to resist unlawful government power, a Boston minister pointed out in 1766, it would have been "difficult, if possible, to justifie the REVOLUTION, and that ESTAB-LISHMENT in consequence of it, upon which his present Majesty sits upon the British throne."[38]

Another constitutional premise for legal rebellion was that a prince who does not govern by law "dissolves those very ties upon which Obedience due to himselfe is founded" and lawfully can be resisted.[39] That doctrine probably first found popular acceptance through the writers of 1642[40] and Algernon Sidney.[41] Although royalist law-

[37] For a discussion of some legal theories see, Reid, *In a Defensive Rage: The Uses of the Mob, the Justification in Law, and the Coming of the American Revolution,* 49 N.Y.U.L. REV. 1043, 1050–69 (1974).

[38] C. CHAUNCY, A DISCOURSE ON "THE GOOD NEWS FROM A FAR COUNTRY." DE-LIVER'D JULY 24th. A DAY OF THANKS-GIVING TO ALMIGHTY GOD, THROUGHOUT THE PROVINCE OF THE MASSACHUSETTS-BAY IN NEW-ENGLAND, ON OCCASION OF THE REPEAL OF THE STAMP-ACT 21 footnote (1766). An English text that same year premised the legitimacy of the Glorious Revolution on the "principle of resistance." BRITISH LIBERTIES, OR THE FREE-BORN SUBJECT'S INHERITANCE; CONTEND-ING THE LAWS THAT FORM THE BASIS OF THOSE LIBERTIES, WITH OBSERVATIONS THEREON; ALSO AN INTRODUCTORY ESSAY ON POLITICAL LIBERTY AND A COMPRE-HENSIVE VIEW OF THE CONSTITUTION OF GREAT BRITAIN lxx (1766). For a British argument that American Whigs were resisting in a manner justified by English precedent see, 39 THE LONDON MAGAZINE OR GENTLEMAN'S MONTHLY INTELLIGEN-CER 441 (1770).

[39] Burnet, *Last Words* [July 1687], in 20 HIST. J. 223, 225 (1977). For the doc-trine applied to the American Revolution see, ANON., A LETTER TO THE REV. DR. COOPER, ON THE ORIGIN OF CIVIL GOVERNMENT; IN ANSWER TO HIS SERMON, PREACHED BEFORE THE UNIVERSITY OF OXFORD, ON THE DAY APPOINTED BY PROCLAMATION FOR A GENERAL FAST 16 (1777). For a recent discussion of the early theory see, H. NENNER, BY COLOUR OF LAW: LEGAL CULTURE AND CONSTITUTIONAL POLITICS IN ENGLAND, 1660–1689, at 171 (1977). In English legal theory this rule was usually expressed in terms of the monarch violating the original contract. *Id.,* at 42.

[40] ANON., THE SOVERAIGNITY OF KINGS: OR AN ABSOLUTE ANSWER AND CONFU-TATION OF THAT GROUNDLESSE VINDICATION OF PSALME 105.15, at 7–8 (1642); W. BISHOP, THE WOUNDED CONSCIENCE CURED, THE WEAK ONE STRENGTHENED, AND THE DOUBTING SATISFIED (1642); J. M[ARCH], AN ARGUMENT OR, DEBATE IN LAW: OF THE GREAT QUESTION CONCERNING THE MILITIA; AS IT IS NOW SETTLED BY OR-DINANCE OF BOTH HOUSES OF PARLIAMENT 8–9 (1642); [H. PARKER] OBSERVATIONS UPON SOME OF HIS MAJESTIES LATE ANSWERS AND EXPRESSIONS 44 [1642]. For discussion see, Schwoerer, *"The Fittest Subject for A King's Quarrel:" An Essay on the Militia Controversy 1641–1642,* 11 J. BRIT. STUD. 45, 68–69 (1971).

[41] C. ROBBINS, THE EIGHTEENTH-CENTURY COMMONWEALTHMEN: STUDIES IN THE TRANSMISSION, DEVELOPMENT AND CIRCUMSTANCE OF ENGLISH LIBERAL THOUGHT

yers questioned the legal validity,[42] the constitutional right
to just rebellion received the sanction of historical and (for
Whigs) legal precedent in the trial, conviction, and execution of Charles I. The king had been accused of violating
not natural law but English law, that is, of violating customary and constitutional law as well as fundamental law. The
"Charge of High Treason" read to Charles at the start of
the trial alleged that he had been "trusted with a limited
Power to govern by, and according to the Laws of the
Land," and breached that trust "out of a wicked Design to
erect and uphold in himself an unlimited and Tyrannical
Power to rule according to his Will."[43]

During the Restoration, a Stuart reaction sought to nul-
lify the precedent of lawful rebellion by inculcating the doctrine of passive obedience as a constitutional maxim.[44] The
attempt was strenuously opposed, and the Glorious Revolution terminated whatever chance it had to obtain legitimacy. If "we have a right to our *property*," Gilbert Burnet
argued in the year James II went into exile, "we must likewise be supposed to have a right to preserve it: for those
rights are by the law secured against the Invasions of the
Prerogative, and by consequence we must have a right to
preserve them against those Invasions."[45] Of course, he ad-

FROM THE RESTORATION OF CHARLES II UNTIL THE WAR WITH THE THIRTEEN COL-
ONIES 43–44 (1959) [hereinafter cited as ROBBINS, COMMONWEALTHMEN].

[42] [J. SPELMAN,] CERTAIN CONSIDERATIONS UPON THE DUTIES BOTH OF PRINCE
AND PEOPLE. WRITTEN BY A GENTLEMAN OF QUALITY, A WEL-WISHER BOTH TO THE
KING AND PARLIAMENT 20 (1642).

[43] A TRUE COPY OF THE JOURNAL OF THE HIGH COURT OF JUSTICE FOR THE TRYAL
OF K. CHARLES I. AS IT WAS READ IN THE HOUSE OF COMMONS AND ATTESTED
UNDER THE HANDS OF PHELPS, CLERK OF THAT INFAMOUS COURT 29 (J. Nalson ed.
1684) [hereinafter cited as JOURNAL OF THE HIGH COURT]. Although even Whig
extremists eventually condemned the execution of Charles I, they continued to
view the civil war as lawful. By his actions Charles, as a Boston clergyman put it,
had "*unkinged* himself," hence resistance to his rule was not rebellion. J. MAYHEW,
A DISCOURSE, CONCERNING UNLIMITED SUBMISSION AND NON-RESISTANCE TO THE
HIGHER POWERS; WITH SOME REFLECTIONS ON THE RESISTANCE MADE TO KING
CHARLES I, at 42 (1750), reprinted in J. MAYHEW, SERMONS (1969).

[44] [A. SELLER,] THE HISTORY OF PASSIVE OBEDIENCE SINCE THE REFORMATION
(1689).

[45] [G. BURNET,] AN ENQUIRY INTO THE MEASURES OF SUBMISSION TO THE SUPREAM
AUTHORITY: AND OF THE GROUNDS UPON WHICH IT MAY BE LAWFUL OR NECESSARY
FOR SUBJECTS, TO DEFEND THEIR RELIGION, LIVES, AND LIBERTIES 4 [1688].

mitted, "if the case is doubtful, the Interest of the Publick
Peace and Order, ought to carry it; but the case is quite
different when the Invasions that are made upon *Liberty*
and *Property,* are plain and visible to all that consider
them."[46] In 1776 the case would be as "plain and visible" as
it had been in 1688.[47]

It has been suggested that after 1714 British Whigs, re-
alizing it could become a Jacobite justification, abandoned
the right of rebellion as a constitutional doctrine.[48] Perhaps
politics changed, but not constitutional theory. On both
sides of the Atlantic men criticized the "disgraceful,"[49]
"horrid,"[50] and "exploded principles of passive obedience
and non-resistance."[51] On the eve of the prerevolutionary
controversy, even a Scots supporter of Lord Bute endorsed
the doctine of lawful revolution,[52] and in 1769 a South Car-

[46]*Id.,* at 5.

[47]A Boston clergyman asserted the Americans' right of rebellion on authority of
"the Laws of God & Men." S. N[OWELL], ABRAHAM IN ARMS; OR, THE FIRST RELI-
GIOUS GENERAL WITH HIS ARMY ENGAGING IN A WAR FOR WHICH HE HAD WISELY
PREPARED 10 [1678]. Pamphlets printed in the colonies reminded people also of
the precedent of the lawful rebellion against King John "because he abused them
of those rights to which they were entitled, as well by the common law, as by the
grants of any former Kings." H. CARE, ENGLISH LIBERTIES, OR THE FREE-BORN
SUBJECT'S INHERITANCE 6–7 (6th ed. 1774) [hereinafter cited as CARE, ENGLISH
LIBERTIES PROVIDENCE EDITION]; H. CARE, ENGLISH LIBERTIES, OR THE FREE-BORN
SUBJECT'S INHERITANCE 6 (5th ed. 1721) [hereinafter cited as CARE, BRITISH LIB-
ERTIES BOSTON EDITION].

[48]Straka, *Book Review,* 83 AM. HIST. REV. 719, 720 (1978) [reviewing J. KENYON,
REVOLUTION PRINCIPLES: THE POLITICS OF PARTY, 1689–1720 (1977)].

[49]Christopher Gadsen in [W. DRAYTON, W. WRAGG, C. GADSEN, AND J. MACK-
ENZIE,] THE LETTERS OF FREEMAN, &C. 127 (1771) [hereinafter cited as [DRAYTON,
et al.,] THE LETTERS].

[50][T. BARTON,] THE CONDUCT OF THE PAXTON-MEN, IMPARTIALLY REPRESENTED:
WITH SOME REMARKS ON THE NARRATIVE 4 (1764).

[51]Speech of the earl of Chesterfield, Lords' Debates of Mar. 9, 1738, 10 THE
PARLIAMENTARY HISTORY OF ENGLAND FROM THE EARLIEST PERIOD TO THE YEAR
1803, at 521 (1813). See also New London Resolves, Dec. 10, 1765, The Massachusetts Gazette and Boston News-Letter, Dec. 19, 1765, at 2, col. 1.

[52]"No friend to liberty will deny, but that cases have arisen, and may arise again,
in which the regular method of opposition, would prove ineffectual to avert im-
pending evils: Kings have supported ministers and measures, and parliaments
have supported them too, to the open violation of national rights. Under such
circumstances, when the ordinary methods of obtaining redress fail, recourse must
be had to extraordinary remedies." [O. RUFFHEAD,] CONSIDERATIONS ON THE PRES-
ENT DANGEROUS CRISES 24 (1763).

olinian could assert with a good deal of accuracy that "[a]ll good writers on government agree that when delegated [government] authority threatens the safety of society, they [the people] have a right to resist, and reduce it within its proper bounds."[53]

So much was written during the 1770s on the topic that there can be no doubt that at the time of the American Revolution, adherents to the majority political party in the colonies thought the principle of lawful rebellion constitutional.[54] Tories might object that provocation was lacking, that American grievances were too slight to invoke the principle,[55] but before historians agree they should check their own objectivity. Whig assessments that their constitutional peril was sufficient justification to resist should be evaluated for what they were: appeals to legal right.[56] If we think the factual case unconvincing, there were contemporaries in London who saw its merits. No less than *Junius* once implied that grievances against the current British government might justify rebellion at home even where those grievances were much more minor than those of the colonies. When the Reverend John Horne declared in 1771 that had he lived in the time of Charles I, he would have rebelled, and that a king "whose actions justify rebellion to his government, deserves death from the hand of every subject,"[57] *Junius* asked him about George III.

I presume he [Horne] is not yet so much a courtier as to affirm that the constitution has not been grossly and daringly

[53] John Mackenzie in [DRAYTON, *et al.*,] THE LETTERS, *supra* note 49, at 110.

[54] For American statements of the doctrine during the controversy see J. LATHROP, INNOCENT BLOOD CRYING TO GOD FROM THE STREETS OF BOSTON 16 (1770); D. GRIFFITH, PASSIVE OBEDIENCE CONSIDERED 19–22 [1776]. The principle had also been stated in Cato's letters, a work popular in the colonies. ROBBINS, COMMONWEALTHMEN, *supra* note 41, at 123–24.

[55] [S. SEABURY,] THE CONGRESS CANVASSED; OR, AN EXAMINATION INTO THE CONDUCT OF THE DELEGATES AT THEIR GRAND CONVENTION (1774); [T. CHANDLER,] THE FRIENDLY ADDRESS TO ALL REASONABLE AMERICANS ON THE SUBJECT OF OUR POLITICAL CONFUSIONS: CAREFULLY ABRIDGED FROM THE ORIGINAL (1774).

[56] *E.g.*, [A. LEE,] A SECOND APPEAL TO THE JUSTICE AND INTERESTS OF THE PEOPLE, ON THE MEASURES RESPECTING AMERICA BY THE AUTHOR OF THE FIRST 86 (1775).

[57] Letter from John Horne, 31 July 1771, in 2 JUNIUS 218 [1772].

violated under the present reign. He will not say, that the laws have not been shamefully broken or preverted;—that the rights of the subject have not been invaded, or that redress has not been repeatedly solicited and refused. — Grievances like these were the foundation of the rebellion in the last century, and, if I understand Mr. Horne, they would, at that period have justified him . . . in deliberately attacking the life of his Sovereign. I shall not ask him to what political constitution this doctrine can be reconciled. But, at least, it is incumbent upon him to shew, that the present King has better excuses than Charles the First, for the errors of his government. He ought to demonstrate to us that the constitution was better understood a hundred years ago than it is at present;—that the legal rights of the subject, and the limits of the prerogative were more accurately defined, and more clearly comprehended. If propositions like these cannot be fairly maintained, I do not see how he can reconcile it to his conscience, not to act immediately with the same freedom with which he speaks.[58]

British Whigs such as Horne would not take up *Junius's* challenge, for they were not so provoked and would not feel sufficient justification as did American Whigs. But the constitutional principle would have been the same. "When," a colonist explained in 1775, "any Governor [invades the Rights and Properties of the Society, or lays aside those Laws that are made for their Security] as He thereby ceases to Govern that People, so that People are discharged from their Obedience to Him, as their Governor, and the reason of their Allegiance being ceas'd, their duty and obligation must likewise cease."[59] Accept the justification, and the Declaration of Independence rested soundly on English and British constitutional theory. The precedents of Charles I and James II led directly to the parliament of George III.

Sixth: Some historians overemphasizing the importance of natural law, have made assumptions about its quality not

---

[58] Junius Letter LIV, 15 August 1771, in *Id.*, at 233–34.
[59] ANON., AN ESSAY UPON GOVERNMENT, ADOPTED BY THE AMERICANS WHEREIN; THE LAWFULNESS OF REVOLUTIONS, ARE DEMONSTRATED IN A CHAIN OF CONSEQUENCES FROM THE FUNDAMENTAL, PRINCIPLES OF SOCIETY 63 (1775) [hereinafter cited as, ANON., AN ESSAY UPON GOVERNMENT].

applicable to eighteenth-century British or American legal theory. They have, for example, assumed the premise, generally incorrect,[60] that natural law was superior to positive law. From that proposition it follows that natural law took precedence over positive law,[61] which implied the further assumption that natural law must have furnished a guide for action. In fact, natural law in eighteenth-century English legal thought was not (as Blackstone pointed out) "perplexed . . . with a multitude of abstracted rules and precepts referring merely to the fitness or unfitness of things, as some have vainly surmised; but has graciously reduced the rule of obedience to this one paternal precept, 'that man should pursue his own happiness.' "[62] That fact, that natural law was not a code for legal conduct, had been appreciated by seventeenth-century English lawyers,[63] and was equally understood in colonial America.[64] The converse was also understood: that natural law was so indefinite it might be employed to support any legal argument[65] and could, if misapplied, be "destructive of all liberty."[66]

[60] R. Cover, Justice Accused: Antislavery and the Judicial Process 27 (1975). But see Hamilton, Farmer Refuted, *supra* note 12, at 87.

[61] Grey, *Unwritten Constitution, supra* note 2, at 853. Grey, however is interpreting eighteenth-century law from evidence of seventeenth-century legal arguments.

[62] 1 W. Blackstone, Commentaries on the Laws of England 40–41 (1765) [hereinafter cited as Blackstone].

[63] "[I]f we all lived according to the Law of Nature, we should need few laws, & fewer Lawyers. *Do as thou wouldst be done unto* were a rule sufficient to rule us all; and every man's Conscience would supply both the place of an Advocate & a Judge." John Davis [Davies], Les Reports Des Cases & Matters En Ley, Resolves & Adjudges En Les Courts Del Rey En Ireland (unpaginated, Preface at 13) (1674) [hereinafter cited as Davis, Les Reports].

[64] 1 Pamphlets of the American Revolution 1750–1776, at 108 (B. Bailyn ed. 1965) [hereinafter cited as 1 Pamphlets]. See *e.g.,* Thomas Hutchinson's concept of natural law. Hutchinson, *A Dialogue Between an American and a European Englishman* (B. Bailyn ed.) in 9 Perspectives in American History 369, 391 (1975).

[65] To premise civic privileges on "the *natural rights of mankind*" could "render the blessings of our excellent constitution universal to the natural Indians of North-America: the Negroes, the Hottentots, the Tartars, Arabs, Cafres and Greenlanders. All of these will have an equal title to the rights and liberties of Englishmen, with the good people of Pennsylvania; for all their constitutions of government are founded on the *natural rights* of mankind." A London newspaper quoted in The Boston Chronicle, Apr. 10, 1769, at 115, col. 2.

[66] Anon., The Late Occurrences in North America, and Policy of Great Britain Considered 3 (1766).

Seventh: Historians supposing that eighteenth-century natural law could guide civic behavior may also have misdefined the word "law" itself. It did not always mean "command" or "will," nor did theorists necessarily associate "law" with sovereignty.[67] The anachronistic attribution of our definition of "law" to statements by Whigs and Tories in prerevolutionary America, has tended to color eighteenth-century law with greater coercive power than it possessed. That fact is more important than it may seem to be with only superficial consideration. It means that we are probably interpreting their words differently than they were intended to be understood. For people to whom "law" is as much custom and community consensus as sovereign command, natural law, even if God's directive, may be less compelling than has been thought.

Eighth: The lesson is not so much that historians have misunderstood the definition of eighteenth-century law as they have not understood its sources. That mistake is another reason they have characterized as "natural law" arguments those making them thought of as constitutional law. Assumptions that the authority of law was derived from the sovereign's command have dominated the historical literature and distort conclusions. Consider the following statement, which its author believed to be a conclusion of fact but was really an incorrect conclusion of law: "From the legal standpoint, this view [that parliament possessed constitutional authority to tax American colonies] was unassailable. It was . . . vulnerable from the historical standpoint, as Parliament had hitherto not exercised all its legal powers, notably that of taxation."[68] The statement makes sense only by nineteenth- and twentieth-century definitions of "constitution" and "law." By applying anachronistic meanings to arguments advanced in the prerevolutionary debates, historians have concluded that colonial Whigs, unable to identify constitutional rights to which Americans were entitled, substituted privileges enjoyed by earlier generations as a re-

[67] See discussion by Henrik Hartog, *post* at 152–55.
[68] G. BEER, BRITISH COLONIAL POLICY 1754–1765, at 311 (1933).

sult of British laxity and recklessly claimed that these privileges had somehow been bequeathed them as constitutional rights.[69] What has not been realized is that rights established by custom and proven by time were legal rights. To contend that uninterrupted enjoyment creates prescriptive title was a legal argument.[70] Americans relying on custom thought they were relying on constitutional, not "natural rights" as has been supposed.[71] "[W]hat has," Arthur Lee maintained, "prevailed from the Beginning of the Colony, without Question or Controul, is Part of the Constitution; and . . . ancient and undoubted Rights are of all others the most sacred and valuable."[72] A committee of the Connecticut legislature, which included future loyalists, asserted the theoretical basis of the constitutional right as correctly as anyone stated it during the 1760s.

These privileges and immunities, these powers and authorities, the colony claims not only in virtue of their right to the

[69] L. LEDER, LIBERTY AND AUTHORITY: EARLY AMERICAN IDEOLOGY 1689–1763, at 125–26 (1968) [hereinafter cited as LEDER, LIBERTY].

[70] Reid, *In Accordance with Usage; The Authority of Custom, the Stamp Act Debate, and the Coming of the American Revolution*, 45 FORD. L. REV. 335–68 (1976).

[A] custom, in the intendment of law, is such an usage as hath obtain'd the force of a law, and is in truth a binding law to such particular place, persons, or things as it concerns; and such custom cannot be established by the king's grant, nor by act of parliament, but it is *jus non scriptum*, and made by the people only of such place, where the custom runs. For where the people find any act to be good and beneficial, and apt and agreeable to their nature and disposition, they use and practice it from time to time, and so by frequent iteration and repetition of the act, a custom is formed, and being used time out of mind, it obtains the force of a law.

J. DAVIES, A REPORT OF CASES AND MATTERS IN LAW, RESOLVED AND ADJUDGED IN THE KING'S COURT IN IRELAND 87 (1762). See also, [Foster,] *The Recorder's Argument*, in THE CASE OF THE KING AGAINST ALEXANDER BROADFOOT 7 (1758); Charge of Justice Edmund Trowbridge, Rex. v. Wemms (1770), in 3 LEGAL PAPERS OF JOHN ADAMS 288 (1965); Grey, *Unwritten Constitution, supra* note 2, at 863–64.

[71] LEDER, LIBERTY, *supra* note 69 at 145–46.

[72] Lee, *Answer to Considerations on Certain Political Transactions of the Province of South Carolina* (1774), reprinted in THE NATURE OF COLONY CONSTITUTIONS: TWO PAMPHLETS ON THE WILKES FUND CONTROVERSY IN SOUTH CAROLINA BY SIR EGERTON LEIGH AND ARTHUR LEE 131, 155 (J. Greene ed. 1970) [hereinafter cited as THE NATURE OF COLONY CONSTITUTIONS]. See also, Carroll, *First Citizen*, reprinted in MARYLAND AND THE EMPIRE, 1773: THE ANTILON—FIRST CITIZEN LETTERS 131 (P. Onuf ed. 1974).

general principles of the British constitution and by force of the royal declaration and grant [the charter] in their favor, but also as having been in the possession, enjoyment, and exercise of them for so long a time, and constantly owned, acknowledged, and allowed to be just in the claim and use thereof by the crown, the ministry, and the Parliament, as may evidently be shown by royal instructions, many letters and acts of Parliament, all supposing and being predicated upon the colony's having and justly exercising these privileges, powers, and authorities; and what better foundation for, or greater evidence of, such rights can be demanded or produced is certainly difficult to be imagined.[73]

Ninth: Another reason why natural law has been accorded undue emphasis by historians of the American Revolution is that few of them are familiar with seventeenth-century English and eighteenth-century British constitutional principles. Encountering an argument by colonial Whigs, the constitutional antecedents of which they do not recognize, many erroneously attribute it to natural law. As this explanation provides the chief reason that natural law has assumed so prominent a place in the mythology of the American Revolution, innumerable instances could be discussed. Rather than enter a lengthy discussion, however, it would serve our purposes better to look at a single example, and the one revealing more than any other is the doctrine of consent.

At first glance the principle that no one could be governed or taxed without giving personal consent seems to come directly from natural-law theory. Some contemporaries thought it might. Many public resolutions and individual

[73] REASONS WHY THE BRITISH COLONIES IN AMERICA . . . (1764), reprinted in 1 PAMPHLETS, *supra* note 64, at 392. Admittedly this argument was more reminiscence of the seventeenth-century English than of the eighteenth-century British constitution. See J. Greene, *Introduction,* in THE NATURE OF COLONY CONSTITUTIONS, *supra* note 72, at 52–53. Yet the importance of customary right in a debate supposingly dominated by parliamentary sovereignty is demonstrated by the fact that some of the strongest arguments against the American case were based on appeals to counter customs. *See* J. TUCKER, TRACT V. THE RESPECTIVE PLEAS AND ARGUMENTS OF THE MOTHER COUNTRY, AND THE COLONIES, DISTINCTLY SET FORTH 27–29 (1775) [hereinafter cited as TUCKER, TRACT FIVE].

writers attributed the maxim of consent to a combination of natural law and the constitution,[74] and a few even stated it in purely natural-law premises.[75] "All men," James Wilson wrote in 1770, "are, by nature, free and equal: no one has a right to any authority over another without his consent: all lawful government is founded in the consent of those who are subject to it."[76] The trouble with this argument, as Wilson may have realized, was that the opposite was just as natural. "[T]he notion," Allan Ramsay pointed out, "of people consenting to their own taxation is contrary to the nature of government, and unsupported by any fact."[77] Also unsupported by any fact is the assumption that when Americans claimed they had a right to consent before being taxed or bound by legislation, they were thinking of a natural right. Were space available, it could be demonstrated that in the overwhelming majority of cases they were not.

Colonists of the 1760s and 1770s had no difficulty understanding the doctrine of consent and perhaps even its historical roots. There were pamphlets delineating an ancestry

---

[74] *E.g.,* "Circular Letter from the House of Representatives of Massachusetts Bay . . . ," Feb. 11, 1768, in SPEECHES, *supra* note 26, at 134; New London Resolves, Dec. 10, 1765, The Massachusetts Gazette and Boston News-Letter, Dec. 19, 1765, at 2, col. 1; [S. DOWNER] A DISCOURSE DELIVERED IN PROVIDENCE, IN THE COLONY OF RHODE-ISLAND, UPON THE 25TH DAY OF JULY 1768. AT THE DEDICATION OF THE TREE OF LIBERTY, FROM THE SUMMER HOUSE IN THE TREE 6 (1768).

[75] Boston Resolves, Sept. 13, 1768, The Boston Post-Boy & Advertiser, Sep. 19, 1768, at 1, col. 2 [hereinafter cited as Boston Resolves]; [P. LIVINGSTON] THE OTHER SIDE OF THE QUESTION: OR, A DEFENCE OF THE LIBERTIES OF NORTH AMERICA. IN ANSWER TO A LATE FRIENDLY ADDRESS TO ALL REASONABLE AMERICANS ON THE SUBJECT OF OUR POLITICAL CONFUSIONS 16 (1774), reprinted in EXTRA NUMBER 52 OF THE MAGAZINE OF HISTORY WITH NOTES AND QUERIES 225–51 (1916) [hereinafter cited as [LIVINGSTON,] THE OTHER SIDE]; John Trenchard, Letter of Dec. 30, 1721, reprinted in THE ENGLISH LIBERTARIAN HERITAGE FROM THE WRITINGS OF JOHN TRENCHARD AND THOMAS GORDON IN THE INDEPENDENT WHIG AND CATO'S LETTERS 108 (D. Jacobson ed. 1965) [hereinafter cited as CATO'S LETTERS].

[76] Quoted in R. HARRIS, A SHORT HISTORY OF EIGHTEENTH-CENTURY ENGLAND 150 (1963).

[77] [A. RAMSAY,] THOUGHTS ON THE ORIGIN AND NATURE OF GOVERNMENT. OCCASIONED BY THE LATE DISPUTES BETWEEN GREAT BRITAIN AND HER AMERICAN COLONIES 48 (1769). For an argument from "nature" that Americans had voluntarily surrendered the right of "consent" see, [S. JOHNSON,] POLITICAL TRACTS. CONTAINING, THE FALSE ALARM. FALKLAND'S ISLANDS. THE PATRIOT; AND TAXATION NO TYRANNY 209–10 (1776).

which, if limited to parliamentary enactments alone, implied a lineage back to time immemorial,[78] with statutory precedents found in various reigns such as those of Edward I,[79] Henry IV,[80] and Henry VIII.[81] For more recent times every lawyer—perhaps most educated people—knew that the constitutional connection between consent and taxation, or consent and legislation was stated in the commons' Petition of Grievances of 1610[82] and reserved as a fundamental guarantee by the Petition of Right of 1628.[83] It was not, however, until the English revolution that the doctrine of consent acquired the meaning it would have in the eighteenth century. The reason is not because people in the 1640s disagreed as to the validity of the doctrine. They disagreed about its application. Charles I claimed a right to exercise legislative powers in situations of emergency, and, without consent of the lords or the commons, to promulgate "law." This assertion of extreme prerogativism compelled common lawyers to redefine parliamentary "consent" as a constitutional absolute, and to deny that there could be occasions when the crown, citing "necessity," could suspend its operation. Those historians who associate "consent" only

[78] A. LEE, AN APPEAL TO THE JUSTICE AND INTERESTS OF THE PEOPLE OF GREAT BRITAIN, IN THE PRESENT DISPUTE WITH AMERICA 4–10 (4th ed. 1775) [hereinafter cited as LEE, APPEAL TO JUSTICE]. For a similar argument, made by an Englishman in a pamphlet reprinted in the colonies see, CARE, ENGLISH LIBERTIES BOSTON EDITION, *supra* note 47, at 58–62. But see, R. ECCLESHALL, ORDER AND REASON IN POLITICS: THEORIES OF ABSOLUTE AND LIMITED MONARCHY IN EARLY MODERN ENGLAND 41–42 (1978).

[79] [H. CARE,] ENGLISH LIBERTIES: OR, THE FREE-BORN SUBJECT'S INHERITANCE, CONTAINING I. MAGNA CHARTA, THE PETITION OF RIGHT, THE HABEAS CORPUS ACT; AND DIVERS OTHER MOST USEFUL STATUTES: WITH LARGE COMMENTS UPON EACH OF THEM 37 (c. 1690); CARE, ENGLISH LIBERTIES PROVIDENCE EDITION, *supra* note 47, at 53.

[80] Quincy, *Observations on the Act of Parliament Called the Boston Port-Bill* . . . (1774), reprinted in MEMOIRS OF THE LIFE OF JOSIAH QUINCY JUN. OF MASSACHUSETTS: BY HIS SON JOSIAH QUINCY 355, 450n (1825).

[81] 25 Henry VIII, cap. 21 (1553).

[82] "Petition of Grievances by the Commons in 1610," 2 Howell, STATE TRIALS 521 (1816).

[83] The Petition of Right, 1628, THE STUART CONSTITUTION 1603–1688: DOCUMENTS AND COMMENTARY 82 (J. P. Kenyon ed. 1966).

with the Levellers,[84] therefore, are mistaken. In truth, the doctrine's constitutionality was acknowledged by leaders on every side of the political controversy. A striking example is furnished by the trial of Charles I. A regicide once asked whether the king ruled by arbitrary will or the people lived "under a government derived from their own consent."[85] Appealing to the same constitutional tradition, Charles asked the regicides by what authority their court assumed jurisdiction to judge and condemn him "without the Consent at least of the *Major Part* of every Man in *England,* of whatsoever Quality or Condition."[86] It will be noted below that the doctrine of consent played a similar role during the Glorious Revolution in England. A final point to be made at this time is to recall its importance for the Glorious Revolution in North America. Enactment without popular consent of prerogative taxation and prerogative legislation was (together with revocation of colonial charters) the major grievance voiced by those Americans, especially in New England, who actively opposed Stuart rule.[87]

The doctrine of constitutional consent was uniformly stated on both sides of the Atlantic during the eighteenth century. In Great Britain it was usually expressed in terms of taxation—"No Money to be Levied but by the common consent"[88]—or of parliamentary representation—"the *King* cannot (God be thanked) take over our Properties from us, without an Act of Parliament; or, in other Words, without

---

[84] Manning, *The Levellers,* in THE ENGLISH REVOLUTION 1600–1660, at 144, 145–56 (E. W. Ives ed. 1968); T. PEASE, THE LEVELLER MOVEMENT: A STUDY IN THE HISTORY AND POLITICAL THEORY OF THE ENGLISH GREAT CIVIL WAR 120, 146n31, 219 (1916).

[85] Edmund Ludlow quoted in J. TANNER, ENGLISH CONSTITUTIONAL CONFLICTS OF THE SEVENTEENTH CENTURY 1603–1689, at 118 (1961).

[86] *Journal of the High Court, supra* note 43, at 48.

[87] T. BREEN, THE CHARACTER OF THE GOOD RULER: A STUDY OF PURITAN POLITICAL IDEAS IN NEW ENGLAND, 1630–1730, at 143–44, 157, 173–74 (1970). See also [Bayard,] *A Modest and Impartial Narrative* (1690), reprinted in NARRATIVES OF THE INSURRECTIONS 1670–1690, at 320, 341–42 (C. Andrews ed. 1915).

[88] A. MARVEL, AN ACCOUNT OF THE GROWTH OF POPERY AND ARBITRARY GOVERNMENT IN ENGLAND 4 (1677).

our own Free-will and Consent." [89] The only difference in
the American colonies was that the consenting institution
was the local assemblies, not parliament. Otherwise the doctrine was as much a constitutional absolute as in the home
islands. [90]

Historians of the American Revolution might have better
understood the constitutional foundations of the doctrine
of consent had they paid closer attention to what was being
said in Great Britain. With few exceptions, [91] anti-American
pamphleteers acknowledged the constitutionality of the
doctrine, [92] even writers in the pay of the ministry. [93] For
example, the man who drafted the Stamp Act wrote (in a
pamphlet contemporaries attributed to George Grenville, the
minister heading the government) that Americans claimed

> the Privilege, which is common to all *British* Subjects, of being
> taxed only with their own Consent, given by their Represen-
> tatives; and may they ever enjoy the Privilege in all its Extent:
> May this sacred Pledge of Liberty be preserved inviolate, to
> the utmost Verge of our Dominions, and of the latest Page of
> our History! but let us not limit the legislative Rights of the
> *British* People to Subjects of Taxation only: No new Law
> whatever can bind us that is made without the Concurrence
> of our Representatives. The Acts of Trade and Navigation,
> and all other Acts that relate either to ourselves or to the
> Colonies, are founded upon no other Authority; they are not

[89] ANON., SOME THOUGHTS ON THE CONSTITUTION; PARTICULARLY WITH RESPECT
TO THE POWER OF MAKING PEACE AND WAR: THE USE OF PREROGATIVE: THE RIGHTS
OF THE PEOPLE, &C. 10–11 (1748).

[90] Message from the Boston Town Meeting to Governor Francis Bernard, June
14, 1768, The Massachusetts Gazette, June 20, 1768, at 2, col. 1; "Extract of a
Letter from a Gentleman in Virginia to his Friend in this City, From the Bristol
Journal, Dec. 2," The Boston Post-Boy and Advertiser, Mar. 17, 1766, at 1, col. 1;
Issue of Dec. 7, 1752, THE INDEPENDENT REFLECTOR OR WEEKLY ESSAYS ON SUNDRY
IMPORTANT SUBJECTS MORE PARTICULARLY ADAPTED TO THE PROVINCE OF NEW
YORK BY WILLIAM LIVINGSTON AND OTHERS 62 (M. Klein ed. 1963).

[91] See *e.g.*, 2 A NEW AND IMPARTIAL COLLECTION OF INTERESTING LETTERS FROM
THE PUBLIC PAPERS; MANY OF THEM WRITTEN BY PERSONS OF EMINENCE 122 (1767).

[92] See argument in "L.," A LETTER TO G. G. STIFF IN OPINIONS, ALWAYS IN THE
WRONG 27 (1767).

[93] [J. MACPHERSON,] THE RIGHTS OF GREAT BRITAIN ASSERTED AGAINST THE
CLAIMS OF AMERICA: BEING AN ANSWER TO THE DECLARATION OF THE GENERAL
CONGRESS 4 (10th ed. 1776).

obligatory if a Stamp Act is not, and every Argument in support of an Exemption from the Superintendence of the *British* Parliament in the one Case, is equally applicable to the others.[94]

Tenth: There is a final consideration to be weighed. It arises from the fact that the word *constitution* was less precisely defined during the eighteenth century than it is for us. Contemporaries could truly say there was no term so little understood.[95] As a result, expressions were used lightly and statements made in a phraseology that has misled later generations. For one thing, it was common to equate the constitution with "natural law," to say "certain essential Rights of the *British* Constitution" were "founded in the Law of God and Nature,"[96] or that the "British Constitution" itself was "grounded on the eternal Laws of Nature".[97] We read these words thinking them appeals to natural law and we may be right. More likely, however, they were boasts about the validity[98] and perfection[99]—perhaps even the immutability—of the constitution upon which they

[94] [T. WHATELY,] THE REGULATIONS LATELY MADE CONCERNING THE COLONIES AND THE TAXES IMPOSED UPON THEM, CONSIDERED 104 (1765) [hereinafter cited as WHATELY, THE REGULATIONS] See also, I. CHRISTIE & B. LARABEE, EMPIRE OR INDEPENDENCE 1760–1776: A BRITISH-AMERICAN DIALOGUE ON THE COMING OF THE AMERICAN REVOLUTION 55–56 (1976).

[95] "There is scarce a word in the English language so frequently used, and so little understood as the word Constitution." 32 THE MONTHLY REVIEW; OR LITERARY JOURNAL: BY SEVERAL HANDS 59 (1765). "This poor word *Constitution* has been more abused than any in the English language. Many have attempted to explain it; few have been satisfactory on the subject." 28 THE MONTHLY REVIEW; OR, LITERARY JOURNAL: BY SEVERAL HANDS 490 (1763).

[96] The Massachusetts Resolves, Oct. 29, 1765, reprinted in PROLOGUE TO REVOLUTION: SOURCES AND DOCUMENTS ON THE STAMP ACT CRISIS, 1764–1766, at 56 (E. Morgan ed. 1959).

[97] Resolves of the Town of Wrentham, Jan. 11, 1773, The Boston Evening-Post (Supplement), May 24, 1773, at 1, col. 1.

[98] "The Laws and Constitution of the Government of England . . . are founded upon these Laws of God and Nature, and on that Account receive all their Value." Quoting a handbill posted in New York City. The Boston Post-Boy & Advertiser, Dec. 30, 1765, at 2., col. 1.

[99] Letter from the Massachusetts House of Representatives to Henry Seymour Conway, Feb. 13, 1768, The Boston Post-Boy & Advertiser, Mar. 28, 1768, at 2, col. 1.

relied. The argument was to extremes, particularly when constitutional right was being defended against parliamentary power. Opposing the Stamp Act "even Lord Camden, in a moment of aberration," described the principle of "no taxation without representation" as a "law of nature." [100] "It is," the Massachusetts house of representatives agreed with Camden, "an essential unalterable right in nature, ingrafted into the British constitution as a fundamental law, and ever held sacred and irrevocable by the subjects within the realm, that *what is a man's own is absolutely his own;* and that no man hath a right to take it from him without his consent." [101]

We are considering more than a matter of words. There is also the meaning of words. Appeals to natural law more often than not were appeals to constitutional law. The town of Boston spoke of "the undoubted natural Rights of Subjects," and we think the reference is to natural law. Instead, Boston's "undoubted natural Rights" were "declared in the aforesaid Act of Parliament," that is the Bill of Rights.[102] They were not abstract, but specific rights, claimed by statute—"*freely* to give and grant their own Money for the Service of the Crown, with their own Consent." [103] We should not be surprised to discover that there was something different than meets the eye. Other participants in the prerevolutionary debates, both individuals writing pamphlets [104] and towns voting resolutions,[105] used the term

[100] Headlam, *The Constitutional Struggle With the American Colonies, 1765–1776*, in THE CAMBRIDGE HISTORY OF THE BRITISH EMPIRE: VOLUME I, THE OLD EMPIRE FROM THE BEGINNINGS TO 1783, at 646, 652 (J. Rose, A. Newton, & E. Benians eds. 1929) [hereinafter cited as Headlam, *Constitutional Struggle*].

[101] Letter from the Massachusetts House of Representatives to the Earl of Camden, Jan. 29, 1768, The Boston Post-Boy & Advertiser, Apr. 4, 1768, at 1, col. 1. See also Letter from the Maryland House of Delegates to the Massachusetts House of Representatives, June 24, 1768, The Massachusetts Gazette [and Post-Boy], July 11, 1768, at 2, col. 2.

[102] I William & Mary, session 2, cap. 2 (1689).

[103] Boston Resolves, *supra* note 75, at 1, col. 2.

[104] E.g. [William Henry Drayton,] A LETTER FROM FREEMAN OF SOUTH-CAROLINA TO THE DEPUTIES OF NORTH-AMERICA ASSEMBLED IN THE HIGH COURT OF CONGRESS AT PHILADELPHIA 44–45 (1774).

[105] *E.g.*, citizens of Massachusetts expressed apprehension that the stamp act "infringed" their "Charter Privileges and natural Rights," but as they claimed

"natural rights" when clearly referring to constitutional rights or rights in common law. One final example may be in order. In 1768, the Virginia house of burgesses claimed that "their ancestors brought over with them intire, and transmitted to their descendants, the natural and constitutional rights they had enjoyed in their native country". Rather than detailing these rights or indicating in what natural phenomenon they would be found, the Virginians said that these "natural and constitutional rights" meant "a legislative authority . . . derived, and assimilated as nearly as might be to that in England."[106] If that was what "natural and constitutional rights" meant, they could have more simply and more accurately been called "constitutional rights" only. Almost invariably, when one examines texts cited as evidence by historians that natural law was the basis of prerevolutionary American legal claims, they prove to contain the words "natural and constitutional," and rely on "constitutional" law alone.[107]

II. The Irrelevance of John Locke

We must continue to stress the negative. There is even more to be said about why historians have looked for "natural law" in the prerevolutionary debates and why what

---

those "natural Rights" as "Descendents from Great Britain" they could not have been thinking of "natural" rights belonging to all mankind, but "natural" British rights, in other words, customary constitutional rights. The Boston Evening-Post, Sep. 30, 1765, at 3, col. 1.

[106] Letter from the Virginia House of Burgesses to the Massachusetts House of Representatives, May 8, 1768, The Massachusetts Gazette, June 27, 1768, at 2, col. 1.

[107] It is also worth noting that to common lawyers, "natural law" traditionally meant "reason" or "reasonable" or "common sense," not a grand metaphysical system of the universe. Thus, it was positive law in the sense that common law unlike constitutional law, was reason as well as custom. Frederick Pollock, *The History of the Law of Nature: A Preliminary Study,* 1 COLUM. L. REV. 11, 20 (1902); S. PRALL, THE AGITATION FOR LAW REFORM DURING THE PURITAN REVOLUTION 1640–1660, at 23–24 (1966); Shepard, *The Political and Constitutional Theory of Sir John Fortesque,* in ESSAYS IN HISTORY AND POLITICAL THEORY IN HONOR OF CHARLES HOWARD MCILWAIN 289, 297–98 (1936). Natural law of reason could also be associated with English equity law. John Trenchard, Letter of Jan. 6, 1721, CATO'S LETTERS, *supra* note 75, at 118.

they have looked for they found. Even those who know nothing of English constitutional history, or of Sir Edward Coke, have heard of John Locke. Moreover, although Locke himself identifies the law of nature with reason,[108] and "when he refers to natural law it is strangely like the English common law,"[109] the prevalent notion has been that he provided a *sui generis* theory of legality that Americans drew upon for most of their ideas[110] and upon which they justified the case for rebellion.[111] Indeed, some scholars need only see something that looks slightly Lockean to spin a theory of total dependence. Daniel Dulany, for example, cited the doctrine of consent and grounded it entirely on constitutional principle.[112] He frequently referred to the British constitution, magna carta, the bill of rights, and the common law, basing all his contentions on legal authority. Yet it is said that "Dulany, in the language of consent, and by reference to the British constitution, really appealed to natural rights." The explanation is Locke, whom Dulany never mentioned, but from whom, of course, he derived his ideas. "In the well-accepted tradition of Locke, such popular consent to taxes was an analytical implication of the natural right of property."[113]

---

[108] Quoted in BECKER, THE DECLARATION, *supra* note 7, at 64.

[109] A. GOODHART, THE LAW OF THE LAND 54 (1966).

[110] Headlam, *Constitutional Struggle*, *supra* note 100, at 656. "His writings furnished an arsenal of the abstractions that have an irresistible fascination for unsophisticated people." Ewing, *The Constitution and the Empire—From Bacon to Blackstone*, in THE CAMBRIDGE HISTORY OF THE BRITISH EMPIRE: VOLUME I, THE OLD EMPIRE FROM THE BEGINNING TO 1783, at 603, 618 (J. Rose, A. Newton, & E. Benians eds. 1929).

[111] Especially as a source for the ideas "put into the Declaration." BECKER, THE DECLARATION, *supra* note 7, at 62. Even lawyers have attributed the Declaration to Locke, Grey, *Unwritten Constitution*, *supra* note 2, at 860; Dana, *The Declaration of Independence*, 13 HARV. L. REV. 319, 328 (1900).

[112] "By these charters, founded upon unalienable rights of the subject and upon the most sacred compact, the colonies claim a right of exemption from taxes *not imposed with their consent*. They claim it upon the principles of the constitution, as once English and now British subjects, upon principles on which their compact with the crown was originally founded." [D. DULANY,] CONSIDERATIONS ON THE PROPRIETY OF IMPOSING TAXES IN THE BRITISH COLONIES, FOR THE PURPOSE OF RAISING A REVENUE, BY ACT OF PARLIAMENT (1765), reprinted in 1 PAMPHLETS, *supra* note 64, at 634 [hereinafter cited as DULANY, CONSIDERATIONS].

[113] CONKIN, SELF-EVIDENT TRUTHS, *supra* note 29, at 34.

It is well to take heed. The argument could easily be misunderstood. The works of John Locke were cited as authority during the prerevolutionary debates, but nowhere near as much as one might think reading the secondary literature. Both lawyer Arthur Lee[114] and nonlawyer Benjamin Franklin,[115] found Locke useful when addressing arguments to the London public, and so did an occasional writer in the colonies.[116] But that fact does not prove the colonial case was of natural law, any more than it proves the British relied exclusively on their constitution. If all the evidence was tabulated and evaluated, the writings of John Locke would be found as often marshaled to support the answer of American Tories as the argument of American Whigs.[117] Admittedly, one loyalist said he quoted Locke's opinion "because it has been often heretofore relied on by the American advocates, as worthy of credit,"[118] a theme repeated by some of the most ardent opponents of colonial claims who called American Whigs Locke's "Disciples"[119] or Locke "their professed director."[120] We can only guess at the implication, but the purpose again seems disparagement.

The major source of Locke's credit as philosopher for rebellious Americans, however, is not British embroidery, but a second word historians have, along with *consent,* misun-

---

[114] LEE, APPEAL TO JUSTICE, *supra* note 78, at 4–5 & 15.

[115] The *Public Advertiser,* Jan. 4, 1770, reprinted in BENJAMIN FRANKLIN'S LETTERS TO THE PRESS 1785–1775, at 169 (V. Crane ed. 1950).

[116] For a particularly strong statement citing Locke as authority for revolution see, The Massachusetts Gazette and Boston Post-Boy and the Advertiser, Sept. 19, 1774, at 3, col. 1.

[117] See, Peter Van Schaack to the New York Provincial Convention 1777, reprinted in THE AMERICAN TORY 44–46 (M. Borden and P. Borden eds. 1972). See discussion, Clark, *Jonathan Boucher's "Causes and Consequences"* in THE COLONIAL LEGACY: VOLUME I LOYALISTS HISTORIANS 89, 109 (L. Leder ed. 1971).

[118] [J. GALLOWAY,] A CANDID EXAMINATION OF THE MUTUAL CLAIMS OF GREAT-BRITAIN, AND THE COLONIES: WITH A PLAN OF ACCOMODATION ON CONSTITUTIONAL PRINCIPLES 15 (1775).

[119] J. TUCKER, A LETTER TO EDMUND BURKE, ESQ; MEMBER OF PARLIAMENT FOR THE CITY OF BRISTOL, AND AGENT FOR THE COLONY OF NEW YORK, &C. IN ANSWER TO HIS PRINTED SPEECH 11–13 (1775); TUCKER, TRACT FIVE, *supra* note 73, at 39.

[120] [A. SERLE,] AMERICANS AGAINST LIBERTY: OR, AN ESSAY ON THE NATURE AND PRINCIPLES OF THE TRUE FREEDOM, SHEWING THAT THE DESIGN AND CONDUCT OF THE AMERICANS TEND ONLY TO TYRANNY AND SLAVERY 34 (3d ed. 1776).

derstood. That word is *contract*. When colonial Whigs spoke of contract, it has generally been assumed they were arguing in a Lockean vein. On rare occasions, perhaps, they were.[121] What is almost always forgotten or not noticed is that Locke's writings contained two contracts.[122] One was the social contract, the most famous theory underpinning Locke's notions of natural law, the other was the original contract, not Lockean at all, but a central dogma in English and British constitutional law since time immemorial.[123]

Considering the misunderstanding that has surrounded the contract as used during the prerevolutionary debates, a rule of interpretation cannot be overemphasized. The term *contract* in the great majority of instances was employed in a constitutional-law sense, not a natural-law sense. When colonial Whigs spoke of contract or of compact, their reliance was on much firmer jurisprudential grounds than John Locke or an appeal to nature. They were using a concept still very much a viable notion in eighteenth-century legal theory[124] as well as the doctrine that, throughout English constitutional history, had more than any other, been utilized by Whigs to limit royal power. Once more, we encounter a practice of constitutionalism stretching back beyond legal memory, to the pledge of King Canute to govern by the laws of Edgar,[125] the promise of William the Con-

---

[121] Sheffield Resolves, Jan. 12, 1773, The Boston Evening-Post, Feb. 15, 1773, at 2, col. 1; ANONYMOUS, AN ESSAY UPON GOVERNMENT, *supra* note 59, at 67. After the revolution began, the social contract became more important when it entered constitutional theory as in section 1, of the *Virginia Declaration of Rights*.

[122] Pole, *Equality in the Founding of the American Republic: A Complex Heritage,* in THE B. K. SMITH LECTURES IN HISTORY: SOCIAL RADICALISM AND THE IDEA OF EQUALITY IN THE AMERICAN REVOLUTION 15, 18 (1976).

[123] R. ACHERLEY, THE BRITANNIC CONSTITUTION: OR, THE FUNDAMENTAL FORM OF GOVERNMENT IN BRITAIN 102 and 108–62 (1727) [hereinafter cited as ACHERLEY, THE BRITANNIC CONSTITUTION].

[124] G. WOOD, THE CREATION OF THE AMERICAN REPUBLIC 1776–1787, at 19 (1969). Blackstone, who denied the existence of a social compact, defined restraint upon executive power in terms of the original or constitutional contract. BLACKSTONE, *supra* note 62, at 47–48; E. BARKER, ESSAYS ON GOVERNMENT 147 (1945).

[125] *Charter of Canute* (c. 1020), in SELECT CHARTERS AND OTHER ILLUSTRATIONS OF ENGLISH CONSTITUTIONAL HISTORY FROM THE EARLIEST TIMES TO THE REIGN OF EDWARD THE FIRST 75–76 (8th ed. W. Stubbs ed. 1895).

queror to continue Anglo-Saxon customs,[126] the coronation charter of Henry I,[127] and the several versions of magna carta.[128]

We need not speculate about the legal-historical knowledge of prerevolutionary Americans. Surely, if nothing else, they knew that Charles I had been executed for violating his compacts with the English and Scottish nations.[129] "There is," he was told on being sentenced to death, "a contract and a bargain made between the King and his people, and your oath is taken: and certainly, Sir, the bond is reciprocal; for as you are the liege lord, so they liege subjects. . . . This we know now, the one tie, the one bond of protection that is due from the sovereign; the other is the bond of subjection that is due from the subject."[130] The contract that had been invoked against the father was later breached by the son.[131] In fact, as the Massachusetts house of representatives would charge, James II could be accused of hav-

[126] Section 7, *The Laws of William the Conqueror,* in SELECT HISTORICAL DOCUMENTS OF THE MIDDLE AGES 7–8 (E. Henderson ed. 1896) [hereinafter cited as SELECT HISTORICAL DOCUMENTS]. There was also William's promise to London. T. PLUCK-NETT, A CONCISE HISTORY OF THE COMMON LAW 13 (5th ed. 1956). See, McIlwain, *The English Common Law Barrier Against Absolutism,* 49 AM. HIST. REV. 23, 25 (1943).

[127] The *"Coronation Charter" of Henry I* (5 August 1100,) in 2 ENGLISH HISTORICAL DOCUMENTS 1042–1189, at 400–02 (D. Douglas & G. Greenway eds. 1953). See also the Charter of King Stephen confirming the laws of Henry I. *Id.,* at 402.

[128] *Magna Carta (1215* A.D.), in SELECT HISTORICAL DOCUMENTS, *supra* note 126, at 135–48; The Great Charter . . . of King Henry the Third, and confirmed by King Edward the First in the Five and Twentieth Year of his Reign, 1 *Statutes at Large* 1–15 (1762).

[129] Contemporary theory had been that the opponents of Stuart royalism did not seek "to make any new contract: our end is to establish the old." Speech of William Noy, Apr. 26, 1628, 3 COMMONS DEBATES 1628, at 97 (R. Johnson, M. Keeler, M. Cole, and W. Bidwell eds. 1977).

[130] C. WEDGWOOD, THE TRIAL OF CHARLES I, at 182 (1964) [hereinafter cited as WEDGWOOD, TRIAL].

[131] James II did "violate and Break the fundamental Laws and Statutes of this Realm, which were the original Contract between him and his People." John Trenchard, letter of June 8, 1723, CATO'S LETTERS, *supra* note 75, at 268. For an American tory's use of this precedent see Dulany, *Antilon,* reprinted in MARYLAND AND THE EMPIRE, 1773: THE ANTILON-FIRST CITIZEN LETTERS 103 (P. Onuf ed. 1974). For a discussion of how the Lords, dealing with James's departure, asked lawyers to define the original contract *see,* M. LANDON, THE TRIUMPH OF THE LAWYERS: THEIR ROLE IN ENGLISH POLITICS 1678–1689, at 229–30 (1970).

ing "broke the original contract of the settlement and government of these colonies," as well as "the original compact with his three kingdoms."[132]

For too long, specific words employed during the pre-revolutionary controversy have not been accorded the scrutiny they deserve. The Massachusetts house spoke of "the original contract of settlement," and we should ask what was meant. Obviously the representatives were not thinking of the compact by which people first organized society. That contract—the Lockean social contract—was seldom intended when the concept was cited in Massachusetts Bay. John Winthrop, founder of the colony, had based his idea of government upon a covenant between the ruler and the ruled.[133] Indeed, whether theoretical or actual, it had been the dominant secular explanation for civic responsibility among the Puritans—"the intellectual origin and rationale of the New England Way in both church and state."[134] Even when employed by clergymen to defend colonial rights against London's encroachments, it was based on constitutional principles, not those of natural law.[135] The two sources of law need not be rigidly divided, however, for the original contract could guarantee natural rights, putting natural law on the firmer ground of constitutionality. "[T]he implied contract I take to be this," an anonymous Bostonian explained.

> That if the adventurers will hazard their lives and properties in acquiring, according to the rules of justice, possessions in the desert regions of America, far remote from their native

[132] Letter from the Massachusetts House of Representatives to Agent Dennys deBerdt, Jan. 12, 1768, in 1 THE WRITINGS OF SAMUEL ADAMS 140 (H. Cushing ed. 1904).

[133] 2 WINTHROP'S JOURNAL "HISTORY OF NEW ENGLAND" 1630–1649, at 238 (J. Hosmer ed. 1908).

[134] D. RUTMAN, WINTHROP'S BOSTON: PORTRAIT OF A PURITAN TOWN 1630–1649, at 278 (1965). See also *id.* at 11–13.

[135] T. PRINCE, CIVIL RULERS RAISED UP BY GOD TO FEED HIS PEOPLE: A SERMON AT THE PUBLIC LECTURE IN BOSTON JULY 25. 1728, at 22 (1728); M. Mather, *Reasons For the Confirmation of the Charters belonging to the several Corporations in New-England* (1689–1690), reprinted in 2 THE ANDROS TRACTS 225 (1869).

land, and encounter all the difficulties and dangers necessarily attending such an enterprise, that then the King and the nation will support and defend them in those possessions. They paying due allegiance to his Majesty, and holding the lands of him upon stipulated conditions; and that they shall lose no part of their natural *rights, liberty and property*, by such removal; but that *they, and all their prosperity for ever, shall as fully and freely enjoy them, to all intents, constructions, and purposes whatsoever, as if they and every of them were born in England.*[136]

This contract, quite obviously, is not the compact Charles I and James II violated, but the one just cited by the Massachusetts house of representatives. It was the original compact that Americans would claim the British breached, justifying the Declaration of Independence and seccession.

The colonial original contract was even less complicated than the original contract between the English and their monarchs. The first American settlers, on one side, pledged to remain subjects of the king. In return they "were to receive protection, and enjoy all the rights and privileges of freeborn Englishmen."[137] This contract has been discussed elsewhere, and there is no purpose repeating facts here, except to note that more than one contract would be debated. The fact is surprising, but the British did not question the existence of the original colonial contract, so much as dispute its specific terms.[138] An exception was Lord Lyttleton, whose brother had been governor of South Carolina, and who placed an anachronistic burden of proof on the colonies by saying they had to prove that the first settlers had made "a new compact" with "the parliament of Great Britain."[139] By contrast, the marquis of Rockingham put the

[136] The Boston Evening-Post, July 1, 1765, at 1, col.2. Similarly see, [LIVINGSTON,] THE OTHER SIDE, *supra* note 75, at 16.

[137] [S. HOPKINS] THE GRIEVANCES OF THE AMERICAN COLONIES CANDIDLY EXAMINED 8 (1766).

[138] Reid, *"In Our Contracted Sphere": The Constitutional Contract, the Stamp Act Crisis, and the Coming of the American Revolution*, 76 COLUM. L. REV. 21–47 (1976) [hereinafter cited as *Contracted Sphere*].

[139] Speech of Lord Lyttleton, "Debate on the Conway Resolutions, House of Lords, 10 February 1766," in THE DEBATE ON THE AMERICAN REVOLUTION 109 (M. Beloff ed. 2d ed. 1960) [hereinafter cited as DEBATE ON THE REVOLUTION]. The

burden of proof on the ministry. Unable to determine that Americans had consented to parliamentary supremacy, he refused to violate the contract. "I wish," Rockingham explained, "to find a consent, and acquiescence in the *governed,* and I choose therefore to have a recourse to what I think an original *tacit compact,* and which usage has confirmed, until the late unhappy financiering project interrupted the union and harmony which had so long prevailed."[140]

Historians may legitimately question whether Lyttleton and Rockingham really believed the contract constitutionally binding, or whether they were indulging in convenient but loose parliamentary rhetoric. What they cannot legitimately do is assert that these men, and the many others citing the "contract,"[141] were natural-law theorists applying the Lockean social compact to solve the American controversy. They were constitutionalists citing a doctrine from the ancient English constitution,[142] certainly antiquarian, yet surprisingly precise to some lawyers[143] and as useful in 1776 as it had been in 1688. Just as Charles I[144] and James

---

rule was anachronistic not only because there had been no "parliament of Great Britain" at the time of first settlements, but because Lyttleton applied eighteenth-century constitutional law to a seventeenth-century event when he contended that "the king alone could not make a new compact with them."

[140] G. GUTTRIDGE, ENGLISH WHIGGISM AND THE AMERICAN REVOLUTION 74 (1966).

[141] *E.g.,* T. POWNALL, THE ADMINISTRATION OF THE COLONIES. WHEREIN THEIR RIGHTS AND CONSTITUTION ARE DISCUSSED AND STATED 50 (4th ed. 1768); [WHATELY,] THE REGULATIONS, *supra* note 94, at 22; [W. BOLLAN,] CONTINUED CORRUPTION, STANDING ARMIES, AND POPULAR DISCONTENTS CONSIDERED; AND THE ESTABLISHMENT OF THE ENGLISH COLONIES IN AMERICA, WITH VARIOUS SUBSEQUENT PROCEEDINGS, AND THE PRESENT CONTESTS EXAMINED . . . 61 (1768); (quoting William Pitt) P. THOMAS, BRITISH POLITICS AND THE STAMP ACT CRISIS: THE FIRST PHASE OF THE AMERICAN REVOLUTION 1763–1767, at 190 (1975). See also other sources cited, *Contracted Sphere, supra* note 138.

[142] "The 'original contract' is not 'the original of government'; it is identified with the coronation oath, an oath to observe the ancient constitution." J. POCOCK, THE ANCIENT CONSTITUTION AND THE FEUDAL LAW: A STUDY OF ENGLISH HISTORICAL THOUGHT IN THE SEVENTEENTH CENTURY 231 (1957).

[143] See discussion of James Wilson, "Speech in the Pennsylvania Convention, January 1775," in DEBATE ON THE REVOLUTION, *supra* note 139, at 178–79.

[144] WEDGWOOD, TRIAL, *supra* note 130, at 182–83.

II[145] could be accused of breaching the original contract, so could the Americans assert that parliament had overstepped the bounds of the covenant, and, though rebels, they were rebelling by legal right.[146] "It is," William Henry Drayton told a South Carolina grand jury, "the voluntary and joint Act of the whole British Legislature, on the Twenty-first Day of December 1775, releasing the Faith, Allegiance and Subjection of America to the British Crown, *by solemnly declaring the former out of the Protection of the latter;* and thereby, agreeable to every Principle of Law, actually *dissolving* the Original Contract between King and People."[147]

III. The Irrelevance of Evidence

We may wonder if there is a self-perpetuating myth surrounding the Declaration of Independence and eighteenth-century natural law that is, in fact, "history" no matter what evidence to the contrary may be uncovered. Perhaps we are too conditioned to answer questions about the Declaration and law by predetermined judgments about what is relevant and what irrelevant. In 1977 an historian, discussing American conceptions of property in the prerevolutionary era,

---

[145] WILLS, INVENTING AMERICA, *supra* note 5, at 55; J. GOUGH, FUNDAMENTAL LAW IN ENGLISH CONSTITUTIONAL HISTORY 1 & 87 (1955); B. KEMP, KING AND COMMONS 1660–1832, at 28 (1957); G. TREVELYAN, THE ENGLISH REVOLUTION 1688–1689, at 77 (1938); Pollock. *The History of English Law as a Branch of Politics*, in F. POLLOCK, JURISPRUDENCE AND LEGAL ESSAYS 185, 209–11 (1961).

[146] The concepts of "contract" and "breach," of course, provided an additional, constitutional, nonnatural-law argument justifying "legal" rebellion. For an early explanation see, W. BISHOP, THE WOUNDED CONSCIENCE CURED, THE WEAK ONE STRENGTHENED, AND THE DOUBTING SATISFIED 31 (1642).

[147] W. DRAYTON, A CHARGE ON THE RISE OF THE AMERICAN EMPIRE DELIVERED BY THE HON. WILLIAM-HENRY DRAYTON, esq; CHIEF JUSTICE OF SOUTH-CAROLINA: TO THE GRAND JURY FOR THE DISTRICT OF CHARLESTOWN 5 (1776). Even after parliament became supreme over the crown, there was a reluctance in Great Britain to admit it was supreme also over law. "[I]t neither has, nor ought to have an arbitrary Power over the Lives, Liberties, or Fortunes of the Subjects; and shou'd they manifestly appear to aim at such an exercrable Design, the whole People may justly call them to Account." J. TOLAND, ANGLIA LIBERA: OR THE LIMITATION AND SUCCESSION OF THE GROWN OF ENGLAND EXPLAIN'D AND ASSERTED . . . 4 (1701).

explained what some lawyers of that time meant by property in terms of natural law.[148] Definitions rooted in common law, we must suspect, are irrelevant. The next year Morton White, writing on the Declaration of Independence was somewhat troubled by the fact "[t]he word 'property' is notoriously vague as well as ambiguous in the literature of natural law."[149] In his case there is no need to speculate. Positive law, both common and constitutional, is irrelevant.

Professor White's book is almost a caricature of the genre of Declaration scholarship criticized in this paper. All of the assumptions mingle freely with all of the platitudes. "[I]t was the British government's invasion of unalienable rights that gave the colonists one of their strongest arguments for resistance and rebellion," he writes, echoing Carl Becker.[150] "[T]he enunciation of 'self-evident' truths in the Declaration of Independence revealed an acceptance of an epistemology of natural law which was basically Lockean and rationalistic in tendency."[151] In fact, one of the chief purposes of White's study is "to reinforce the view that Locke's moral rationalism played a crucial part in the Declaration of Independence."[152]

It is instructive how strongly the mythology of the Declaration of Independence governs the imagination of historians. To cling to it undiluted, and to keep natural law somehow relevant to the American Revolution, they treat evidence, proof, and causation as irrelevant. In his probing

[148] W. Scott, in Pursuit of Happiness: American Conceptions of Property from the Seventeenth to the Twentieth Century 36–39 (1977).

[149] M. White, the Philosophy of the American Revolution 284 (1978) [hereinafter cited as White, Philosophy of the Revolution].

[150] *Id.* at 215.

[151] *Id.* at 48. The Declaration was important "in catapulting the word 'self-evident' out of the pages of Locke and into the language of American politics." *Id.,* at 61.

[152] *Id.* at 94. "[T]he Declaration appealed to a Lockean rationalism in ethics." *Id.* at 52. In the other book under review, Garry Wills sought to prove the opposite: that Locke was not important. Wills, Inventing America, *supra* note 5, at 169–75. "All I assert is that we have no reason to keep assuming that a Lockean orthodoxy explains the early formation of Jefferson's political thought." *Id.* at 175. For doubts if Wills proves all his case see, Morgan, *The Heart of Jefferson,* N.Y. Rev. of Books 38 (August 17, 1978).

study, using the canons of historical methodology, Gary
Wills shows how even the contemporary insignificance of
the Declaration has been obscured by the mythology. It simply was not considered important at the time, a minor document, the drafting of which was assigned to a junior member of the Continental Congress who happened at that
moment to be in Philadelphia, and which some delegates
did not even take the trouble to sign. Yet White, seeking
"the principles that supposedly justified the Revolution,"[153]
limits himself to that document as evidence of the "philosophy of the American Revolution." Indeed, he does not
consider the entire Declaration, but only about one-fourth,
for the three-fourths discussing constitutional violations by
the mother country apparently is irrelevant, the preamble
with its nonlegal, rhetorical flourishes contains the philosophy. What results may pass muster as philosophy, but as
history it is a crabbed interpretation of the past, that makes
one think of glosses upon the glossators, annotations upon
the annotators. Reality seems lost along with the irrelevancy
of evidence. "I have," White boasts, "expounded the elements of Locke's moral rationalism, and I have shown how
they influenced the Jefferson of the Declaration."[154] The
difficulty with the book is summed in that phrase, "the Jefferson of the Declaration." For, even if we all agreed that
the philosophy of the American Revolution can be found
entirely in the Declaration of Independence, how can the
search be limited to Thomas Jefferson and a few other individuals? It is not even the "Jefferson of the Declaration."
It is rather the Jefferson-of-the-Declaration-that-might-
have-been, for White concentrates much attention on Jefferson's "Rough Draft,"[155] that is, on what Jefferson wanted
Congress to say, including words, phrases, and arguments
Congress voted it did not want to say. The technique might
have relevance if the purpose is to ask what Congress had

---

[153] WHITE, THE PHILOSOPHY OF THE REVOLUTION, *supra* note 149, at 136.
[154] *Id.*
[155] WHITE, PHILOSOPHY OF THE REVOLUTION, *supra* note 149, at 160, 165–66,
245–51.

in mind by studying passages excised from Jefferson's draft and questioning why they were expurgated. Instead, the mythology of the Declaration is so dominant in this book, White's canon of relevance is the opposite of our expectations. "I cannot help feeling," he writes, "that what Jefferson *intended* in the so-called philosophical part of the Declaration on the subject of life was better expressed in the Rough Draft than in the final version."[156] In other words, White says that what "Jefferson intended," is more relevant to learning the philosophy of the American Revolution, than what a majority of congress voted, even though without that majority adopting the Declaration of Independence, it would have been nothing but a statement of private views.[157] "I emphasize that much of my interpretation relies on the Rough Draft," White confesses, and his reason is that he thinks that in the Rough Draft "the influence of Burlamaqui and even that of Locke is more evident than in the final version."[158] Put another way, because we all know the Declaration was Lockean, the more Lockean the version, the more it is authentic.[159]

IV. The Irrelevance of Law

We may be grateful to Morton White for clarifying some ideas about which historians have been confused,[160] yet still

[156] *Id.* at 212.

[157] Garry Wills, writing history, takes up this very point by reminding us that Jefferson was writing for a constituency, not for himself. The Declaration meant nothing until adopted, and therefore had to reflect ideas respected in congress by expressing "the delegates, 'common sense of the subject'—not by voicing a 'Lockean' orthodoxy in the preamble, but by making a hard list of specifics that would pass the objections of men with great experience at testing such claims." WILLS, INVENTING AMERICA, *supra* note 5, at 79–80.

[158] WHITE, THE PHILOSOPHY OF THE REVOLUTION, supra 149, at 255.

[159] "I have found no scholar who argues that the congressional changes altered Jefferson's message in any substantial way. In fact, most critics think that Congress—with the possible exception of the paragraph on slavery—improved his draft, sharpened its meaning, trimming nothing but rhetorical excess or exaggerated claims." WILLS, INVENTING AMERICA, *supra* note 5, at 307.

[160] *E.g.*, the meaning of "alienable" and "valuable." WHITE, THE PHILOSOPHY OF THE REVOLUTION, *supra* note 149, at 197.

ask questions concerning the relevance of evidence and the irrelevance of law.[161] Perhaps the mythology of the Declaration has become so persuasive the document can be interpreted by special canons of relevancy that make irrelevant the familiar rules of historical methodology. Yet, even within the context of the myth, questions are created that would not even exist were law taken into account. Consider, for example, that if one looks at evidence from other years, there appear to be two Thomas Jeffersons. One is White's "Jefferson of the Declaration," discovered by reading only the preamble and ignoring the remainder, a man who seemingly believed in unalienable rights and natural law. The other is the Jefferson of reality, who insisted all law is mutable, all rights alienable.[162] We must not expect these two jurisprudentially opposed Jeffersons will be reconciled. As long as law remains irrelevant to historians of the Declaration, the right questions will not be asked because no one knows the real Jefferson.

It may be for this reason, because mythology has obscured reality, that the Declaration of Independence has a capacity for posing puzzles that should not be puzzling. Toward the end of his book, Morton White wondered about "the ultimate ambiguity of the American revolutionary mind: its failure to come to a single conclusion on the role of government with regard to man's natural rights."[163] From the perspective of the legal historian, this statement sums up much of what is objectionable about the mythology pursued by the school of Becker and White. It degenerates into fiction. White is asking a question that is not legitimately an historical question. Based on a false assumption of law, compounded by an erroneous historical technique, it asks natural law to provide answers about "the revolutionary mind" that, had it cared about the matter, "the revolu-

---

[161] Thus White discusses the eighteenth-century dichotomy between "mere power" and "authority" as defining the morality of an action when it was more concerned with the meaning and legitimacy of law. *Id.* at 190–94.

[162] D. BOORSTIN, THE LOST WORLD OF THOMAS JEFFERSON 209–13 (1948).

[163] WHITE, THE PHILOSOPHY OF THE REVOLUTION, *supra* note 149, at 256.

tionary mind" would have sought in positive law. What is the evidence for expecting that the role of government in the eighteenth century should have been stated in terms of "man's natural rights" rather than constitutional rights? The fault alone is not due to concentrating all attention on the Declaration and misreading its legal premises. The basic mistake is to use the Declaration at all. It provides ambiguous answers because it was never intended to answer the questions it is asked.

If historians would heed the message of *Inventing America,* they might go less astray. Three lessons are taught. One is that the Declaration's purpose was to lay the legal foundation for an alliance with France.[164] A second is that the Declaration, and especially its preamble,[165] was not regarded as important during the Revolution. And third, the Declaration was not, and was never intended to be, either a statement of philosophy or political theory. It was, pure and simple, a legal document, claiming and executing a constitutional right.[166]

Unfortunately, there is more to legal interpretation than acknowledging the legal nature of an instrument or event. The relevance of evidence must also be considered before deciding that we understand the Declaration of Independence. To assume, as White has, that John Locke was the source of Jeffersonian philosophy, or, as Wills has, that Jefferson was influenced by Francis Hutcheson and Thomas Reid, tells us mainly about Thomas Jefferson. It furnishes very little evidence proving what the Continental Congress understood phrases and provisions in the Declaration to

---

[164] WILLS, INVENTING AMERICA, *supra* note 5 at 327–29. John Dickinson must have thought so. He explained why he did not sign the document by saying: "Foreign aid would not be obtained by the declaration, but by our actions in the field, which were the only evidence of our union and vigour that would be respected." Dickinson, *Vindication,* reprinted in J. HAZELTON, THE DECLARATION OF INDEPENDENCE: ITS HISTORY 353, 354 (1905).

[165] WILLS, INVENTING AMERICA, *supra* note 5, at 65–66.

[166] In strict legal terms, the right was exercised when the Congress adopted the motion that the colonies were independent states. The Declaration "was a paper issued subsequent to an action in order to explain that action." WILLS, INVENTING AMERICA, *supra* note 5, at 334.

mean. The document was not adopted and made official by Jefferson. It was adopted and made official by a majority of the congressional membership. If its meaning is to be found it must be from their understanding and their intent. Jefferson's perceptions of David Hume and Jean Jacques Burlamaqui are relevant to the meaning of the document only to the extent his congressional colleagues knew of these perceptions and endorsed them with their votes.

We must not demand too much. Precise knowledge of law cannot be expected and mistakes in accuracy can be anticipated,[167] but the mistakes would become less serious if historians acknowledge it is law and constitutionalism, not abstract philosophy or morality, that is being discussed. Just for historians to be aware might help avoid some of the most obvious errors, even if awareness takes in nothing more than the elementary doctrines of the ancient English constitution.[168] Then, perhaps, no one would wonder why (1) the delegates to the Continental Congress thought even after they had authorized George Washington to take command of the army surrounding Boston, they still could remain subjects of George III;[169] (2) men could "profess devotion to the law while openly defying it";[170] and (3) what "basically conservative men like Dickinson and Jay hope[d] for in a patently illegal venture."[171] We would know that it was because (1) the British, not they, had altered the customary constitution, and they were asking not for new but old rights, that (2) parliament and the ministry in London, not they, defied the ancient law, and that they did not de-

---

[167] For example, Wills repeats Richard B. Morris's stale, inaccurate charge that John Adams conducted the defense in the Boston Massacre trials to protect the Whigs of Boston, not his clients. *Id.* at 23. In fact, John Adams acted in the best interests of the defendants. Reid, *A Lawyer Acquitted: John Adams and the Boston Massacre Trials*, 18 AM. J. LEGAL HIST. 189–207 (1974).

[168] For example, knowledge of the original contract might not have changed the judgment that Jefferson borrowed his theory of expatriation from Richard Bland, but it would have avoided the mistake of thinking it *sui generis* with Bland. WILLS, INVENTING AMERICA, *supra* note 5, at 82–83.

[169] *Ibid.*, at 50–51.

[170] *Ibid.*, at 55.

[171] *Ibid.*, at 56.

fine "law" as the historian posing the question defines it, and that (3) conservatives could rebel because the Revolution was not illegal.[172]

There is work yet to be done. We may concede the Declaration is more legal than we thought, but still we do not know how legal. All attention has been focused on the preamble, the rhetoric of the Declaration, the part that Becker, White, and Wills think alone is significant. Historians must turn to the substance of the Declaration, the charges directed by congress against George III, and they must realize it is an indictment they are reading. So too it would be well to recognize that the counts of that indictment were not American complaints spelling out dissatisfaction with British rule. They were English complaints inherited from a century and a half of Whig struggles against the crown.[173]

The familiar may become too familiar. An American historian or lawyer, reading a list of counts charging the king of England with "raising and keeping a standing army" without legislative consent, "quartering soldiers contrary to law," and arming a faction loyal to the crown, immediately may recognize that these words come from the Declaration of Independence. That historian or lawyer would be only partly correct. These offenses were attributed to George III, true enough, but more to the point, they were expressly charged against James II in the Bill of Rights of 1689. The Declaration of Independence was repeating, not originating them. Historians should also cease ignoring other milestones of English constitutionalism, especially the Petition of

[172] As a lawyer once said of Charles I: "He hath met in the field with two contrary Armies of his own Subiects [*sic*], and yet that Army which he went to destroy, and advanced their colours against him, was more loyall than that which [he] himselfe commanded." [H. PARKER,] OBSERVATIONS UPON SOME OF HIS MAJESTIES LATE ANSWERS AND EXPRESSIONS 25 (1642).

[173] As was the technique of counting violations of constitutional rights. The impeachments of Clarendon and Strafford, for example, alleged constitutional offenses, as did the "indictment" the Massachusetts house returned against Governor Bernard. See, Petition of the House of Representatives to the King, to Remove Sir Francis Bernard Forever from this Government, June 27, 1769, in SPEECHES, *supra* note 26, at 189.

Right of 1628. The constitutional grievance of taxation imposed without the consent of elected representatives, and the constitutional grievance of rendering the military independent of civil authority by conducting trials in peacetime under martial law, were raised as issues and settled as rights in the Petition 148 years before they were reiterated in the Declaration of Independence.

When the constitutional roots of the American indictment of George III are evaluated, historians will learn that each count, with possibly three exceptions,[174] stated a constitutional grievance previously litigated and established as an offense in British constitutional law. The assertion may be thought too strong, for some of the counts, such as those accusing George III of "establishing . . . an arbitrary government" in Quebec, and of making war on his people, appear to be peculiar to the America quarrel with the mother country. In fact, there was precedent among English constitutional grievances for the first charge, while the second was supported by both English constitutional precedent and, with lesser authority, by recent British constitutional theory. A precedent to the Quebec grievance was stated by the house of commons in 1667. One of the articles of treason exhibited in parliament against Edward Hyde, earl of Clarendon, accused him of introducing "an arbitrary government in his majesty's foreign plantations."[175] It was the same charge levied in the Declaration against George III,

---

[174]Counts in the Declaration that may have been peculiar to the colonial case were (1) refusal to extend judicial jurisdiction to the back country, (2) restrictions on immigration and international trade, and (3) placemen.

[175]*Article #9, Impeachment of Clarendon,* in 1 THE LAW AND WORKING OF THE CONSTITUTION: DOCUMENTS 1660–1914, at 156 (W. Costin and J. Watson eds. 1952). The first article exhibited against Sir Thomas Wentworth, earl of Strafford, charged "That he hath designed to subvert the fundamentall lawes of England and Ireland, and to introduce an arbitrary and tyrannicall form of government, and to advise the king to establish it by violence and armes." *Articles against the Earl of Strafford,* Nov. 20, 1640, reprinted in 4 A COLLECTION OF SCARCE AND VALUABLE TRACTS, ON THE MOST INTERESTING AND ENTERTAINING SUBJECTS: BUT CHIEFLY SUCH AS RELATE TO THE HISTORY AND CONSTITUTION OF THESE KINGDOMS. SELECTED FROM AN INFINITE NUMBER IN PRINT AND MANUSCRIPT, IN THE ROYAL, COTTON, SION, AND OTHER PUBLIC, AS WELL AS PRIVATE, LIBRARIES; PARTICULARLY THAT OF THE LATE LORD SOMERS 209 (2d ed. 1810).

and one of the most serious constitutional grievances that
could be made in English constitutional law.[176] The grievance of making war had been one of the constitutional justifications for trying and executing Charles I. He had, the
"Charge of High Treason, and other high Crimes," alleged,
"Traiterously and Maliciously Levied War against the present Parliament, and the People therein represented."[177]
Much as American Whigs would say in the Declaration of
Independence that George III had "plundered our seas,
ravaged our coasts, burnt our towns, and destroyed the lives
of our people," the English parliamentarians asserted that
Charles I "hath caused and procured many Thousands of
the free People of this Nation to be slain, and by Divisions,
Parties, and Insurrections within this Land, by Invasions
from Foreign Parts, endeavoured and procured by him,
and by many other evil ways and means, He . . . hath
. . . maintained and carried on the said War both by Land
and Sea."[178] In addition to this clear English precedent,
American Whigs (for the principle that a king criminously
could "make war" on his people) could have relied on commentaries on the contemporary British constitution.[179] An
instance is provided by Roger Acherley of the Inner Temple, the leading constitutional theorist on the Hanoverian
succession, who published in 1722 the first edition of his
treatise entitled *The Britannic Constitution.* In that book, Ach-
erly listed four acts of "arbitrary" power that, when performed by the monarch of Great Britain, would both violate

[176] The grievance against "arbitrary" government may possibly have been the
best articulated principle of English constitutionalism. *See,* Reid, *In Legitimate
Stirps: The Concept of "Arbitrary," the Supremacy of Parliament, and the Coming of the
American Revolution,* 5 HOFSTRA L. REV. 459–99 (1977).

[177] *Journal of the High Court, supra* note 43, at 30.

[178] *Id.* at 30–31.

[179] An American Whig, relying upon Grotius but saying the rule "exactly
adapted to the Constitution of *England,*" pointed out that "even where the Power
of declaring War is lodged solely in the Prince" it "must be understood to relate
only to foreign War." *The Independent Reflector,* Aug. 16, 1753, reprinted in THE
INDEPENDENT REFLECTOR OR WEEKLY ESSAYS ON SUNDRY IMPORTANT SUBJECTS
MORE PARTICULARLY ADAPTED TO THE PROVINCE OF NEW YORK BY WILLIAM LIV-
INGSTON AND OTHERS 322 (M. Klein ed. 1963).

the original constitution of the kingdom, and justify rebellion.[180] They were (1) suspending laws, (2) taxation without consent of parliament, (3) maintaining standing forces in time of peace without consent of the two estates, and (4) to make war on his own people, "or to *Violate* their *Liberty,* by Imprisonments, or to *Invade* their Property, by taking from them their Freeholds, or other Goods or Estates, or the Profits of them, &c."[181] Aspects of each of these four constitutional justifications were alleged in the Declaration of Independence.

V. Conclusion

This study could go on and on. It would, however, be well to draw it to a close, not only because the evidence is overwhelming and far too lengthy to be considered in one chapter, but because the mythology of the Declaration will probably prove stronger than all the proof that can be mustered from eighteenth-century reality. When even lawyers tell us that the Declaration of Independence rests on natural law, historians cannot be blamed for adhering to the popular tale. What they do not tell is how French or Spanish colonials in 1776 would have claimed natural-law rights to jury trial, to judges with tenure *quamdiu se bene gesserint,* to civil control of military actions, to taxation by consent, and to freedom from standing armies, quartering of soldiers in private homes, and arbitrary government. These are the rights claimed in the Declaration of Independence. If natural rights, we may assume they belonged to all mankind. They did not; they belonged only to those who had customarily possessed them from time immemorial. Only the British could make that claim, for they were English

---

[180] The legal principle according to William Livingston was "a Right to defend" the citizen's "Share in the supreme Power." *Id.* at 322. According to Acherley it was "the Principle of Self-Preservation [which] hath furnished to every Man, a Right to Defend himself, and his Possessions, against the Ministers of Arbitrary Power, and to avoid the *Slavery* of him, and his Posterity." ACHERLEY, THE BRITANNIC CONSTITUTION, *supra* note 123. at 93.

[181] *Ibid.,* at 9.

constitutional principles, sanctioned by English constitutional history, and guaranteed by English common law.[182] Far from being a statement of abstract, natural principles, the Declaration is a document of peculiarly English constitutional dogmas.

It is necessary to do more than demythify our story of the Declaration. We must discover how wrong it has been. The bill of indictment against George III did not contain "only the most *obvious* complaints" or "constitutional infringements,"[183] it contained grievances indisputably constitutional and known on both sides of the Atlantic to people better versed than are we in English constitutional history and contemporary British constitutional law.[184] We may be puzzled by the eighteenth-century constitution,[185] but that is no reason to assume that contemporaries were also puzzled. "[K]nowledge of the true Spirit of our Constitution,"

[182] Recently a lawyer has denied these were claimed by the Declaration as legal rights, pointing out that "the Declaration did not characterize these actions [depriving Americans of these rights] as illegal, or suggest that an important ground of objection to them was their inconsistency with the British constitution." Grey, *Unwritten Constitution, supra* note 2, at 891n230.

[183] WILLS, INVENTING AMERICA, *supra* note 5, at 59.

[184] In 1769 a London journal listed 11 grievances Americans had against current British rule. While one or two of these grievances were expressed in terms more familiar to the British audience than to American realities (for example, the charge of raising a revenue by prerogative), they all reappeared in the Declaration of Independence. 39 THE GENTLEMAN'S MAGAZINE AND HISTORICAL CHRONICLE 291 (1769).

[185] This is true, not only for reasons suggested in this article. There is much work to be done. The word "law" needs to be defined and so does the term "fundamental law." It is a very common error for lawyers and historians to treat "constitutional law" and "fundamental law" as if they were synonymous. Sometimes they were, but not often. Constitutional law, for example, was not immutable. In the year of the Declaration the following argument, attributed to Lord Holt, was published in London. "Weigh then the *reason* why Englishmen are not bound by laws made by members of their choosing; it is not because a charter has said it; it is not because the usage has authorized it; it is [not] even because the constitution requires it; nay, and for a farther yet and still better reason. If James or Charles had *abolished* parliaments, we should still have had a *right now* to demand their restoration; if there had never been a parliament from that time to this." ANON., A DIALOGUE ON THE PRINCIPLES OF THE CONSTITUTION AND LEGAL LIBERTY, COMPARED WITH DESPOTISM; APPLIED TO THE AMERICAN QUESTION; AND THE PROBABLE EVENTS OF THE WAR WITH OBSERVATIONS ON SOME IMPORTANT LAW AUTHORITIES 89 (1776).

Boston's committee of correspondence boasted, "has spread to the remotest parts of the Province."[186] It was a claim with which others, including John Adams agreed. "The great Principles of the Constitution, are intimately known," Adams wrote in his diary, "they are sensibly felt by every Briton—it is scarcely extravagant to say, they are drawn in and imbibed with the Nurses Milk and first Air."[187] We need not wonder about accuracy. As significant as what American Whigs knew about constitutional law, was what they thought. They thought constitutional law not a myth and were at least familiar enough with the ancient English constitution so that, when they read the Declaration of Independence, they did not think of natural law, John Locke, or Scots philosophy. They recognized constitutional principles relevant to their cause.

[186] Letter from Boston Committee of Correspondence to Westborough, Jan. 19, 1773, quoted in Bushman, *Massachusetts Farmers and the Revolution*, in SOCIETY, FREEDOM AND CONSCIENCE: THE AMERICAN REVOLUTION IN VIRGINIA, MASSACHUSETTS, AND NEW YORK 77, 80 (R. Jellison ed. 1976).

[187] 1 LEGAL PAPERS OF JOHN ADAMS 230 (L. Wroth and H. Zobel eds. 1965). But see statement of dissenters from town resolves of Petersham, Jan. 4, 1773, quoted in R. BROWN, REVOLUTIONARY POLITICS IN MASSACHUSETTS: THE BOSTON COMMITTEE OF CORRESPONDENCE AND THE TOWNS, 1772–1774, at 134 (1970).

PART II

The Revolution in Law

Accounting for Change
in American Legal History[*]

∽ Robert W. Gordon ∾

PROFESSOR Nelson's *Americanization of the Common Law* records the conclusions of a mighty research project. The author has undertaken a comprehensive account of the changes in Massachusetts law over a period of 70 years. Anyone who has ever been tempted to tackle a project of this magnitude has been humbled quickly enough by the immense problems of assembling the sources. Legal records, especially those of the colonial period, are typically mountainous in bulk, difficult of access and untracked by previous researchers. Nelson has overcome this obstacle, however: he has read not only all the published case reports and statutes for his period, but also "all available manuscript material, including unpublished judicial opinions, lawyers' notes, and, most commonly, records of pleadings, judgments, and other papers incorporated into official court files" (p. vii). This exhaustive coverage of the sources[1]

---

[*] A review of William E. Nelson, THE AMERICANIZATION OF THE COMMON LAW: THE IMPACT OF LEGAL CHANGE ON MASSACHUSETTS SOCIETY, 1760–1830 (Cambridge, Mass., 1975). This essay originally appeared in 51 N.Y.U.L. REV. 686 (1976). It is reprinted with minor changes by permission of the *New York University Law Review*.

[1] This is as good a place as any to complain about the production of this book. The Harvard University Press has not only bunched all the footnotes in the back—

means that when Nelson mentions creditors' remedies or pleading rules, we can be extraordinarily confident that he is not guessing the shape of a larger bulk, but knows the thing itself; we learn what there is to know.[2] Moreover, this mass of detail has been succinctly and lucidly reported.

Yet, although Nelson traverses every inch of ground, he has chosen some odd boundaries for his study. The "law" in this work consists largely of the rules applied by courts. We learn a lot about criminal law, contracts, debtor-creditor relationships, land and water use, corporations and master-servant rules. In a few contexts, Nelson gives us glimpses of the law in action as well. In his discussions of civil procedure, for example, he considers jury discretion and the practices followed by litigants in framing responsive pleadings; in analyzing criminal law, he reports the types of offenses for which people were prosecuted. Otherwise, the author pays practically no attention to aspects of the legal order other than its formal rules. For instance, he ignores changes in the structure and functions of the legal profession, or in the social origins or political affiliations of the judiciary.

Most legal historians would have chosen the same emphasis. In Nelson's book, however, the limitations of the traditional materials of legal history are notably perverse because Nelson's goal is far different from that of traditional historians.[3] He seeks to relate legal change to "more basic changes in American thought and society" (p. vii). To that end, he seeks to fit his account into a framework of general social change, a framework he expects will help to explain specific incidents of legal change and will be illustrated by them.

---

especially annoying in a book aiming to serve as a guide to its sources (p. vii)—but has printed footnote numbers in brackets in the same type size as the body of the text, thus breaking up sentences without even rewarding the reader with a footnote at the bottom of the page.

[2] In this respect Nelson's study goes beyond its predecessor as the most complete record of 18th century Massachusetts practice since the superb edition of the LEGAL PAPERS OF JOHN ADAMS (L. Wroth and H. Zobel eds. 1965).

[3] *See* text accompanying note 31 *infra*.

That effort represents both the book's greatest ambitions and its deepest flaws. The shortcomings, as I see them, are the author's monolithic view of the nature of social change and his often unsupported connections between social change and transformations in legal rules. Those basic points in Nelson's study are so oversimplified that they lead repeatedly to a distorted and idiosyncratic interpretation. The following analysis takes up each of these problems in turn.

I

The book begins with a characterization—a sort of still photograph—of Massachusetts in 1760 as a society almost frozen in stasis: a collection of tightly-knit corporate communities—stable, homogeneous, harmonious, religious. Such a society would not seem to possess any notable internal dynamic, and in Nelson's account it does not. Rather, it is the American Revolution, portrayed in this book as a mysterious event originating from outside the community, which seizes this peaceful society and sets off its rapid metamorphosis into a polar opposite society—atomistic, acquisitive, competitive, materialistic, secular, relativistic, utilitarian. As the society mutated, so did its law. A legal system devoted in the eighteenth century to the maintenance of what Nelson calls "ethical unity" and of economic and social stability, became, by the 19th century, simply a forum for competition among diverse interest groups seeking power and wealth.

This view of prerevolutionary society depends heavily on Michael Zuckerman's study of Massachusetts, *Peaceable Kingdoms*.[4] That work, perhaps more than any other analysis of the 18th century, stresses the existence of communitarian consensus in what the author believes to have been the only important unit of social life—the town. Other historians argue that that picture of consensus better describes

[4] M. ZUCKERMAN, PEACEABLE KINGDOMS: NEW ENGLAND TOWNS IN THE EIGHTEENTH CENTURY (1970).

the world of 1720 than of 1760, by which time the Christian corporate communities of New England were breaking up under the tensions created by generational conflicts, new settlers competing for land, and the religious schisms of the Great Awakening.[5] Nelson's fidelity to the Zuckerman thesis is, in fact, rather remarkable in view of the criticism that thesis has provoked,[6] and of Nelson's often differing interpretations (*e.g.*, of the significance of litigation in prerevolutionary Massachusetts).[7]

The real problem with Nelson's pre- and postrevolutionary social paradigms, however, is not that they reflect the minority view among historians, but that he rigidifies the structure of social change. While there was obviously an overall pattern of change from provincial corporate communitarianism to the individualism of Jacksonian America, it is absurd to suppose that this pattern was replicated in every detail of social life.

For example, Nelson repeatedly contrasts the religious, other-worldly values of the eighteenth century with the pecuniary ones of the nineteenth, an opposition that limits his

[5] *See, e.g.*, R. Bushman, From Puritan to Yankee: Character and the Social Order in Connecticut, 1690–1765, at 186–95, 235–38, 257–88 (1967); A. Heimert, Religion and the American Mind: From the Great Awakening to the Revolution 2–14, 88–93, 129–30, 136, 251–60 (1966); K. Lockridge, A New England Town: The First Hundred Years: Dedham, Massachusetts, 1636–1736, at 79–163 (1970); 1 W. McLoughlin, New England Dissent, 1630–1833, at 329–488 (1971).

[6] For criticisms especially relevant to law in provincial Massachusetts, see Murrin, *Review Essay*, 11 History and Theory: Studies in the Philosophy of History 226, 245–72 (1972), and Wroth, *Review Essay: Possible Kingdoms: The New England Town from the Perspective of Legal History*, 15 Am. J. Legal Hist. 318 (1971).

[7] Zuckerman, *supra* note 4, at 89–92. Nelson adverts to this matter in a footnote (p. 185 n.5), taking the position that the presence of litigation does not mean that consensus was not still "the ideal toward which Massachusetts communities strived." He says that litigation may in fact have been an integrative force, tending to strengthen "social unity and stability," and finally, that "the lawsuits that were brought could not have been resolved if they had been destructive of the underlying ethical consensus in Massachusetts." One can only conclude that, although Zuckerman and Nelson may both be right to argue that provincial Massachusetts was a consensus society, a writer who takes the absence, and one who takes the presence, of litigation as an index of consensus probably do not have the same conception of "consensus."

ability to perceive the complex interrelationship between ethics and economics in both societies. In Puritan New England, people emphatically refused to distinguish money-making endeavors from religious life. They thought it entirely proper for men to labor in their callings to increase their stock of wealth, but, when this activity produced an increasingly luxury-loving society, they experienced confusion and guilt. As Perry Miller put it, "the wrong thing," acquisitiveness, "was also the right thing."[8] Indeed, the revivalism of the Great Awakening may have been the most intense where settlers had achieved the greatest commercial success.[9] There are similar conflicts at the base of the Jacksonian character. No people as purely economically oriented as Nelson's social types of the Jacksonian era could have responded as deeply as Jacksonians did to a rhetoric of yeoman virtue, simplicity and frugality.[10]

Nelson draws another rigid dichotomy between ethical unity and ethical relativism. Massachusetts, by his description, changed from a society whose members were expected to subscribe unanimously to one set of religiously-derived values to one in which values were believed to be wholly subjective (p. 115). This change is illustrated by the withdrawal of the state's legal system from enforcement of a unitary ethical standard. Gradually deviations from the standard were no longer punished under the criminal law, and institutions for promoting compliance with accepted values—including the established churches—lost support. Like the ethics/economics dichotomy, this one corresponds crudely to differences between provincial and Jacksonian societies. Yet it completely fails, for example, to account for the evangelical impulse behind the disestablishment of churches. Pietists, more than rationalists, urged the state to disestablish religion on the ground that a voluntary system of religious worship and financial support would help to

[8] P. Miller, The New England Mind: From Colony to Province 51 (1967).
[9] Bushman, *supra* note 5, at 188–91.
[10] *See* M. Meyers, The Jacksonian Persuasion: Politics and Belief 12–17, 115–18, 132–35, 152–53 (1957).

eliminate religious conflict (at least among Protestants) and would encourage the spread of Christianity.[11] In fact, perceptive visitors like Alexis de Tocqueville[12] and Philip Schaff[13] concluded that voluntarism had contributed to establishing a degree of cultural homogeneity unapproachable in European society.

These simplified social categories do no harm as long as they are left as dicta, or as incidental commentaries on the main text. Occasionally, they even help to explain the legal data. That is true, for example, of Nelson's valuable treatment of changes in contract law from an eighteenth-century system in which community notions of fair exchange generally determined the terms of an obligation to a nineteenth-century system which enforced the parties' express intentions (pp. 54–61, 136–43). Trends in criminal law also fit Nelson's general thesis of secularization. He finds that, starting in the 1780's, crime gradually ceased to be viewed as sin: prosecutions for minor sexual offenses, for missing church and for Sabbath-breaking, dwindled. At the same time, prosecutions for theft increased. "By the turn of the century," he says, "the criminal was no longer envisioned as a sinner against God but rather as one who preyed on the property of his fellow citizens" (p. 118).

Generally, however, the rigidity of Nelson's categories leaves him in the predicament of a biologist with a collection of unadjustable microscopes. If the fixed focus isn't just right for the object, the image comes through fuzzily. For example, Nelson explores property law chiefly through the categories of communitarianism and individualism. This is an unhappy choice for analyzing any society. Nelson sees rules restricting property uses as communitarian and rules

[11] *See generally* McLoughlin, *The Role of Religion in the Revolution: Liberty of Conscience and Cultural Cohesion in the New Nation*, in ESSAYS ON THE AMERICAN REVOLUTION 197, 247–55 (S. Kurtz & J. Hutson eds. 1973).

[12] 1 A. DE TOCQUEVILLE, DEMOCRACY IN AMERICA 300–14 (P. Bradley ed. & H. Reeve transl. 1945).

[13] P. SCHAFF, AMERICA: A SKETCH OF ITS POLITICAL, SOCIAL, AND RELIGIOUS CHARACTER 73–82 (P. Miller ed. 1961).

expanding such uses as individualistic. But the relationship of ideology and practice is frequently more complex; it is not unusual for framers of property rules to argue that individual fulfillment is maximized by strict regulation of some property uses or that the community as a whole will profit from leaving other uses unregulated. Furthermore, since any system specifying property rights inevitably both recognizes and restricts such rights, Nelson has placed himself in the position of trying to describe differences between eighteenth- and nineteenth-century property law by reference to elements common to both periods. He is further entangled by his desire to fit property law into his general framework of social change—a change from communitarianism to individualism.

Difficulties appear as soon as Nelson starts feeding the evidence through the categories. We learn that in provincial Massachusetts, "[r]ights in property were not granted for the benefit of the individual; on the contrary, property rights received legal protection only to the extent that a person used his property consistently with the community's interests" (p. 51). Property was, therefore, subject to extensive regulation (pp. 51–52). For example, the community sought social stability by restricting competition for uses of property (pp. 47–54). We might expect to be told that post-revolutionary property law expressed the growth of individualistic ideology by lifting these anti-competitive restraints. Such a trend is indeed discernible by the time that the *Charles River Bridge* case[14] is decided by the Massachusetts court in 1829 (pp. 161–63). But on the contrary, immediately after the revolution the courts *expanded* the kinds of first-user property rights that the law was willing to protect from the incursions of competitive, would-be users (pp. 121–26). This development puzzles Nelson (p. 126), be-

[14] Proprietors of Charles River Bridge v. Proprietors of Warren Bridge, 36 U.S. (11 Pet.) 419 (1837), *aff'g* 24 Mass. (7 Pick.) 344 (1829). The Court held that the first proprietors of a bridge over the Charles River did not possess a monopoly over that waterway.

cause it reveals not only that his categories are too rigid but also that they are fundamentally unsound. As Nelson himself observes:

> the postrevolutionary rules allocating property did not result in increased individual liberty; they merely identified the individuals who would enjoy it. For every person who gained liberty by obtaining protection of a property right, some other person usually lost at least an equivalent amount of liberty (p. 126).

If specification of property rights is always this sort of zerosum game, it is hard to see how any particular regime of property rules could ever be more individualistic than any other.[15]

The same analytic confusion pervades Nelson's treatment of postrevolutionary public works that devalued neighboring properties—projects such as the enlargement of jail yards and the improvement of public roads (pp. 131–32). Nelson says that these actions signify that "private property" had come to be seen as "a value of less importance than promotion of the will of a democratic majority" (p. 130). This comment is an effort to preserve his general thesis of the growth of individualistic attitudes in the nineteenth century by redefining individualism to embrace the political aggregation of individual wills into a "democratic majority." Confusion deepens when, two pages later, he undertakes to summarize trends in property law as a whole:

> [In the view of the Massachusetts court, a] rapacious, and authoritarian crown, which threatened the liberty and stability of Massachusetts communities, had been replaced by the ma-

---

[15] Yet Nelson attempts to explain that expansion of property rights by noting that the postrevolutionary generation equated "the protection of property with the preservation of liberty" (p. 126).

Arguably, however, property rights were expanded because people were becoming more sophisticated about the variety of resources susceptible to commercial exploitation, and believed that conferring monopoly rights was a necessary incentive to potential exploiters. This argument is both plausible and consistent with Nelson's general observations about the role of law in promoting economic growth (pp. 145–64).

joritarian and egalitarian democracy of the Age of Jackson. The interests of community and of selfish individualism had changed sides. *Absolute and total protection of the owner in his enjoyment of property no longer seemed necessary to the interest of community;* instead, the individual now appeared as an obstruction to continued social progress, liberty, and equality— a perception that emerged with particular clarity in cases involving the limits of jail yards. By 1830, in short, private property was ceasing to be seen as an institution that promoted community values and was becoming instead a tool for the aggrandizement of the individual (pp. 132–33) (emphasis added).

What is going on? We were once told that eighteenth-century law restricted property uses in the interests of community; now we hear that it gave owners "[a]bsolute and total protection." Now nineteenth century law is cast in the role of restricting property in the interests of community. The judges had come to think of property as a vehicle for selfish individualism, and thus believed they had to control it for the sake of community values.

Yet just as the reader has reconciled himself to this revised perspective, Nelson pulls another switch. He cheerfully relates how these same judges gradually *privatized* the law of corporations and of contracts, releasing market behavior from the constraints of governmentally defined purposes. He concludes that "[t]he prerevolutionary legal system, in which community was the primary social value, had largely been destroyed. A new system emphasizing rugged individualism as its fundamental value had begun to take its place" (p. 143).

These contradictions derive, I think, from Nelson's insistence that the legal system, at any given time, must express some single set of values. As he moves from subject to subject, therefore, he is driven to assert the dominance first of one set of values and then of the other. Several excellent studies of law and public policy in the 19th century American states, however, suggest that state policy embodied both individualistic and communitarian norms. The content of both norms was considerably transformed as they were used to sanction novel forms of public support for business enterprise; as different factions came to dominate state politics, the ideologies of power-holders and of their opponents naturally tended to stress whichever individualistic or communitarian elements of commonly shared norms suited their interests.[16] Nelson may be detecting the influence of these ideological shifts. But explaining the rules in these terms would require strict attention to the chronology of events, particularly to political events outside the legal system, and would require abandonment of the thesis of universal and undirectional social change.

Nelson's simplification of social categories also causes him to miss subtleties of interpretation. For example, in his discussion of liquor license regulation, he describes how sessions courts in the early 1820's routinely resisted petitions from townsmen praying for reduction in the number of liquor licenses, but started to grant such petitions in the late 1820s and early 1830s. He analyzes this trend as part of the growing tendency to subordinate private property values to the "will of a democratic majority" (p. 130). Yet the early temperance movement in Massachusetts is probably better understood as an attempt by a declining Federalist-Calvinist elite to "re-establish prestige by 'lifting' the rude mass to styles of life enunciated by an aristocratic moral authority."[17]

[16]*See* O. HANDLIN AND M. HANDLIN, COMMONWEALTH: A STUDY OF THE ROLE OF GOVERNMENT IN THE AMERICAN ECONOMY: MASSACHUSETTS, 1774–1861 (rev. ed. 1969); L. HARTZ, ECONOMIC POLICY AND DEMOCRATIC THOUGHT: PENNSYLVANIA, 1776–1860, at 3–33, 173–75, 306–15 (1948); J. HURST, LAW AND THE CONDITIONS OF FREEDOM IN THE NINETEENTH CENTURY UNITED STATES 7, 30–32, 37–40 (1956); H. SCHEIBER, OHIO CANAL ERA: A CASE STUDY OF GOVERNMENT AND THE ECONOMY, 1820–1861, at 26–28, 90–94, 353–56 (1969); Horwitz, *The Transformation in the Conception of Property in American Law*, 1780–1860, 40 U. CHI. L. REV. 248, 248–51 (1973).

[17]J. GUSFIELD, SYMBOLIC CRUSADE 42 (1963). A social historian of the town of Springfield has concluded that even by the 1840s, when the temperance movements became more broadly based, they remained "confident, benevolent, inclusive, and assimilative" towards the immigrants they were trying to reform—behav-

Similarly, Nelson sees the great *Dedham Church* case[18] as evidence that the legal system had grown indifferent to the enforcement of religion and was trying instead to deal with church property disputes by adhering strictly to secular rules of property law (pp. 128–29). But strict property law did not actually resolve any of the issues in the case. The case may, therefore, represent something more interesting—a desire to strengthen the authority of ministers in Massachusetts by widening their corporate constituencies and thus ensuring that *parish* majorities, even if they left the faith of the church's founders, would be able to retain its property.[19]

II

The basic datum of Nelson's study, what he terms the "law," is the legal rule, especially as applied by a court. But the historian who asserts, as Nelson does, that study of the norms expressed in legal rules tells us something about the contemporary society must explain at some point what he thinks that something is. "[T]he historical task," Nelson agrees, requires "the articulation of social theory as well as the narration of recorded facts" (p. ix). The biggest disappointment of this book is that it fails to articulate a viable social theory. Rather, its implicit theories of the relationships between legal rules and social change are either incoherent or implausible. In fact, these theories derive from what students in American law schools have learned to call "policy analysis"—extrapolation of the likely social conse-

---

ior more conformable to Nelson's eighteenth- than to those nineteenth-century types. *See* M. FRISCH, TOWN INTO CITY 36–38 (1972).

[18] Baker v. Fales, 16 Mass. 488 (1820). This case involved a dispute over succession to church property between a majority of church members (who were, however, a minority in the parish as a whole) who adhered to the Trinitarian principles of the church's founders, and a parish majority of Unitarians (who had called a Unitarian minister to the church over the objections of the church members). The Unitarians won.

[19] *Cf.* 2 MCLOUGHLIN, *supra* note 5, at 1193–95.

quences of the adoption of a legal rule, using no evidence
but the rule itself.[20]

Policy analysis, as usually practiced, relies upon a simple
utilitarian model of the relationship between legal rules and
social behavior. Social actors in this model look to the rules
as their primary or even sole source of rewards and penalties. Their attention is riveted on the courts, so they may
promptly react to any change in the rules. Finally, social
actors are presumed to be rational—which is another way
of saying that their behavior is expected to accord with the
policy analyst's projections.

Nelson does not make extravagant claims for this
method. His use of it is appropriately tentative. Presumably,
however, he would not use it at all unless he thought it had
some explanatory or at least heuristic value. Its application
to eighteenth-century contract law, however, shows that, far
from generating workable research hypotheses, the method
leads to nothing but trouble. One example will suffice to
illustrate the difficulties with this approach.

[20] The following paragraph exemplifies the growing trend to mix a bit of economic analysis with policy analysis:

> But prerevolutionary contract law probably furthered ethical unity and stabil-
> ity in the allocation of wealth and status at the expense of economic efficiency.
> Although careful empirical research would be necessary to confirm any cor-
> relation, it seems likely that the people who gain most in freely negotiated
> contracts are those with the greatest entrepreneurial skills, while those who
> lose most are those with the fewest skills. Two important entrepreneurial skills
> are an ability to predict future market trends and a knowledge of current
> market values; a man with these skills is better able than a man without the
> skills to make investments at a lower cost that are likely to satisfy future mar-
> ket requirements. To the extent that a legal system seeks to maximize eco-
> nomic growth and development, it should allocate resources to people who
> possess such skills. The legal system of prerevolutionary Massachusetts prob-
> ably retarded economic growth by impeding the efforts of such men to ac-
> quire additional resources (pp. 62–63).

This paragraph, quite aside from its breathtaking ideological premises about who
wins in a free market, vividly demonstrates the limited utility of this analytic
method for historical inquiry. I cannot imagine what archives might be used to
assist in the "careful empirical research" needed to support the correlation. In any
event, the passage's assumptions are poorly suited to the circumstances of eighteenth century commerce, which was carried on through networks of kinship and
religious affiliations, and in which the paramount entrepreneurial skill was knowing whom to trust. Not for nothing was wealth in that world called fortune.

Nelson describes the various writs available to plaintiffs seeking contractual or quasi-contractual remedies in provincial Massachusetts and makes a convincing case that the system of writs imposed obstacles to compensating plaintiffs for their full expectancy when executory agreements were breached. To oversimplify somewhat, unless a party took the trouble to write out (and perhaps file with a justice of the peace) his agreement in advance, and then performed his side of it, the writs available limited the other party's obligation to a reasonable or customary return for benefits conferred (pp. 54–61). Nelson's descriptive passage is, as usual, clear and compact. His conclusions, however, are less impressive. From the formality required for court enforcement of promises that might be unequal, Nelson infers that

> [t]o the extent that it impeded change in the allocation of wealth, the law of contract may also have furthered ethical unity. A person who loses money in speculative transactions or in transactions entered into with imperfect knowledge often feels cheated. Sensing that the person who gained at his expense did so by failing to disclose relevant information, he may tend to feel an animosity that may long linger, only to arise under circumstances disruptive of community unity. By impeding speculative bargains and bargains whose terms did not reflect community norms of fair exchange, prerevolutionary law reduced the likelihood of such animosity and may thus have promoted social unity. By further allowing bargains in which there were opportunities for overreaching to be made only in the presence of others and under circumstances that promoted careful deliberation, contract law may similarly have reduced the likelihood of social rancor (p. 62).

To the extent that Nelson suggests that the system of contract remedies affected economic behavior, the assertion seems unprovable. In fact, available evidence supports the contrary view. For example, legal rules certainly did not deter trade or speculation in land. Engaging in any sort of commerce in the eighteenth century entailed speculation; a merchant could not even accept a bill of exchange without

considerable risk.[21] It is impossible to say whether there
would have been more speculation but for the restrictive-
ness of the writs. I think it is more likely that the hostility
of the official legal system to enforcement of promissory exchanges helped to ensure that most exchanges would remain unaffected by the rules. As Morton Horwitz has
pointed out,

> [b]usinessmen [in the eighteenth century] settled disputes in-
> formally among themselves when they could, referred them
> to a more formal process of arbitration when they could not.
> . . . [T]hey endeavored to find legal forms of agreement
> with which to conduct business transactions free from the
> equalizing tendencies of courts and juries.[22]

Although Nelson might admit that his rules are not always accurate guides to behavior, he might urge that they
do say something about what contemporaries found desir-
able. What is bad or inadequate evidence for social or economic history may still be good evidence for the study of
values and ideologies. If this is Nelson's position, I would be
happier if he advertised it more prominently, since it is
rarely clear whether his conclusions about the social significance of legal rules relate to attitudes or to practices. At any
rate, if the rules are evidence of attitudes, we need to know
whose attitudes. It will not do to adopt an a priori position
that legal rules embody the deepest-felt, commonly-held
norms of a society, or even that they embody the values of
an important elite. Some rules may survive because they are
irrelevant to anyone but an occasional litigant; no force has
been at work to alter or abolish them. Others may be "symbolic," registering the pressure of a group with just enough

---

[21] *See* R. Zemsky, Merchants, Farmers, and River Gods 193 (1971).

[22] Horwitz, *The Historical Foundations of Modern Contract Law,* 87 Harv. L. Rev.
917, 927 (1974). The most important of these legal forms was the penal bond with
conditional defeasance, which Nelson himself calls a "highly flexible commercial
instrument" (p. 61). Because of informal devices like the penal bond, and the
disposition of merchants to work outside the common law writ system, the common law of contract fails even dimly to reflect commercial practice until the very
late eighteenth century in England. *See* Thorne, *Tudor Social Transformation and
Legal Change,* 26 N.Y.U.L. Rev. 10, 19–21 (1951).

influence to get its values declared in law, but not enough to have them enforced against the rest of society.[23]

Nelson's own account of the legal system of provincial Massachusetts should inspire extreme caution in anyone tempted to draw inferences about social attitudes from that system's rules. Effective law-finding power was delegated to juries, a situation in which Nelson says that "legal change and development are imperceptible." He further notes that "[e]xplicit rules of law," which counsel argued to the juries, "remain unchanged, while substantive law is still extremely flexible in its ability to adapt itself to social needs in individual cases" (p. 29). It is, therefore, difficult to determine what the operative common law rules were, much less whether they reflected the attitudes of Massachusetts society. Nelson suggests that juries usually followed the law as urged on them by counsel or by the court, and rejected only "whatever parts of that law were inconsistent with their own views of justice and morality or with their own needs and circumstances" (p. 30). But what were those inconsistencies? And supposing juries mostly followed the rules, where did the rules come from? According to Nelson, they were copied out of form and precedent books, or cited straight from English cases and texts; they were "adhered to . . . with a simple-minded rigor and consistency," and were rarely modified by statute or by judicial decision (p. 19). It requires some bravery to deduce prevailing social norms from rules like these, except on the desperate hypothesis that even mechanically borrowed rules would not be used unless they served *some* social need. Perhaps the social need they served was simply that of giving the impression to provincials that they lived under a fixed system of law—an impression easily given by almost *any* set of rules with a colorable common law origin.

The problem of determining what social attitudes are expressed in provincial law becomes still more complicated if one challenges Nelson's application of the Zuckerman the-

---

[23]*Cf.* M. EDELMAN, THE SYMBOLIC USES OF POLITICS 22–43 (1964).

sis[24] to the world of the 1760s. If provincial society were
static and homogeneous, organized around a stable consensus on values, then we could sensibly suppose that formal
legal institutions helped to maintain equilibrium by discour-
aging deviance and by reaffirming shared values. Kenneth
Lockridge has suggested, however, that society in 1760 was
increasingly "polarize[d] . . . along lines of wealth, interest,
and opportunity," and its politics dominated by a struggle
between "rural reactionaries and a frightened elite . . .
pushed as never before to justify its existence."[25] If he is
correct, it is entirely possible that, far from expressing a stable consensus, the legal rules may embody one class's attempts to promote, or to resist, change.[26] Similarly, if John
Murrin is right that Massachusetts was becoming "angli-
cized" in the late eighteenth century, and that one of the
signs of this was increasing professionalization of bench and
bar, then the rules may reflect little more than lawyers' be-
witchment with English models.[27]

[24] *See* text accompanying notes 4–5 *supra*.

[25] Lockridge, *Social Change and the Meaning of the American Revolution*, in COLO-
NIAL AMERICA: ESSAYS IN POLITICS AND SOCIAL DEVELOPMENT 490, 510, 515 (2d ed.
S. Katz ed. 1976).

[26] Discussing enforcement of laws against moral deviance, Nelson comments:
The source of most of these stringent standards lay in the Puritan beginnings
of New England. Although Puritanism had lost much of its forcefulness by
the 1760s, juries of the period, *perhaps only as a matter of reflex,* continued to
give effect to puritanical traditions (p. 37) (emphasis added) (footnote omitted).
Also, pointing to the importance of the oath in provincial procedure, Nelson concludes:
The colonial approach to evidentiary questions rested in large part, then, on
a conception of truth that we do not share. The conception—that truth would
emerge not from a weighing of credibilities and probabilities but from the
sanctity of an oath—looked backward to earlier times, in which God-fearing
men had attached enormous importance to a solemn oath. *To the extent that
such notions persisted,* they reduced somewhat the power of juries to determine
facts both by keeping evidence from them and by reducing their freedom in
weighing the evidence that they heard (pp. 25–26) (emphasis added).
These exquisite hedges register Nelson's awareness of, but do not solve, the problems that changing values pose for his view that law represented social consensus.

[27] Murrin, *The Legal Transformation: The Bench and Bar of Eighteenth Century Massachusetts,* in COLONIAL AMERICA: ESSAYS IN POLITICS AND SOCIAL DEVELOPMENT
415 (1st ed. S. Katz ed. 1971).

The point is that it is impossible to decide what social reality a legal rule represents—how most people behave, how most people think, how one group thinks, how nobody but lawyers think—without some attention to a great web of processes. That web includes the social functions of litigation in the culture; nonjudicial sources of coercive and normative direction such as families, churches and employers; the extent of differentiation of legal from other norms and occupations; and the role of the courts in government and politics.[28]

Nelson's sections on procedure, judicial control of juries, pleading reform and revision of appellate process are especially valuable because they provide some insight into the shape of the web connecting law and society. Nelson shows that in provincial Massachusetts various devices available in England to control juries—special pleadings, instructions, postverdict motions—were left undeveloped or unused. Parties usually tried cases under the general issue; instructions were cursory or even conflicting when several judges delivered charges *seriatim;* and postverdict motions provided no effective sanction against juries who ignored instructions (pp. 21–28).

After the revolution all this changed. By 1820, a series of procedural reforms had shifted the lawfinding function from the jury to the judge. Trial was before a single judge, and trial de novo before the full bench of the Supreme Judicial Court was abolished. This reform had the effect not only of simplifying jury instructions but also of placing another level of review—full court review on a bill of exceptions—above the trial process. At the same time, the courts

---

[28] It is instructive to contrast Nelson's book in this respect with the classic account of law in seventeenth-century Massachusetts, G. HASKINS, LAW AND AUTHORITY IN EARLY MASSACHUSETTS (1960), which really does succeed in placing the legal order in the context of the total culture—its religious and political norms and institutions, social structure, economy, etc. It may be that the much greater differentiation of legal activities from other kinds of social activities in the eighteenth century led Nelson to believe that law could be studied as a relatively autonomous phenomenon. That makes sense. What does not work is the attempt to re-connect the relatively autonomous field to the rest of social life by the mechanical apparatus of "policy analysis."

began to develop supervisory mechanisms, expecially motions after verdict, for the relief of litigants whose juries had failed to decide in accordance with the instructions or the evidence (pp. 166–70).

Equally dramatic changes overtook the rules of pleading. In his most detailed and carefully documented chapter, Nelson shows that the Massachusetts courts moved gradually after the revolution to rid common law pleading of its extreme technicality and formalism. The courts began by freely allowing amendment for trivial defects of form, and then went on to overlook the pleading mistakes of parties who brought the wrong writ, so long as the basis for the action was clear. They also loosened up defensive pleading, slowly promoting a unitary defensive plea. Eventually, Nelson argues, their impatience with technicality led the judges to the point where they perceived substantive bases of obligation beneath the ancient procedural categories of the writs, and as they perceived these bases they began to articulate them, using their new authority to develop law on their own. Substance and procedure became distinct categories in their minds: the pleading process came to be understood simply as an instrument for giving notice of the essential elements of a claim (pp. 77–88).

These developments naturally simplify the task of the historian attempting to extrapolate social consequences from legal rules. The rules were increasingly the work of American judges, rather than excerpts from English books, and they were far less vulnerable to subversion by juries.

Legal procedures, however, represent only a few of the strands connecting the legal and social systems. For the most part, Nelson ignores the other strands, or substitutes for them the suppositions of policy analysis. For example, a short account of the postrevolutionary economic changes that turned Massachusetts into an "industrialized, market economy that reached into the interior of the state" leads into the assertion that "[f]ollowing such a transformation in the economy, change was inevitable in the rules of law" (p. 147). Nelson certainly demonstrates that changes in the rules occurred. He does not, however, show why such change was "inevitable": he does not indicate what newly forged links had made commercial practice and common law courts interdependent. Furthermore, the critical question—how is it that judges and entrepreneurs both came to perceive *courts* as important places to resolve disputes and as important agencies for the promotion of social change?— remains unexplored.[29] It is insufficient to regard the view as the inevitable product of commercialization or of industrialization. Some of the available evidence weakens that presumption. For example, English judges and businessmen apparently did not share the perception of the utility of courts for industry; England lagged far behind the United States in developing legal devices to facilitate corporate enterprise. Yet England's entrepreneurs found they could function without such devices, and did.[30]

III

There is a danger that readers will take away the wrong impression from the peculiar combination of virtues and defects of this book—its magnificence as research into the history of legal doctrine and procedure and its tendentiousness as social explanation. Perhaps readers will conclude that lawyer-historians should stick to technical legal history in the traditional mode. As one who is convinced that the older mode of historiography—with its focus upon the "de-

[29] I once worked at trying to answer this question for New York in the early nineteenth century, and had hoped that Nelson's book would throw some light on it for Massachusetts. A promising beginning has been made towards discovering how *judges* arrived at this perception in Horwitz, *The Emergence of an Instrumental Conception of American Law*, 1780–1820, in 5 PERSPECTIVES IN AMERICAN HISTORY 287 (1971).

[30] For one of the very few treatments of the relationship between law and economic change in Europe, see Landes, *The Structure of Enterprise in the Nineteenth Century*, in 5 RAPPORTS, COMITÉ INTERNATIONALE DES SCIENCES HISTORIQUES, XI CONGRÈS INTERNATIONALE 107 (1960). A splendid recent study by Richard Danzig treats the relationship between law and social change in England. Danzig, *Hadley v. Baxendale: A Study in the Industrialization of the Law*, 4 J. LEGAL STUDIES 249 (1975).

velopment" of the internal details of the common law—led all too often to anachronism or to triviality, I can only celebrate the present shift towards a merger of legal and general history.[31]

My criticism centers not on Nelson's approach to fuse legal and general history but rather on his execution of that approach. It seems to me perfectly appropriate to write legal history as the intellectual history of the formation and transformation of thought-systems in treatises and the case-law—some very exciting work of this kind is afoot—so long as one respects the historicity of the materials and does not try to assimilate them to language and categories of present professional concerns (such as policy or microeconomic analysis). Legal history that tries to relate doctrine to the rest of social life is, however, a much more problematic enterprise, one requiring both much more monographic work on small-scale problems and more sophisticated social theories of law than the field has as yet produced. Nelson's book exposes very clearly the weaknesses of the mechanical linkages between legal rules and social behavior. If the book manages to get that point across, its weaknesses will prove as instructive as its considerable strengths.

[31] Nelson has made some very sensible and illuminating remarks on this subject in Nelson, *Legal History*, ANNUAL SURVEY AM. L. 625 (1974).

Revising the Conservative Tradition:
Towards a New American Legal History*

ᔓ Stephen B. Presser ᔕ

Introduction

DARK AND Doestoyevskyan is the world of Morton
Horwitz. In *The Transformation of American Law*, Professor Horwitz portrays nineteenth-century private law as a
battleground where God and the Devil fight over the soul
of man. Legal principles are subverted (p. 99), "class bias"
prevails (p. 188), and "gross disparities of bargaining
power" are brushed behind a facade of "neutral and formal
rules" (p. 201). In sum, legal power is ruthlessly exercised
to bring about economic redistributions, by powerful
groups who carefully "disguise" their activities from the majority of Americans (p. 266). When all of this is over, the
forces of goodness and morality in private law have been
completely thrashed by emergent entrepreneurial and commercial groups, who manage "to win a disproportionate
share of wealth and power in American society" (p. xvi).
Horwitz's primary purpose in writing this book was to

---

*A review of Morton J. Horwitz, *The Transformation of American Law 1780–1860*
(Cambridge, Mass., 1977). This essay originally appeared in 52 N.Y.U. L. REV. 700
(1977). It is reprinted by permission of the *New York University Law Review*.

correct an error made by "consensus" American historians, who ignored the redistributive effects of private law doctrines. These historians, who Horwitz believes were writing to provide an historical pedigree for the New Deal (p. xiii), "discovered" the long American tradition of governmental and legal activity to regulate and promote the economy.[1] They failed, however, to ask: "in whose interests were regulations forged?" This question Horwitz now attempts to answer. Primarily addressed to general American historians, the book employs a minimum of complex legal terminology.[2]

From other writings of Horwitz[3] and from hints thrown out here (pp. xiii, 266), a second aim can be discerned. Horwitz seeks to correct what he believes to be a misconception held by most lawyers and some legal historians—the notion that American law has a valid claim to political and moral neutrality. Most of this book is an analysis of the private law doctrines with which every lawyer and law student is familiar. Horwitz draws the legally trained reader in, and then forces him to reexamine the foundation of "scientific" reason on which the case-method system of instruction is founded. This is a disturbing enterprise, and if Horwitz's views on the law and legal change gain acceptance, we may soon see a major modification in the way legal history is taught in the law schools. This, in turn, may lead to some basic changes in the way lawyers think and act about law.

While it contains some problems on the polemical level, Horwitz's view of legal history is brilliantly conceived and should affect the teaching and writing of legal history for

---

[1] Horwitz refers expressly to "the Handlins and Hartz" (p. xiii). The reference is to O. HANDLIN AND M. HANDLIN, COMMONWEALTH: A STUDY OF THE ROLE OF GOVERNMENT IN THE AMERICAN ECONOMY: MASSACHUSETTS, 1774–1861 (rev. ed. 1969), and L. HARTZ, ECONOMIC POLICY AND DEMOCRATIC THOUGHT, PENNSYLVANIA, 1776–1860 (1948).

[2] For example, Horwitz manages to discuss the "holder in due course" doctrine without once calling it by name (pp. 213, 224).

[3] *E.g.*, Horwitz, *The Conservative Tradition in The Writing of American Legal History*, 17 AM. J. LEGAL HIST. 275, 277–78 (1973) [hereinafter Horwitz, *The Conservative Tradition*].

some years to come. In the remainder of this review, I will summarize Horwitz's argument as I understand it, explain why I think its impact will be substantial, and finally explore some of the limits of Horwitz's analysis.

I. Law as a Capitalist Tool: American Legal Development 1780–1860

A. A New Kind of Judging

Chapter I is derived from Professor Horwitz's seminal article, *The Emergence of an Instrumental Conception of Law, 1780—1820*.[4] Unlike the rest of the book, which is principally concerned with the use of nineteenth-century law to promote economic development, Chapter I focuses on political theory.

Horwitz believes that a fundamental change in attitudes toward substantive legal doctrines came about as a result of the American Revolution. In the eighteenth century, he argues, the law (or at least the English common law) was thought to be a fixed set of divinely inspired principles, which judges accepted on faith and applied in a consistent and unvarying manner. The war with England, however, forced Americans to rethink their institutions to bring the workings of government into line with the theories of popular sovereignty and social contract that were used to explain and justify the Revolution and the state and federal

---

[4] 5 PERSPECTIVES AM. HIST. 287 (1971), *reprinted in* D. FLEMING & B. BAILYN, LAW IN AMERICAN HISTORY 287 (1971). Chapter II first appeared as Horwitz, *The Transformation in the Conception of Property in American Law, 1780–1860*, 40 U. CHI. L. REV. 248 (1973). Chapters III, IV and V are published for the first time here. Portions of Chapter VI appeared as Horwitz, *The Historical Foundations of Modern Contract Law*, 87 HARV. L. REV 917 (1974). Chapter VII is new and Chapter VIII originally appeared as Horwitz, *The Rise of Legal Formalism*, 19 AM. J. LEGAL HIST. 251 (1975). The articles have undergone some editing for inclusion in this volume and seem to be more accessible than when they first appeared. The increase in readability is nearly offset, however, by the damnable and execrable practice (common to the volumes in Harvard's *Studies in Legal History* series) of placing all the footnotes at the end of the book.

constitutions.[5] It became impossible to view the English common law in the same manner as before Independence. Some English doctrines, such as the common law crimes of seditious libel and malicious shooting, were clearly inconsistent with new conceptions of American liberty, reflecting values more appropriate to a monarchical or feudal society.[6]

Moreover, if the substantive common law was a product of a hierarchical and probably corrupt[7] Old World, then perhaps the English common law judges were not simply applying unvarying rules of divine reason. This realization, Horwitz maintains, emancipated American judges from the slavish bonds of common law precedent and freed them to function as quasi-legislators, fashioning a new American common law consonant with the social and economic needs of the young Republic (pp. 18–19, 22–23).

Chapter I suggests the promise of a flowering of American law sprouting from the fertile soil of Enlightenment rationalism. In American courts, freed from nonsensical trappings of English justice like wigs and feudal doctrines, a new law based on equity and liberty could take shape. In his following chapters, Horwitz argues that this promise went unfulfilled.

B. Property Law

Horwitz begins by describing the transformation in the conception of property, using the doctrines of riparian rights as his paradigm. First, he shows how American courts in the colonial and early national periods enforced the doc-

[5] For a general discussion of this trend, see W. NELSON, THE AMERICANIZATION OF THE COMMON LAW: THE IMPACT OF LEGAL CHANGE ON MASSACHUSETTS SOCIETY, 1760–1830 (1975), and G. WOOD, THE CREATION OF THE AMERICAN REPUBLIC, 1776–1787 (1969).

[6] For a discussion of libel, see *Hitherto Unpublished Correspondence Between Chief Justice Cushing and John Adams*, 27 MASS. L. QUAR. 11 (1942), and on malicious shooting, see State v. Campbell, Charlt. T.U.P. 166 (Ga. 1808).

[7] *See* B. BAILYN, THE IDEOLOGICAL ORIGINS OF THE AMERICAN REVOLUTION 144–59 (1967); M. BLOOMFIELD, AMERICAN LAWYERS IN A CHANGING SOCIETY, 1776–1876, 18–20 (1976).

trine of "natural flow," which barred riparian owners from interrupting the flow of water to others. This preserved the stable, quiet situation of the past, permitting only agricultural or domestic uses while occasionally allowing the operation of grist mills. Other uses could be enjoined as nuisances (pp. 35–36).

When judges sensed, however, that economic progress demanded the encouragement of new forms of manufacturing based on water power, the natural flow rule was replaced by the doctrines of "prior appropriation" and "prescription." These new doctrines encouraged the initial investments necessary to put up new mills by permitting the first mill owner to continue using the flow, even if this interrupted the natural flow to his fellow riparians, and even if his use of the water prevented a similar use by them (pp. 34, 36, 42–43).

Finally, in a manner that Horwitz characterizes as Machiavellian (p. 34), the prescription and prior appropriation theories were in turn abandoned, when judges sensed that economic progress required a new rule. They were succeeded by "reasonable use" doctrines, which required courts to balance conflicting uses, ultimately permitting new owners to come onstream and jeopardizing the initial investments encouraged by the abandoned doctrines. By this time, "quiet enjoyment" and "absolute dominion," the basic principles of eighteenth-century property law, had been all but forgotten in the push for efficiency and material progress.[8] Property, once valued for its own ascriptive nature, became merely a tool of economic growth.

C. Tort Law

A similar transformation occurred in tort law. Eighteenth-century doctrines, such as "strict liability" in nuisance, had imposed a high cost for interfering with the tranquility or livelihood of another. In the nineteenth century,

---

[8] The adjustment of common law doctrines to favor economic progress is also illustrated by Horwitz's discussion of the mill acts and the waste and dower doctrines (pp. 47–58).

these doctrines were replaced with new legal concepts, like negligence. When the negligence doctrine was fully developed, by the mid-nineteenth century, it permitted substantial interference with the property of another, so long as the interfering actor adhered to an accepted standard of care. The move from nuisance to negligence was accomplished in fits and starts. For instance, Horwitz describes the modification and eventual destruction of nuisance law by the public-nuisance exception,[9] statutory justification,[10] and the exceptions for consequential or remote injury (pp. 71-74, 83). In their efforts to protect "infant" industry, ostensibly for the benefit of the public at large, the courts eventually extended the limited liability afforded by the statutory-justification doctrine to both franchised and unfranchised entrepreneurs, resulting in the "triumph" of modern negligence. The new American transportation and manufacturing establishment found its liability in nuisance virtually eliminated, so long as its activities were undertaken with "due care" (pp. 97-99).

Examining the consequences of these new tort doctrines, Horwitz stresses that the encouragement of industry was achieved at great cost. First, removing the damage remedies provided by the old doctrines placed what Horwitz believes is a disproportionate share of the cost of manufacturing and transportation development on landowners and artisans who were no longer assured recovery for injury. Had development been encouraged by direct subsidies through taxation, the cost of development would have been spread over a greater segment of the population, and the process would have been much more open to public discussion and scrutiny (pp. 99-101). Second, judges used the new legal rules of public nuisance, consequential damages, and negligence to restrict the traditional power of juries to award damages according to their sense of fairness and equity.

---

[9] This doctrine denied any private right of recovery where the general public was injured (pp. 76-78).

[10] This doctrine permitted the holders of state franchises, such as turnpikes or canals, to cause damage when acting pursuant to a statutory plan (pp. 78-80).

Judges' notions about how best to promote industrialization became more important than jurors' sense of justice (pp. 80–84).

D. The Law of Competition

The development of laws regulating competition provides still another variation on the theme of nineteenth-century common law's transforming itself to meet judicially perceived commercial needs. At the beginning of the nineteenth century, the spirit of Jeffersonian egalitarianism had seeped into the courts, and judges tended to reject the Blackstonian rule that certain "public" enterprises, like transportation, could secure injunctive relief to prevent competition. Soon, however, judges became convinced that the inducement of exclusive franchises and injunctive protection would increase investment in new transportation technologies. Thus, in *Livingston v. Van Ingen*,[11] the New York Court for the Correction of Errors held that Livingston's monopoly on steamboat transportation was entitled to injunctive relief against competitors.[12] The use of the injunctive remedy, of course, insulated the question of protection of monopolies from jury intervention.

As still newer technological developments became available, some legal theorists began to see that the recently entrenched monopolies might themselves have to be destroyed to make way for progress. And so the third stage of the nineteenth-century common law of competition came about. Horwitz uses as the paradigm for this stage the great *Charles River Bridge* case,[13] which, he argues, "represented the last great contest in America between two different models of economic development" (p. 134). The first model, which was rejected in *Charles River Bridge,* was the notion that "certainty of expectations and predictability of legal consequences" were of paramount importance (p.

[11] 9 Johns, 507 (N.Y. 1812).
[12] *Id.* at 589–90.
[13] Charles River Bridge v. Warren Bridge, 24 Mass. (7 Pick.) 344 (1829), *aff'd,* 36 U.S. (11 Pet.) 341 (1837).

134). Therefore, once the state granted a transportation franchise, as Massachusetts had to the Charles River Bridge Company, that investment had to be protected from competition. The competing model, which prevailed in the case, held that "fair and equal competition" was the best means to promote economic progress.[14]

The real winners in the *Charles River Bridge* case, those who stood to benefit the most from this second transformation of competition doctrine, were the railroads. Because the Supreme Court had affirmed the states' power to license competing public works, the railroads no longer had to fear that some state-franchised canal or bridge company could enjoin their operation. The stage was set for the explosion in railroad development that followed (pp. 137–39).

E. The Lawyer-Merchant Alliance

Obvious questions are raised by this description of the American common law's fashioning and dismantling of legal rights in the service of economic growth. How was it that judges could be so obviously inconsistent in their adherence to legal doctrines? How could rational men so cavalierly condone the creation and destruction of important legal rights? Horwitz answers these questions with his theory of the lawyer-merchant alliance.

In colonial times, Horwitz explains, lawyers chiefly served the interests of landed wealth. The common law rules enforced in the courts were suited to this service, and were not particularly hospitable to other areas of economic exchange, such as trade, finance, and manufacturing (pp. 140–41). As a consequence, merchants employed their own mechanisms for dispute settlement, like arbitration and penal bonds. The common law even encouraged this self-regulation by permitting the practice of "struck" juries— juries composed solely of members of the merchant class.

After about 1790, however, the merchant and entrepreneurial classes began to seek advice from lawyers in such

---

[14]*Id.* at 462.

matters as marine insurance and speculation in state securities (pp. 140–41, 174). This shift in their clientele encouraged lawyers (and thus courts) to focus more closely on commercial interests. Toward the end of the eighteenth century, two developments occurred that accelerated the shift in the nature of the lawyers' practices and subsequently changed the substantive nature of the common law. First, a split developed in the merchant community as different types of commercial enterprise began competing for wealth and influence. In marine insurance, for example, distinct groups of underwriters and insured formed even as early as 1790. Prior to that time, shipowners had combined haphazardly to insure each other as a means of mutual risk-pooling. After 1790, however, separate insurance companies, devoted solely to underwriting, began to emerge. The effect of specialization in the commercial community was to diminish the role of self-regulation, since the increasing fragmentation of interest made consensus difficult to achieve. This drove merchants to litigation, and thus gave lawyers and courts a more prominent role in the settlement of commercial disputes.

The second late eighteenth-century development pinpointed by Horwitz as affecting the relation between the bar and commercial interests was the growing tendency of courts to consolidate their law-declaring function. Jury discretion became strictly limited to matters of fact; all questions of law were reserved for the court. Cutting back the role of the jury, Horwitz argues, enhanced the prospects for certainty and predictability of judicial decisions, thus promoting merchant resort to the courts. At the same time, the courts' consolidation of their law-declaring function explains the increasing hostility to extra-judicial dispute settlement, manifested by refusals to enforce arbitration awards or to permit struck juries.

The increasing judicial hostility to merchants' settling their own disputes did not, however, reflect a more general hostility to merchants. In his most provocative stroke, Horwitz argues that the exact opposite inference should be made. Perhaps seeing where the future of lucrative legal practice lay, the courts embarked on a program of writing a procommercial common law. According to this view, the transformations of tort, property, and competition doctrines explored above occurred because the lawyers and judges shifted from protecting the landed gentry of the eighteenth century to promoting the emerging entrepreneurial, transportation, and manufacturing interests of the nineteenth century. This procommercial transformation of the common law was most striking in the area with the most immediate impact on trade—the law of contracts. Horwitz forcefully maintains that, despite ostensible justification in the needs of the whole society, the procommercial transformation in contracts disproportionately benefited the newly blessed merchant and entrepreneurial interests.

F. Contract Law

Eighteenth-century rules of exchange required that bargains be "fair" and generally permitted courts to set aside transactions that resulted in harshness to one of the parties. These doctrines well suited an economy in which complicated long-distance executory exchanges were rare, prices and trade patterns were stable, and the community had a good sense of "fair" prices for virtually all items.[15] With the advent of speculation in state securities after the Revolution, and with the beginnings of national commodities markets after about 1815, however, the American economy underwent fundamental change. In this more complex market society, it was important that merchants be able to rely on getting the exchanges for which they bargained.

For this reason, Horowitz argues, the rules of contract damages were rewritten to shift from the equitable eighteenth-century theory of fair exchange to the nineteenth-century model of expectation or "benefit of the bargain." A new central organizing principle, the "will theory" of contract, was articulated by nineteenth-century judges to bring

---

[15] *See* W. NELSON, *supra* note 5, at 54–63.

about this change. The relevant inquiry shifted from the community's sense of what a fair bargain in a similar contractual situation would be to the parties' "intent" as set forth in their particular arrangement. Old ideas about the existence of "objective" values of goods were discarded by judges and legal theorists and new ideas and techniques took their place (pp. 173–85). These new concepts, still the basis of modern contract law, included the supremacy of express over implied contracts, the refusal to set aside contracts in law or equity for inadequacy of consideration, and the widespread acceptance of the rule of *caveat emptor.*

By mid-nineteenth century, Horwitz argues, a further transformation in contract law had begun. The will theory, which relied on the intention of the parties, was becoming less useful as an instrument for meeting the increased needs for certainty and predictability in the expanding American market. So the will theory gave way to a new "objective" theory of contract, which focused on the practices and desires of the commercial group itself. Somehow, states Horwitz, judges managed to disguise this "class legislation" (p. 192), and a new law of commercial contracts was written to favor sophisticated insiders at the expense of consumers and laborers (p. 200).

According to Horwitz, the greatest victory of the lawyer-merchant alliance was this objective theory, specifically its acceptance of the fiction that equal bargaining power existed in virtually all business arrangements. Judges like Lemuel Shaw were prepared to assume that their contract model existed in the real world, and that when a laborer took a job with a railroad he held out for wages that truly reflected the risks of fellow-servant negligence (p. 210). Horwitz believes that the pressure to transform contract law to incorporate the rules of the marketplace led judges to redefine all economic relationships in terms of contract, and to assume that the rules of the marketplace governed in many situations in which they actually did not.

Seduced by the intellectual (and business) appeal of these new contract notions, judges began to undermine the body of eighteenth- and nineteenth-century tort law, which had imposed reciprocal duties and obligations wholly apart from contract. Eventually, it became possible to ignore the law of torts when the parties had arrived at some arrangement that could be characterized as a "contract." Judges were fully prepared to allow parties to "contract" away their tort law rights and, in ambiguous cases, equally prepared to erect presumptions to that effect. This triumph of contract over tort law in the mid-nineteenth century meant that the law would henceforth ratify any form of inequality that the market system produced (p. 210).

G. Legal Formalism

For these commercial doctrines to triumph, Horwitz believes, their political implications had to be disguised to an extent that has completely escaped contemporary historians. The chief instrument of deception was the fiction that in implementing commercial doctrines, judges were merely applying "scientific" general principles of law. This attitude, Horwitz argues (pp. 245–50), occurs as early as 1842 in Chief Justice Story's opinion in *Swift v. Tyson*.[16] In *Swift*, Story overruled New York decisions on the basis of a "general" commercial law that, Story said, the federal courts were qualified to expound authoritatively.[17] In Horwitz's view, *Swift* was designed to impose procommercial doctrines on reluctant state courts (p. 250), but in light of the prevailing anticommercial attitudes in the states, it was premature.

Horwitz's final chapter details the eventual victory of the attitudes reflected in *Swift v. Tyson*. In the first half of the nineteenth century, the ease with which early nineteenth-century private law decisions dispensed with contrary precedent had bothered some of the more conservative and "scientifically minded" treatise writers. These commentators felt that, for law to call itself a science, it was at least necessary for rules and doctrines to be consistently applied (p. 258).

[16] 41 U.S. (16 Pet.) 1 (1842).
[17] *Id.* at 12–14.

In the beginning of the nineteenth century, this conservative attitude was reflected in the law as well as the treatises, although its ambit was restricted to a strain of constitutional law doctrines that protected vested rights from public appropriation (p. 255). The *Dartmouth College*[18] case is a fine example of this trend. Private law, however, had played fast and loose with vested rights, and seemed to set them aside with impunity.[19] By about 1850, according to Horwitz, the lawyer-merchant alliance, having secured most of the things it wanted out of private law, made the tactical decision to freeze legal doctrines where they were. The adherence to precedent required by this strategy dovetailed nicely with the treatise writers' "scientific" attitudes, and with the lawyers' aspirations to the mantle of nonpolitical professionals. So it was that the conservative doctrines of public law began to merge with private law. By the middle of the century, the same notion of protection of vested rights prevailed in both private law and constitutional cases, and the inventiveness of early nineteenth-century private law was no more. No longer would judges rewrite the rules of property, torts, and contracts to conform with their notions of social policy. Now, with the advent for "formalism," *stare decisis* would be the rule, the inherent redistributive dangers of an expansive private law would be diminished, and the lawyer-merchant alliance would be able to consolidate its gains. This is where Horwitz leaves the laws of the nineteenth century.

II. The Impact of Horwitzian Legal History: The Law Students' Perplexity Diminished

A. Law Students and Legal History

To law students, law professors seem like lighthouses. Lighthouses, as Dean Prosser pointed out, are no good for fog. They whistle, they blow, they ring bells, they flash

---

[18] Trustees of Dartmouth College v. Woodward, 17 U.S. (4 Wheat.) 517 (1819).

[19] Examples include the cases involving mill acts, water rights, nuisance, and negligence. *See* pp. 703–04 *supra*.

lights, they raise hell; but the fog comes in just the same.[20] Most law students, especially those in their first year, are bombarded with holdings and dissents; they watch the prestidigitations of their teachers with awe, but to no apparent avail. There are too many conflicting doctrines and policies from too many seemingly discrete bodies of law.

For a few lucky ones, the light begins streaming in the window a few days or hours before the final exam and these few begin to perceive the outlines of some principles for the resolution of problems in particular courses. They get A's on their individual exams, but very few ever find a way of relating their courses to each other. Few are able to see the law as more than different lines of precedent found under different key numbers.

And so, from out of their fog, law students view legal history. They find bits and snatches of it in their casebooks, but it is usually related to doctrinal problems, like the origin of particular writs underlying forms of action in contracts and torts, or the evolution of the courts of equity and common law in legal process or civil procedure. As Professor Calvin Woodard noted ten years ago, this focus on the "origin" and "development" of the institutions of the Anglo-American common law seems narrow and remote to the twentieth-century law student.[21]

Hence the recent push for a new synthesis in legal history, a new "field theory" that will bring to the teaching of legal history something of value to modern law students.[22] Something is needed that will make law students and practitioners appreciate that legal history may be an "antidote to the provincialism inherent in the insularity of the twentieth century,"[23] something that will provide an organizing focus for discrete substantive courses on law.

---

[20] Prosser, *Lighthouse No Good*, 1 J. LEGAL EDUC. 257, 257 (1948).

[21] Woodard, *History, Legal History, and Legal Education*, 53 VA. L. REV. 89, 105 (1967).

[22] For a discussion of "field theories" in nineteenth-century legal history, see Holt, *Now and Then: The Uncertain State of Nineteenth-Century Legal History*, 7 IND. L. REV. 615 (1974).

[23] Woodard, *supra* note 21, at 113.

There is an emerging consensus among legal historians that the future of legal history does not lie in tracing the evolution of narrow legal topics.[24] Legal historians have been censured for their past concentration on the internal logic or lack of logic in pleading, procedure, and case law—for their insistence on staying within the "box" of lawyers' legal history.[25] Thus, the new generation of legal historians has been urged to concentrate on societal factors outside the law which have actually been responsible for the course of American legal history. Instead of the development of legal institutions, in short, legal historians should study and teach about the influence of extra-legal environmental factors and human or personality factors on the law.[26]

B. A New Perspective on Legal History: Horwitz's Method

In *The Transformation of American Law,* Horwitz offers his alternative to the "conservative tradition" of legal historiography reflected in Dean Roscoe Pound's *The Formative Era of American Law.* Pound suggested that the nineteenth-century common law judges arrived at their decisions simply on the basis of tradition, honesty, and application of "reason," unaffected by the economics of emerging capitalism or the political issues of the day.[27] One of the central themes that shapes Horwitz's work is that Pound's tenacious "taught legal tradition" is a myth.[28] Few, if any, legal historians would seriously advance Pound's perspective today, and "Pound-pounding"[29] has been a favorite indoor sport for legal historiographers for almost forty years.[30] Until Horwitz, however, no one had built the case against Pound with such richness, complexity, and power. As Horwitz

[24]*See* Boorstin, *Tradition and Method in Legal History,* 54 HARV. L. REV. 424, 434 (1941); Gordon, *Introduction: J. Willard Hurst and the Common Law Tradition in American Legal Historiography,* 10 LAW & SOC. REV. 9 (1975).

[25]Gordon, *supra* note 24, at 11.

[26]Woodard, *supra* note 21, at 116.

[27]R. POUND, THE FORMATIVE ERA OF AMERICAN LAW 83–84 (1st ed. 1938).

[28]*See* Horwitz, *The Conservative Tradition, supra* note 3, at 277–78.

[29]The noun "Pound-pounding" is the creation of Carole S. Presser.

[30]Criticism perhaps began with Boorstin, *supra* note 24, and it reached its latest and most elegant expression in Gordon, *supra* note 24.

leads us from level to level, it becomes increasingly clear that what went on in nineteenth-century law was not the work of "reason" alone.

At the first level, Horwitz describes substantive legal doctrines. Here, by showing how new doctrines were radically grafted onto old,[31] and by demonstrating the variable nature of property and contract rights in the nineteenth century,[32] he makes a powerful case against Pound's theory of the internal consistency of legal doctrine. Horwitz, like Crosskey before him,[33] shows that even simple legal words like "contract"[34] and "negligence"[35] could be given completely dissimilar meanings at different times.

Working at a second level of analysis, Horwitz explores judges' intellectual processes in order to explain the inconsistencies of their decisions. This bit of judicial intellectual history has two foci: the ideologies of judges, and their choices of theoretical models to implement those ideologies. The individual ideology component is used to explain such diverse matters as James Kent's morally based defense of usury laws (pp. 242–43) and the rejection of the "reasonable use" test for percolating waters by judges conditioned to "laissez-faire" and "rugged individualism" (pp. 105–08). According to Horwitz, a judge's ideology may lead him to select a particular model of legal analysis, which model then tends to circumscribe the result the judge is able to reach. Thus, judges in the middle part of the nineteenth century, who were strongly influenced by the prevailing economic philosophy, chose to interpret ambiguous problems

[31] For example, Horwitz notes that in Livingston v. Van Ingen, 9 Johns. 507, 589–90 (N.Y. 1812), the New York Court for the Correction of Errors treated a franchise as a form of property to be protected by the common law (pp. 123–24).

[32] For example, Horwitz uses the shifts in contract theory from objective to subjective and finally to a new objective theory to illustrate the vagaries of nineteenth-century commercial law (pp. 161–73, 180–85, 188–201).

[33] *See* W. CROSSKEY, POLITICS AND THE CONSTITUTION IN THE HISTORY OF THE UNITED STATES 352–57 (1st ed. 1953).

[34] The word "contract" has defined a mode of transferring title (pp. 162–63) as well as a method of ensuring expectation damages (pp. 173–77).

[35] The word "negligence" has meant nonfeasance (pp. 85–87) as well as misfeasance or carelessness (pp. 94–99).

through a contract mode of analysis, rather than a tort model. This choice of analytical framework made it much less likely that judges would impose liability for tortious acts, because they would presume that parties had (at least impliedly) defined their rights and liabilities according to a contract with risks rationally analyzed and appropriately compensated.[36]

Carrying the analysis still further, Horwitz shows how different theoretical models within the chosen doctrines profoundly influenced results. In the law of competition, he argues, judges' differing models on how best to promote economic development (as expressed in the *Charles River Bridge* case) led to opposite holdings.[37] In the law of insurance, those judges using the "actuarial risk" model were prepared to enforce liability against insurers when judges adhering to an earlier model of "implied warranties" would not (pp. 226–37). In the law of contract, taking "implied contract" or "express contract" as the model could result in widely disparate damage judgments (pp. 170–72, 180, 185–86).

Moving to a third level, Horwitz seeks to demonstrate how changes in the character of business and legal practice resulted in different judicial modes of analysis. Each new business practice—the organization of national commodities markets (pp. 173–80), the technology of water power (pp. 40–41, 49–52), the strategies of dispute settling among merchants (pp. 145–59, 167–70)—influenced lawmakers and shaped legal doctrine. Lying behind all of these developments is Horwitz's posited lawyer-merchant alliance, which made the law's broadscale push for economic progress possible. Of course Horwitz is not the first to suggest that economics was the major shaping force in nineteenth-century legal history.[38] In this book, however; he has contributed

---

[36] *See* text accompanying note 15 *supra.*

[37] *See* text accompanying notes 13–14 *supra.*

[38] *See, e.g.,* L. FRIEDMAN, A HISTORY OF AMERICAN LAW (1973); W. HURST, LAW AND THE CONDITIONS OF FREEDOM IN THE NINETEENTH CENTURY UNITED STATES (1956).

the fullest analysis to date of the characteristics of the economic environment and their effect on the intellectual concepts of nineteenth-century lawmakers.

Horwitz's intellectual history draws not only on cases and economic history; he gives special weight to the influence of legal treatises.[39] Roscoe Pound noted the influence of the treatise tradition in shaping legal development in the nineteenth century, but Pound saw the process mainly as one of consistent logical refinement.[40] Horwitz's interpretation is quite different. He shows how some treatise writers' solutions to legal problems were influenced by a conservative desire to return to the simpler values of the past, while others sought to move the law forward by combining principles from disparate doctrines in a distinctly activist manner (pp. 181–83). Still other treatise writers, like Gulian C. Verplanck and John Milton Goodenow, are shown to have altered the very nature of the way men thought about law and to have been responsible for the shift to judicial policymaking and the procommercial character of the law (pp. 15–16, 181–83). Instead of a neutral development, then, the treatise tradition becomes for Horwitz a major factor in forging the lawyer-merchant alliance.

All these themes coalesce in the discussion of Joseph Story, whom Horwitz seems to regard as the most important nineteenth-century jurist. At this level, Horwitz is writing a sort of judicial biography and is seeking to correct earlier writing on Story.[41] Horwitz has Story participating at every stage of nineteenth-century legal development and shows how the philosophy of Story's opinions mirrored most of the changes in law. In the early years of the cen-

---

[39] For Horwitz's views on the importance of the treatise writers, see Horwitz, *Treatise Literature*, 69 LAW. LIB. J. 460 (1976). For an excellent recent article on nineteenth-century American legal history, also drawing on the treatise literature, see White, *The Intellectual Origins of Torts in America*, 86 YALE L.J. 671 (1977).

[40] R. POUND, *supra* note 27, at 138–67.

[41] *E.g.*, G. DUNNE, JUSTICE JOSEPH STORY AND THE RISE OF THE SUPREME COURT (1971); J. MCCLELLAN, JOSEPH STORY AND THE AMERICAN CONSTITUTION (1971). For Horwitz's criticism of these works, see Horwitz, *The Conservative Tradition, supra* note 3, at 283–94.

tury, Story wrote from an eighteenth-century natural law perspective in *United States v. Coolidge*,[42] which announced the inevitable existence of a federal common law of crimes.[43] A few years later, however, Story's treatise on conflict of laws adopted a positivistic position and announced that each independent sovereignty was free to make its own laws.[44]

Horwitz suggests that Story's leading opinion on riparian rights, *Tyler v. Wilkinson*,[45] is a transparent attempt to reconcile a welter of conflicting doctrines, while leaving some freedom for courts to reassess riparian rights as the needs of the times changed (pp. 38–39). Nevertheless, Story in his *Dartmouth College*[46] and *Charles River Bridge*[47] opinions, again reflecting prevailing sentiments, indicates his belief that the state could not cavalierly meddle with private property. When Story ultimately writes *Swift v. Tyson*[48] in 1842, it seems, on the surface at least, as if he has returned to the discredited natural law viewpoint. In *Swift*, he announces the existence of a general law of commerce for which the federal courts are to be the ultimate authority,[49] much like his earlier opinion on federal jurisdiction over common law crimes.

Story's seeming judicial schizophrenia can be explained. For Horwitz, Story's early work on conflict of laws and his opinion in *Coolidge* mark an attempt to promote America's political development, while his later opinion in *Swift* is aimed at encouraging economic progress. Like his brethren generally, Story embraced a flexible jurisprudence when economic initiatives required encouragement, but staunchly defended vested property rights when the security of in-

---

[42] 25 F. Cas. 619 (D. Mass. 1813) (No. 14,857), *rev'd,* 14 U.S. (1 Wheat.) 191 (1816).

[43] *Id.* at 619.

[44] J. STORY, COMMENTARIES ON CONFLICT OF LAWS § 7 (1st ed. 1834).

[45] 24 F. Cas. 472 (C.C.D.R.I. 1827) (No. 14,312).

[46] 17 U.S. (4 Wheat.) 250, 335–37 (1819).

[47] 36 U.S. (11 Pet.) 341, 504–05 (1837) (dissenting opinion).

[48] 41 U.S. (16 Pet.) 1 (1842).

[49] *Id.* at 17–18.

vestment demanded protection. While Story could occasionally be out of step with other judges in his perception of the country's best interests,[50] no one outdid him in attempting to formulate a new American law designed to ensure commercial progress. What motivated Story? That he was a bank president, as well as a Supreme Court Justice, and thus a charter card-carrying member of the lawyer-merchant alliance[51] is presumably of some significance for Horwitz.

With this comprehensive examination of doctrinal development, intellectual history, economic reality, and judicial biography, Horwitz has built the strongest case against Pound to date. No one who seeks to write in this area will be able to ignore this book, and Horwitz's hypotheses about the scope and the nature of doctrinal change have been so carefully constructed that it is difficult to imagine their being convincingly refuted in the near future. In short, the book is a tour-de-force and may well be, as its jacket triumphantly proclaims, "[o]ne of the five most significant books ever published in the field of American legal history."[52]

C. The Relevance of Horwitz

The basic lessons Horwitz offers are first, that diverse forces—moral, political, and economic—go into making the law, and second, that the law does *not* develop along strictly logical lines. Moreover, Horwitz's work teaches that different cultural forces are prominent at different times as the character of society itself changes. Thus, vastly dissimilar areas of substantive law often develop in parallel fashion, and radical shifts occur as new values take prominence in the minds of judges. The course of the law, then, is not a straight-line development but, as is true of societies gener-

[50] His opinion in *Coolidge,* 25 F. Cas. 619 (D. Mass. 1813) (No. 14,857), was reversed, 14 U.S. (1 Wheat.) 191 (1816), and he dissented in *Charles River Bridge,* 36 U.S. (4 Wheat.) 250 (1819).

[51] *But see* G. DUNNE, *supra* note 41, at 141-44 (1970) (Story's bank presidency viewed as a quasi-public service).

[52] The comment is attributed to Professor William E. Nelson, New York University. Professor Nelson circumspectly did not list the other four; neither will I.

ally,[53] one of staged growth. Ultimately, legal history in the Horwitz mold can demonstrate that American law is a reflection of different philosophies of American life and that the meaning of law must be understood in this broader cultural context.

To a great extent, Horwitz begins where law schools leave off. The modern contract doctrines of "consent," "bargain," and "consideration" are still preeminent (or at least ambient);[54] property is still viewed as a tool of the individual in the marketplace; "free competition" is the goal of antitrust law; and "negligence" is central to torts. In illuminating the cultural derivations of these various doctrines, an approach like Horwitz's could go far towards burning away the fog that shrouds our law students.

If any consensus on the goal of legal education exists today, it is that law students should be imbued with the sense that law is "much more than a complex of rules for settling disputes between litigants in court."[55] In George Haskins' summation, law "is both an anchor to tradition and a vehicle for change—a pressure upon social organization and a device for accommodating new and emerging forces."[56] Legal history like that wrought by Horwitz can sharpen students' awareness of law's use as a vehicle for social change, and thus complement learning in the substantive law courses that seek to demonstrate uses of the law in society.

The unique role that courses or writings in legal history can have is to delineate "social purpose."[57] It is through the study of history that overarching cultural ideals are made more intelligible. The notion that legal history should be

[53] W. ROSTOW, THE STAGES OF ECONOMIC GROWTH (2d ed. 1971).

[54] *See generally* Henderson, Book Review, 124 U. PA. L. REV. 1466 (1976). The exaggerated report of the demise of these doctrines is to be found in G. GILMORE, THE DEATH OF CONTRACT (1974). For a sample of the controversy Gilmore has prompted, see Speidel, *An Essay on the Reputed Death and Continued Validity of Contract*, 27 STAN. L. REV. 1161 (1975).

[55] Haskins, *The Legal Heritage of Plymouth Colony*, 110 U. PA. L. REV. 847, 850 (1962).

[56] *Id.* at 851.

[57] The phrase "social purpose" is used by George Haskins in opposition to the other function of law, maintaining "social organization." *Id.*

primarily concerned with the discovery, articulation, and evaluation of the values that have shaped and guided the legal past is the central insight and organizing principle of Horwitz's book. By comparing and contrasting the legal doctrines which were spun out in response to the change in ideologies from the eighteenth to the nineteenth century, Horwitz dramatizes the spectrum of needs and interests that American law has served in the past. By stressing what he believes to be the "disproportionate" share of American wealth and power that some groups received from nineteenth-century law, and by showing precisely which legal changes achieved this misallocation, Horwitz invites legal reform, or at least debate in the classroom. By suggesting that legal doctrines represent political and moral choices, he makes it difficult for the student of law to approach legal problems as matters of purely logical analysis.

A little more than a decade ago, it seemed to a perceptive observer of American law and life that American legal history was a "Dark Continent."[58] "Decades pass," he wrote, "and, while lawyers, judges, and law professors repeat platitudes about their glorious professional past, they find no respectable place for legal history in their extensive curricula."[59] The problem, as this critic saw it, was that the history of American private law—the body of doctrines taught to law students and practiced by most lawyers—remained unexplored,[60] and thus the materials for passing on American legal history to law students were unavailable. Horwitz, Willard Hurst, William Nelson, Lawrence Friedman, G. Edward White, and others are now supplying these materials,[61] and, if Horwitz's success at Harvard is not atypical, the time may be coming when law students will not consider their legal education complete without a course in legal history. But should the interpretations supplied by

[58] D. Boorstin, The Americans: The National Experience 444 (1965) [hereinafter D. Boorstin, The Americans]. Boorstin, who is now best known as a generalist-historian of American culture, began his work in legal history. *See* D. Boorstin, The Mysterious Science of the Law (1941); Boorstin, *supra* note 24.

[59] D. Boorstin, The Americans, *supra* note 58, at 444.

[60] *Id.*

[61] For a discussion of Willard Hurst's contribution, see Gordon, *supra* note 24,

Horwitz be the ones passed on to this new generation of
legal history students?

III. Evaluating the Revision: Horwitz's Alternative
To the Conservative Tradition

A. The Polemical Challenge

The Transformation of American Law persuasively demonstrates that nineteenth-century judges altered legal doctrines in a manner that promoted certain social policies,
usually economic development. To this extent, Horwitz suc-
ceeds in his effort to show that nineteenth-century lawyers
and judges were neither objective nor politically neutral.[62]
In a society that purports to be governed by the popular
will on most nonconstitutional issues, the place of the judge
is a tenuous one. The basic justification for the institution
in America seems to have been that judges would decide
cases impartially and would act as agents of the entire populace, in whose best interests they were to resolve
disputes.[63] Some states subject judges to election to keep
them responsive to the people, but in other states and the
federal system, good behavior tenure gives a measure of political independence that needs to be justified in a democratic society. If Horwitz is correct about the ideological
struggles that went on in nineteenth-century law, and also
correct in asserting that judges tipped the legal scales to
give emerging entrepreneurial and manufacturing groups
a disproportionate share of wealth and power in American
society, then perhaps the judicial institution has proved inconsistent with basic American democratic beliefs. If there

---

and on American legal history generally, see L. FRIEDMAN, *supra* note 38, G.
WHITE, THE AMERICAN JUDICIAL TRADITION (1976), and W. NELSON, *supra* note 5.
In addition to the authors mentioned in the text, see M. BLOOMFIELD, *supra* note
7, and W. HOLT, ESSAYS IN NINETEENTH CENTURY AMERICAN LEGAL HISTORY
(1976).
    [62] Unless, of course, one is prepared to assume that the goal of economic growth
is an "objective" or "politically neutral" goal.
    [63] G. WOOD, *supra* note 5, at 453–63.

is a polemical message in Horwitz, then, it might be that we should redress the imbalances in private law created by nineteenth-century judges and should either restructure the institution of judging, or frankly acknowledge that it is not as objective as it purports to be.

Standing alone, however, *The Transformation of American Law* is not enough to support a movement for radical legal reform. Although Horwitz is brilliant and provocative, the case has not yet been made that the weak and relatively powerless segments of American society were legally overwhelmed by nineteenth-century anti-democratic judges.

As I understand it, the argument for judicial betrayal of the masses depends on the fact that the judges fostered commercial doctrines and attitudes in the face of a clearly dominant "precommercial consciousness" particularly among rural and religious Americans. These people, who presumably made up the majority of American society, are pictured by Horwitz as resisting the judicial implementation of the rules of the market economy and as being the economic losers when those rules were enforced (pp. 253–54).

B. "Losers" as Winners

Horwitz himself concedes that the group he regards as losers were still a powerful force (p. 210). Furthermore, he occasionally acknowledges changes in nineteenth-century law that clearly favored their interests. The good-faith possession statutes, widely passed in the first half of the nineteenth century, offered some measure of protection to occupying claimants whether or not they had good legal title. Although one such law was invalidated by the Supreme Court,[64] and Chancellor Kent blasted good-faith possession laws in his *Commentaries,*[65] Horwitz concedes that the laws remained in effect in most states (pp. 61–62). While the statutes did serve to protect speculating sellers, they also must have been a great benefit to small farmers and squatters.

---

[64] Green v. Biddle, 21 U.S. (8 Wheat.) 1 (1823).
[65] 2 J. KENT, COMMENTARIES ON AMERICAN LAW *337–38 (4th ed. 1840).

Similarly, Horwitz admits that, at least in Massachusetts, courts eventually cushioned the impact of the infamous mill acts (pp. 52–53). Interpretation of the acts in the early part of the century had favored mill owners over other riparians; the owners were permitted to flood neighboring properties and amortize their damages, resulting in a forced loan from those whose lands were damaged. In 1830, however, the Massachusetts legislature responded to dissatisfaction with the mill acts by permitting the recovery of permanent damages. In the next few years, says Horwitz, the Massachusetts courts read the mill acts more narrowly, resulting in greater damage liability for mill owners who flooded adjoining property (p. 52). The beneficiaries of this trend, of course, were not the entrepreneurial mill owners, but their agricultural neighbors.

While most private law doctrines that were litigated in the appellate courts support Horwitz's thesis of merchant and entrepreneurial ascendancy in the law, there must have been many other legal developments in the nineteenth century that had little to do with these groups. For example, *The Transformation of American Law* tells us relatively little about the effects of legislative action, although Horwitz occasionally hints that state legislatures were pressured into passing legislation antithetical to commercial interests (pp. 211, 243). Other action by state legislatures may have had a significant social impact on American life in realms apart from economics.[66] If we were able to add up the impact of the court decisions Horwitz reviews, and somehow compare this with the impact of other forms of law on nineteenth-century society, we might find that the overall result was very different from that which Horwitz's court decisions alone reveal.

Finally, even if Horwitz is correct in viewing nineteenth-century legal development as a tale of great gains by mer-

---

[66] *E.g.,* R. M. Cover, Justice Accused 63–82 (1975) (legislative action to free slaves); L. Friedman, *supra* note 38, at 182 (liberalization of divorce laws); Presser, *The Historical Background of the American Law of Adoption,* 11 J. Fam. L. 443, 465–89 (1976) (legislation permitting legal adoption of children).

chants and entrepreneurs, it does not necessarily follow that these gains came at the expense of other groups such as farmers and consumers. Horwitz does not give us any examination of "free-riders"—the filtering down of economic gains to society generally.[67] For all we know, most of the consumers and farmers, in absolute terms, were better off after the nineteenth-century legal changes than before. In addition, Horwitz's assertion that definable "classes" in American society could be characterized as "gainers" or "losers" in legal development may be wrong. Perhaps in nineteenth-century America, particularly in the West, people moved so freely from one occupational group to another that attempts to draw sharp distinctions between "farmers" and "merchants" distort social reality. Twentieth-century social classifications may be anachronistic in the nineteenth century.[68]

C. Alternative Interpretations

Horwitz's work is most impressive not because it demonstrates the ascendance of any particular group in the law, but because it suggests that the development of American law reflects a continuing struggle between competing economic and social interests. Just as modern American law is composed of different doctrines promoting both certainty or predictability *and* equity, perhaps the American law of the nineteenth century is also a mass of doctrines with contrary purposes. Horwitz makes relatively few references to American private law development in places other than the eastern seaboard. From preliminary work on western law, however, one gets the impression that western private law doctrines and even styles of judicial reasoning may have

[67] This is not properly a criticism of Horwitz, since a major macro-economic study would have been beyond the scope of his undertaking.

[68] Horwitz may have a better case for his proposition in the Northeast, from which he draws much of his data, than in the rest of the country. On the notion of fluid society in nineteenth-century America, see D. BOORSTIN, THE AMERICANS, *supra* note 58, at 113–61.

differed sharply from those in the East.[69] When American legal historians are able to synthesize data on *all* American private law in the nineteenth century, their conclusions may be that the course of American legal history is far more diverse than that presented in *The Transformation of American Law.*

Even if developments in other parts of the country are relatively insignificant, and even if Horwitz is correct about the freezing of legal doctrines in a procommercial mode, his conclusions about the triumph of the merchant-lawyer elite and its *disproportionate* gains may not hold. While nineteenth-century legal change promoted economic development and commerce, it may well have done so not to protect any one favored segment of the economy, but to promote economic and social mobility generally. In the limited sense that the law may have provided equal economic opportunity for those willing and able to learn the techniques of commerce and for those able to employ native intelligence, inventiveness, and shrewdness, the law may have been much more democratic than Horwitz suggests. If one can take nineteenth-century legal commentators at face value,[70] one can read some of Horwitz's evidence as supporting this legal fostering of the development of native abilities. Thus, Gulian Verplanck's insistence in his *Essay on the Doctrine of Contracts* that contractors be permitted to capitalize on "peculiar advantages of skill, shrewdness, and experience"[71] may reflect a desire to encourage those with na-

[69] For example, Daniel Boorstin has suggested that the rule of prior appropriation in water rights, which Horwitz believes went out of favor in the early nineteenth century, was still alive in the West in 1866 when it was codified in federal law. *Id.* at 80. Boorstin believes that the principle of priority continued strong in western law until the end of the nineteenth century. *Id.* In addition, it has been argued that "formalism" was not dominant in the West in the late nineteenth century, and that the whole idea of ascendancy and decline of instrumentalist jurisprudence is open to question. Scheiber, *Instrumentalism and Property Rights: A Reconsideration of American "Styles of Judicial Reasoning" in the Nineteenth Century,* 1975 WIS. L. REV. 1, 12–17.

[70] Admittedly, a dangerous assumption. *See, e.g.,* Katz, *Looking Backward: The Early History of American Law,* 33 U. CHI. L. REV. 867, 881–82 (1966).

[71] G. VERPLANCK, AN ESSAY ON THE DOCTRINE OF CONTRACTS: BEING AN INQUIRY HOW CONTRACTS ARE AFFECTED IN LAW AND MORALS 135 (1825).

tive talent to rise in stature according to their abilities. Similarly, one can read the New York Court for the Correction of Errors' opinion that Livingston and Fulton were entitled to an injunction to protect their steamboat monopoly as a way "to compensate genius for introducing, extending, and perfecting, the invention of others."[72] The whole trend in water rights and negligence cases that promoted the development of industry at the expense of landed wealth may, in fact, be as much a weakening of the *rentier* interest as it was a blow to the small farmers. In short, before we can safely generalize we need to know more about who the real winners and losers were in nineteenth-century legal development.

Part of our difficulties may be solved if Horwitz, or another legal or economic historian, is able to link up the theories discussed here with the actual social composition of the merchant and entrepreneurial class. One immediate problem is that we need to know more about the supposed split in the commercial interest that Horwitz says developed in the early nineteenth century (p. 154). Horwitz discusses this split only in the context of marine insurance (pp. 228–37) and his discussion seems to suggest that there, at least, the law eventually promoted the interests of the insured, not the insurers. Since the insured were arguably smaller enterprises, this instance of the merchant "split" may have resulted in the law's favoring less powerful economic interests. If this result can be generalized to other areas of the merchant community, it may be difficult to read nineteenth-century law as a well organized movement of the most powerful interests to crush the weakest.

Finally, to test whether some groups in American society managed *disproportionate* gains in nineteenth-century law, one ought really to compare the American legal experience with that of other countries. Horwitz provides some hints in his references to English developments. Horwitz's model of an increasingly stratified society seems to fit England much

[72] Livingston v. Van Ingen, 9 Johns. 507, 547 (N.Y. 1812) (argument of counsel); *see id.* at 560 (opinion of Yates, J.).

better than America, and contemporary English law does seem to have given certain groups a disproportionate influence to a greater degree than did American law.[73]

Both English and American law appear to show a reworking of commercial law to favor merchant interests.[74] But it appears that the merchant interest, at least in the area of marine insurance, was more homogeneous in England than in America. American law favored tenants, by permitting them to profit from their improvements as early as 1829 (pp. 55–56). In England, tenants had to wait until the 1880's to win comparable rights.[75] Similarly, the English rule for breach of title warranty in a land sale was less favorable to tenant farmers (or the "industrious citizen or mechanic") than the American rule (pp. 58–62).[76] Nineteenth-century English tort law did not encourage the instrumental uses of property to the extent American law did. England enforced strict liability in trespass after America had begun to implement the negligence doctrine (p. 94), and English courts apparently tended to give damages in nuisance actions with more consistency than did American courts.[77] Finally, in the beginning of the nineteenth century the English courts were restraining competition through the granting of injunctions to franchise holders at a time when American courts favored competition (p. 122). In short, while both English and American law promoted commercial developments through commercial law, the English law of property, torts, and competition appeared to favor vested

[73] *Compare* D. BOORSTIN, THE AMERICANS, *supra* note 58, at 65–90 *with* W. WILLCOX, THE AGE OF ARISTOCRACY 1688 TO 1830, at 256–61 (3d ed. 1976).

[74] On the process in England, see Horwitz's references to the work of Lord Mansfield in the late eighteenth century (pp. 18, 114, 142–44, 148, 155, 168, 170–71, 174, 178–80, 189–94, 214, 219 & 227).

[75] W. ARNSTEIN, BRITAIN YESTERDAY AND TODAY 145 (3d ed. 1976).

[76] The American position was implemented at first through litigation that expressly rejected the English rule, and later, after the English rule was apparently adopted by the courts, through "good faith possession" statutes (pp. 58–62).

[77] This is suggested by Horwitz's observation that it was only *after* 1865 that English courts "acknowledge[d] that a process of weighing utilities and not the mere existence of injury was necessary for deciding whether a particular use of land constituted a nuisance" (p. 75).

property interests to a greater degree than the American law did. In the nineteenth century at least, it seems plausible that English law tended to produce greater disproportionate wealth and power (in the landed property class), than American law did (in a merchant and entrepreneurial class).

Conclusion

None of the criticisms advanced here disprove the Horwitz thesis, of course, but before legal scholars accept his alternative to the conservative tradition in legal history, more must be learned about the social and economic effects of the doctrines that Horwitz analyzes. There is a chapter in Doestoyevsky's *The Brothers Karamazov,* [78] in which Christ returns to earth, to sixteenth-century Seville, and is lectured by the Grand Inquisitor on the shortcomings of Christian teaching. The Grand Inquisitor points out to Christ that men are perfectly willing, indeed eager to live by bread alone, and that the organized church has done them a tremendous favor by offering them sustenance in return for their freedom. Free choice between good and evil, explains the Grand Inquisitor, is a terrible burden and men are happier if they can be supplied miracle, mystery, and authority by the church. Doestoyevsky leaves the reader wondering whether the Grand Inquisitor and the organized church were simply lusting after power or were really rendering a service to mankind. In *The Transformation of American Law,* Professor Horwitz poses similar questions about the development of nineteenth-century American law. Was legal change benign and in the best interests of all, or was it a clandestine grab for power and wealth? Is the law, like the Grand Inquisitor, hiding its lack of objectivity behind a screen of mysterious rules and doctrines? With Doestoyevskyan passion, Horwitz has argued that nineteenth-century law was an instrument of injustice. As with the Russian master, when one finishes Horwitz's book, one isn't quite sure.

[78] F. DOSTOYEVSKY, THE BROTHERS KARAMAZOV 227–44 (Signet Classics ed. 1957).

Losing the World
of the Massachusetts Whig*

∽ Hendrik Hartog ∾

IN A DEFIANT STANCE[1] is the fifth book John Reid has published in a little more than a decade.[2] He has written two biographies of important nineteenth-century judges, two studies of Cherokee legal institutions, and now this, his first book on the legal context of the American Revolution. These are not insignificant subjects. His learning is immense. And Professor Reid writes with rhetorical grace and a personal voice that are immediately recognizable. Yet he remains a relatively elusive figure in American legal scholarship. Most of his work has been favorably reviewed by the

---

*A review of John P. Reid, *In a Defiant Stance: The Conditions of Law in Massachusetts Bay, the Irish Comparison, and the Coming of the American Revolution* (University Park, Pa., 1977). This essay originally appeared in 54 IND. L. J. 65 (1978). It is reprinted by permission of the *Indiana Law Journal*.

[1] J. REID, IN A DEFIANT STANCE: THE CONDITIONS OF LAW IN MASSACHUSETTS BAY, THE IRISH COMPARISON, AND THE COMING OF THE AMERICAN REVOLUTION (1977) [hereinafter IN A DEFIANT STANCE].

[2] CHIEF JUSTICE: THE JUDICIAL WORLD OF CHARLES DOE (1967); AN AMERICAN JUDGE: MARMADUKE DENT OF WEST VIRGINIA (1968); A LAW OF BLOOD: THE PRIMITIVE LAW OF THE CHEROKEE NATION (1970); A BETTER KIND OF HATCHET: LAW, TRADE, AND DIPLOMACY IN THE CHEROKEE NATION DURING THE EARLY YEARS OF EUROPEAN CONTACT (1976).

specialists whose interests intersect with his own; but his books have only infrequently been presented as important to the ordinary legal reader.[3]

The problem may be that John Reid remains committed to a monographic tradition which maintains that one obligation of scholarship is to study and apprehend specific and limited subjects. He lacks that flair for the "big think," for the tendentious argument or the portentous exclamation which a generation of television watchers might demand from their scholarship, if not from their cereal. It is not that he is a modest man; nor are his books shaped by a narrow and dogmatic belief in the particularity of human experience. Professor Reid's works are graced with comparative insights, with allusions and references to modern analogies, with a concern for the social context of law. But John Reid has never claimed that his work can explain "everything." One senses that he would rather the pleasures of a fox, of knowing some things, than those of a hedgehog, in an age when hedgehogs get all the glory.[4]

Professor Reid's new book is a comparative study of the conditions of law and of imperial control in prerevolutionary Massachusetts Bay and in oppressed—or unsuccessfully revolutionary—Ireland. The point of this exercise is not to establish a general model of the role of law in revolution, although the comparative study of revolutions is a well-established theme in modern social science. Several generations of historical sociologists, political scientists, anthropologists, and even historians have drawn scholarly sustenance from metahistorical notions of "revolution" drawn from or applied to the French Revolution, the American Revolution, and the more recent political upheavals of the twentieth century.[5] What Professor Reid is after in his

---

[3] But see, Nelson, Book Review, 44 U. Chi. L. Rev. 911 (1977).

[4] See I. Berlin, The Hedgehog and the Fox (1954).

[5] Of such scholarly enterprise, George Lichtheim once wrote,

To suppose, . . . that "the phenomenon of revolution" can be meaningfully discussed in suprahistorical terms such as "violence," or related to mythical events ("Cain slew Abel and Romulus slew Remus"), is to obliterate several centuries of thought starting with Vico if not Machiavelli. This is not conser-

comparison of Ireland and Massachusetts is very different, though. For him it is the failure to shake off English rule in Ireland that focuses and shapes his vision of the American success. That English legal institutions could be mobilized as effective tools of repression in Ireland at the same time that they were so eminently unsuccessful in prosperous Massachusetts Bay raises the central empirical question that *In a Defiant Stance* answers: How did they (the revolutionary Whigs of Massachusetts Bay and other colonies in British North America) get away with it?

Since World War II, historians of the American Revolution have made the question of motivation—of why "they" did it—the central concern of study.[6] Professor Reid, by contrast, takes the presence of adequate motivation as a given and asks the reader to consider what an easy time of it the Americans had in making their revolution. Not a single Whig was ever forced to stand trial for sedition or treason, no matter how outrageous his attack on English authority.[7] As a result, American patriots were robbed of those martyrs who could "inspire the young or embolden the hesitant." But "no colonist could be a martyr to a law unable to touch him."[8]

The leading American Whigs could go about the business of making a revolution without fear of arrest or attack by imperial authority because it was they—the Whigs—who controlled the effective legal institutions of colonial society. To act as an agent of the crown left one at the legal mercy of any merchant or Whig aggrieved by one's actions. British officers and customs officials who attempted to enforce imperial law could expect to be sued for damages before a jury. And even if the superior court of judicature—the highest court of the province—ruled that a royal official could not incur private-law liability in the exercise of his

---

vative empiricism but mere dogmatism—as doctrinaire as anything produced by the most extreme rationalists.

　　　　　　　　　See G. LICHTHEIM, TWO REVOLUTIONS 118 (1967).

[6] See text accompanying *infra* note 38.

[7] IN A DEFIANT STANCE, *supra* note 1, at 3.

[8] *Id.* at 5.

public responsibilities, juries were free to rule otherwise. "The law was emphatic: a motion for a new trial could not be granted on the ground that the jury had disregarded the court's instruction. In Massachusetts the civil jury's verdict was truly final."[9] Likewise, local justices of the peace could not implement the Quartering Act when British troops first landed in Boston. That statute obliged local justices of the peace to procure various supplies for the enlisted men:

> It was an extremely unpopular law and the justices of Boston refused to enforce it. General Thomas Gage thought they were afraid of the whig crowd. We may think they were following their whig predilections. Yet it is possible that we as well as Gage would be wrong. The magistrates may have been afraid, not of the whig mob but of the whig jury. It is unlikely that even a militant tory justice would have dared requisition candles or firewood without first being certain he was immune from an action of conversion or trover. . . . The magistrate did not worry that the owner would not be reimbursed. He worried that the owner would sue him for the seizure even if reimbursed [by the army]. The payment by the military might be a good defense at law, but the plaintiff could always avoid a ruling on the issue by denying the fact, thus bringing the question before a whig jury. The imperial government might enforce its quartering statutes in Ireland, but in America even its friends could be frozen into political inactivity by the thought of a Massachusetts jury.[10]

Professor Reid's point is not that the revolutionary Whigs of Massachusetts Bay and elsewhere were manipulating legal institutions and subverting the authority of English law. To the contrary, it is his contention that the institutional practices of eighteenth century Massachusetts reflected a legitimate, although no longer dominant, theory of English law. The "conditions" of law in Massachusetts were not yet those of a modern centralized state. Authority was diffuse and decentralized; the legitimacy and the potency of local legal institutions were not dependent on the support and

---

[9]*Id.* at 31 (footnote omitted).
[10]*Id.* at 42 (footnote omitted).

the acquiescence of a central authority.[11] The terms of a positivist jurisprudence that considers law as nothing but the command of a sovereign and unitary state could have had only a limited meaning in prerevolutionary Massachusetts.[12] (By contrast, those terms might have had a general but not absolute applicability in England itself after the Glorious Revolution of 1688.)[13] In fact, Professor Reid demonstrates that imperial officials could not act in a society of hostile local institutions, that they were helpless without the support and acquiescence of local "law."

The thesis of *In a Defiant Stance* is that the legal context of the American Revolution was shaped by the unequal conflict between two competing conceptions of law: a Whig law of local institutions and an imperial law of parliament and of the provincial agents of the crown.[14] "In Massachusetts Bay the struggle was less between the governed and the governors than between different levels of government."[15] In contrast to Ireland, where any revolution would have to be made *against* the law—the symbol of English oppression—in Massachusetts Whigs made a revolution by enforcing *their* law, even to the point of assembling and utilizing a mob.[16] That a mob no less than a civil jury,[17] a grand jury,[18] or a governor's council[19] could be perceived and justified as a legitimate legal institution might seem to call into question the reality of a Whig theory of autonomous local institutions. If the mob is as legitimate as any other institution—is

[11] *See* Reid, *In Legitimate Stirps: The Concept of "Arbitrary," the Supremacy of Parliament and the Coming of the American Revolution*, 5 HOFSTRA L. REV. 459 (1977).

[12] Local customary rights did retain a fragile existence in parts of England throughout the eighteenth century; *see* Thompson, *The Grid of Inheritance: a comment*, in FAMILY AND INHERITANCE: RURAL SOCIETY IN WESTERN EUROPE, 1200 – 1800 328–60 (J. Goody, J. Thirsk, and E. Thompson eds. 1976).

[13] See text accompanying *infra* notes 47–51.

[14] *In a Defiant Stance, supra* note 1, at 66; in a similar vein, see D. BOORSTIN. THE GENIUS OF AMERICAN POLITICS 66–98 (1953).

[15] *In a Defiant Stance, supra* note 1, at 161.

[16] *Id.* at 160–173.

[17] *Id.* at 27–40.

[18] *Id.* at 41–54.

[19] *Id.* at 7–16.

in fact perceived as a public institution—is not that theory nothing more than a mere cover for defiance[20] or violence,[21] as other historians have charged? That Professor Reid successfully meets this charge, that he persuasively argues for a vision of the mob as a partially legal, "constitutional" institution,[22] is only one of the achievements of this book. It is, however, a lesser achievement when compared to the general picture of legal conflict within a society of largely autonomous local institutions, which is the main burden of the work. In *In a Defiant Stance*, the familiar events of the Revolution are placed in a strange context, in which strange institutions act in peculiar ways; and it is Reid's skill in leading us into this suddenly unfamiliar world of "our" revolution that marks the true significance of this book.

The Reality of Whig Law

A diagram of the public institutions of eighteenth-century Massachusetts would differ little from the institutional diagram of a modern American state, the subject matter of a high school civics lesson. There was an executive; there was a legislature; the judicial system was organized in the familiar pyramidal design, with a superior court of judicature at the apex, county courts of common pleas and of general sessions of the peace in the middle, and the lowly courts of individual justices of the peace at the bottom.[23]

[20] H. ZOBEL, THE BOSTON MASSACRE (1970).

[21] R. BROWN, STRAIN OF VIOLENCE (1975), 41–66.

[22] This achievement was presaged by his essay, *In a Defensive Rage: The Uses of the Mob, the Justification in Law, and the Coming of the American Revolution*, 49 N.Y.U.L. REV. 1043 (1974), and in the works of Pauline Maier and Gordon Wood; see Maier, *Popular Uprisings and Civil Authority in Eighteenth Century America*, WM. & MARY Q. (3d ser.) 3 (1970), and Wood, *A Note on Mobs in the American Revolution*, 23 WM. & MARY Q. (3d ser.) 635 (1966).

[23] *See* 1 LEGAL PAPERS OF JOHN ADAMS xxxviii–lii (L. Wroth and H. Zobel eds. 1965).

How representative of other colonies in North America Massachusetts was in this regard (as well as many others) has been a question of serious and continuing debate among historians. See Allen, *The Zuckerman Thesis and the Process of Legal Rationalization in Provincial Massachusetts*, 29 WM. & MARY Q. (ser. 3) 443 (1972) and Zuckerman, *Michael Zuckerman's Reply*, 29 WM. & MARY Q. (ser. 3) 461 (1972).

In the first chapters of *In a Defiant Stance,* Professor Reid enlarges and highlights portions of the diagram, that institutional "map" of Massachusetts Bay, showing how elements of the system operated in the context of the revolutionary conflict. Viewed as aspects of a system—the perspective of a Tory—those elements did not operate very well. Thomas Hutchinson wrote at one point that, "It was not easy to devise a system of subordinate government less controlled by the supreme, than the governments in the colonies."[24] The Governor's Council existed not to effect executive action but to neutralize and where possible destroy it. The civil traverse jury, as we have seen, was free of any obligation to obey the dictates of any judge. The grand jury could declare army barracks a "nuisance,"[25] indict political enemies, and most importantly, exercise a veto over the actions of Tory prosecutors. As a result, "New England Whigs did not fear arrest even for serious offenses of the type that would have left their Irish counterparts rotting in dungeons or swinging from gallows."[26]

To Tories and to the modern viewer alike the actions of these institutions appear lawless; in countermanding the orders of imperial law, local institutions were undermining respect for law in general. Without respect for a central state authority there could be no legitimacy anywhere.[27] Whigs naturally disagreed, not just because they would have severed "their" institutions from those of the British empire, but also because they saw one purpose in any legal process as being to provide an alternative to violence and self-help. According to Professor Reid, it was their restraint rather than their audacity which most impressed Whigs when they reflected on their actions.[28] In manipulating their institutions they managed to defend their rights and assert their

---

[24] IN A DEFIANT STANCE, *supra* note 1, at 8.
[25] The actual declaration of barracks as a nuisance by justices of the peace occurred in Albany, New York. *Id.* at 45.
[26] *See Id.* at 46.
[27] *Id.* at 63.
[28] *Id.* at 65–73.

constitutional arguments without lynchings, without large-scale property damage,[29] and without terrorism. It was only the control they exercised over local institutions which kept Massachusetts Bay from becoming another Ireland.

Yet there was more to the "Whig theory of law" than just a convenient justification for the exercise of institutional discretion in a political crisis. Professor Reid understandably focuses on the ways Massachusetts institutions performed in the extraordinary events of the years between 1763 and 1775. But if we were to look closely at the ways those institutions handled their ordinary business, it would soon be obvious how incomplete that "system" was and how realistic Whig assumptions of local autonomy were in the context of eighteenth-century Massachusetts.[30]

By any modern standard, the Massachusetts legal "system" was no system at all; the very idea of describing Massachusetts local institutions as aspects of a system is as anachronistic as an assertion of Whig law would be today. Consider the administration of justice through the county courts of general sessions of the peace. Between 1692 and the 1780's the legislature and the superior court had only the most rudimentary control over the court structure of the province. The act of 1692 which established the county courts declared that sessions courts could hear any case relating to the conservation of the peace. No attempt was made to define or delimit what that meant. Instead, the legislature limited itself to a schedule for the meetings of the various county courts and descriptions of how appeals might be carried to the superior court, the process of jury selection, and the requisite format for appeals from the criminal judgments of individual justices of the peace.[31]

The whole history of county sessions courts prior to the

---

[29] The great exception to this claim, an exception which worried and disturbed the Whigs themselves, was the sacking and burning of Thomas Hutchinson's house. *Id.* at 76, 83.

[30] The following four paragraphs are drawn substantially from my article, Hartog, *The Public Law of a County Court; Judicial Government in Eighteenth Century Massachusetts*, 20 AM. J. LEG. HIST. 282 (1976).

[31] Act of 1692–93, Ch. 33, 1 Mass. Bay Province Laws 72.

Revolution was marked by a singular lack of legislative attention. Occasional acts were passed specifying the terms of a particular criminal offense cognizable by sessions courts, but until the late 1780s the General Court (the Massachusetts legislature) never tried to direct the activities of the courts. The General Court might indicate areas of province-wise concern through legislation which the courts were in theory bound to enforce. But even that formal power of the legislature over the local court might be ignored when it suited the interests of the court.

In September 1768, for example, the owners of a milldam in Malden petitioned the Middlesex County sessions court to be relieved from their obligation to build a passageway ensuring the free passage of fish downstream, an obligation defined and reinforced by a steady stream of legislation throughout the eighteenth century. The owners of the dam recognized that there was a provincial statute which explicitly ordered them to maintain a right of way for fish, but they asked the court to excuse them both from compliance and from liability "because the Petit. do not think themselves obliged by Law to make such passage way . . . ," and they asked the court to appoint a committee of three disinterested persons to investigate the "necessity" of such a construction. The court agreed and appointed a committee, which made the following report:

> [T]o open a passage way in the same Dam would be a much greater Damage to the Publick than the Fish that might [pass] through the Same Passage Way would be of Advantage, as it appears that there would be but few, if any.

This report was accepted by the whole court, and the prayer of the petition was granted. The petitioners had asked the court to balance a clear legislative directive against the presumed benefits of not enforcing that statute. The petitioners had argued that statutory law, the law of the General Court, need not be the "law" of the Middlesex sessions court.[32] Though lacking in the political context of

[32] Hartog, *supra* note 30, at 314–15.

revolutionary conflict, one can hardly imagine a more direct assertion of the autonomy of local "Whig" law.

Or, consider the entire court system, as a system. Despite the apparently integrated hierarchical structure through which we might expect the superior court of judicature to assert its authority over the lesser judicial agencies of the province, in all ordinary civil or criminal cases, "appeal" meant not a review at a higher level of the legal basis for a decision but rather a new trial. Only in some regulatory cases could a decision of the sessions court be reviewed on certiorari, and even that was a matter of some controversy as late as the 1760s. By the early eighteenth century the principles of certiorari—of control of local institutions through a review of the record by central agencies—was well established in England. But in eighteenth-century America appeal still had less to do with the functional integration of a legal system or the control of administrative discretion than with the financial ability of litigants to change the legal level of their dispute.[33] There was no system, only a variety of discrete and distinctive institutions.

Whig law was more than just a politically motivated response to the demands of an imperial and centralizing authority; rather, it was a largely accurate description of working institutions. Implicit within that description there remained at least a residual recognition of the ultimate authority of the British parliament. But central authority was ineffectual—a fact best demonstrated by the course of the prerevolutionary crisis itself—so long as the troops were not called in. And the Whig theory of law was grounded both in a perception of the autonomy of local legal institutions as independent recipients of constitutional power and authority, and in a realistic appreciation of the relative ineffectuality of all governmental institutions whether local or central.

[I]n the Anglo-American tradition of government . . . government did not have vast bureaucratic armies of officials to

[33]*Id.* 285–86, 314–15.

enforce its laws, but instead relied on its subjects to aid the few officials who did exist in their task of law enforcement.[34]

There was no police force during those days; constables and sheriffs did not do what today would be called police work. The constables' job was to summon jurors, not to keep the peace. The sheriff and his deputies were available for making arrests, though not trained for much except serving writs. For maintaining peace Massachusetts law depended upon citizen participation.[35]

Institutions of government could not function at all without the involvement and the participation of local publics. And in so far as local institutions could hope to perform their "jobs"—the maintenance of peace and order, the suppression of crime and violence, the administration of public works, and so forth—they needed to enlist the support and the interest of their constituencies. In the absence of effective instruments of centralized control, in the absence of a positivist monopoly of violence by the state, a "Whig" model of decentralized, locally responsive institutions might have been the only available model for reasonably effective government.[36]

The Reasonableness of Revolution.

In a Defiant Stance is unmistakeably a "neo-Whig" book; it depends on a foundation of scholarship built up by Bernard Bailyn and other so-called neo-Whig revolutionary historians of the 1950s and 1960s.[37] Yet, it is not just another

---

[34] W. NELSON, THE AMERICANIZATION OF THE COMMON LAW 34 (1975).

[35] IN A DEFIANT STANCE *supra* note 1, at 77.

[36] *See Id.* at 77–78.

[37] To say that much of Reid's argument is dependent on a Bailynesque view of Whig motivation is not to say that Professor Reid is an acolyte at a neo-Whig shrine. Indeed, I believe that the origin of this book lies in his dissatisfaction with the treatment accorded the legal arguments of the colonists by professional historians. I was a student in Professor Reid's course in "Legal Thought in American History" at New York University in the fall of 1972, and much of that course was devoted to the development of a perception of the appropriateness of the legal rhetoric used by the Whigs in the revolutionary crises, a perception which Bernard Bailyn, with his focus on the intense and seemingly irrational nature of colonial anger and fears, had earlier rejected. See text accompanying *infra* notes 42–52.

monograph, an exercise of "normal science" within a dominant "paradigm." And to understand John Reid's contribution to the modern historiography of the Revolution, we should begain by briefly summarizing what a "neo-Whig" interpretation contributes to the historian's understanding of the events of the American Revolution.

Beginning from a perception of both the inadequacy of earlier economic determinist (often called "progressive") models of revolutionary motivation and of the relative mildness of British actions during the revolutionary crisis, historians of the 1950s and 1960s argued that the actions of the revolutionaries were rooted in a consistent and long-lived world view which justified their belief in the corruption and the conspiratorial designs of the leaders of the British empire. The American Revolution grew out of the commitment of many colonists to "old Whig" political values which had led an underground life in England ever since the Glorious Revolution of 1688.[38] Because of that commitment, conservative pillars of provincial society might respond radically to events which would not seem to us to justify such a response. Extreme actions, and ultimately revolution, became justifiable and predictable because colonists believed that they were arguing with the English over what was constitutive of their political and social order.

Underlying this explanation of the motivation for revolution is a judgment that social or economic "causes" cannot explain the decisions to revolt. Historians have been unable

---

[38] At the heart of this theory were the convictions that man in general could not withstand the temptations of power, that power was by its very nature a corrupting and aggressive force, and that liberty was its natural victim. The protection of liberty against the malignancy of power required that each of the various elements in the polity had to be balanced against one another in such a way as to prevent any of them from gaining ascendance over the rest. A mixed constitution was the means by which this delicate balance was to be achieved, but power was so pervasive and so ruthless that nothing was safe from it.

J. GREENE, THE REINTERPRETATION OF THE AMERICAN REVOLUTION (1968), 38–9. *See also* B. BAILYN, THE IDEOLOGICAL ORIGINS OF THE AMERICAN REVOLUTION (1967), B. BAILYN, THE ORIGINS OF AMERICAN POLITICS (1968), Bailyn, *Central Themes of the American Revolution,* in ESSAYS ON THE AMERICAN REVOLUTION 3 (S. Kurtz and J. Hutson eds. 1973).

to distinguish loyalists and patriots from one another by class analysis. The society which earlier historians had posited as wracked by social conflict (else why a revolution?) was found on closer examination to be by and large rather dull and provincial. Extremes of wealth and poverty existed and were growing, but most men and women lived in an agrarian world that at least as compared with England lacked a rigid or even a very perceptible class structure. The franchise was by any contemporary standard remarkably wide. And though there were political hierarchies and political elites, the signs of deference that superiors might exact from inferiors were both limited and culturally legitimated.

The achievement of Bernard Bailyn and other neo-Whigs was to force historians to honor and take seriously the explanations given by the revolutionaries themselves for their actions. Neo-Whig history has given us a consistent and compelling picture of a system of values and beliefs, of a theory of political behavior, that would explain the radical and revolutionary actions of fundamentally conservative and unrevolutionary men. It has demonstrated the seriousness of Whig beliefs, that the contentions and the justifications of the Whigs were not "mere" superstructure, rationalization, or propaganda, as earlier progressive historians had believed.

What they have not been able to demonstrate, on the other hand, is that the Whigs in Massachusetts and elsewhere really had anything to worry about. Neo-Whig historians have honored the seriousness of the revolutionaries' commitment to their beliefs; they have not taken seriously the beliefs themselves. In spite of their insistence on the meaningfulness of revolutionary ideology, neo-Whigs, like the progressive historians who preceded them, do not really take the language of the revolutionaries as expressing anything more than a psychological reality.

To progressives, language was often just a smokescreen that could only hide the real action going on elsewhere;[39]

---

[39] See CARL BECKER, THE DECLARATION OF INDEPENDENCE (1942) (the "ideas" of the revolution as abstract, Lockean philosophy), and A. M. SCHLESINGER, PRELUDE

to Bernard Bailyn, the language of the revolutionaries was an expression of an understandable and culturally validated paranoia.[40] Both views assume the ultimate unreality of the actual arguments. To say that responses to events are understandable only in the context of a particular and highly specific set of beliefs, as neo-Whigs do, is to impute a kind of dogmatism that we might hesitate to apply to ourselves. More importantly, such an assumption draws attention away from the meaningfulness of the constitutional conflict itself. For neo-Whigs, as for progressives, a dispute over constitutional principles is both abstract and highly artificial. For both of them the terms of the British constitution were clearly and finally determined by the Glorious Revolution.

Yet the central fact of the British constitution was that it might change at any time. As John Reid has written elsewhere, "An unwritten constitution must be interpreted

functionally, in terms of the existing legal institutions whose functions and procedures as they develop over centuries are accepted by both popular and professional consensus."[41] Imperial authorities might have believed that the terms of parliamentary control of the colonies had been settled by the Glorious Revolution. But they could not claim that debate over the British constitution was abstract or irrelevant

TO INDEPENDENCE: THE NEWSPAPER WAR ON GREAT BRITAIN, 1764–1776 (1958) (the "ideas" of the revolution as clever propaganda).

[40]. . . . American resistance in the 1760's and 1770's was a response to acts of power deemed arbitrary, degrading, and uncontrollable—a response, in itself objectively reasonable, that was inflamed to the point of explosion by ideological currents generating fears everywhere in America that irresponsible and self-seeking adventurers—what the twentieth century would call political gangsters—had gained the power of the English government and were turning first, for reasons that were variously explained, to that Rhineland of their aggressions, the colonies.

Inflamed sensibilities—exaggerated distrust and fear—surrounded the hard core of the Anglo-American conflict and gave it distinctive shape. These perceptions and anxieties made accommodation at first difficult and then impossible. . . .

Bailyn, *Central Themes of the Revolution,* in ESSAYS ON THE AMERICAN REVOLUTION 13 (S. Kurtz and J. Hutson eds. 1973).

[41] Reid, *In a Defensive Rage: The Uses of the Mob, the Justification in Law, and the Coming of the American Revolution,* 49 N.Y.U.L. REV. 1043, 1088 (1974).

or distanced from the society in which that debate occurred. The constitution was a description of the organization of society, and the constitution encompassed in detail and concretely all aspects of legal order and structure. Debate over the nature of the constitution was in essence a debate over the political nature of the society in which one lived.

It is in this context of the constitutional justification of revolutionary motivation that John Reid's contribution to the historiography of the revolution becomes most apparent. As we noted earlier, *In a Defiant Stance* is in the first instance a discussion of *how* the revolutionaries got away with it, a discussion of the legal technology of rebellion in Massachusetts Bay. It explicitly incorporates a neo-Whig conception of motivation into an analysis of the "conditions of law" that ensured Tory frustration.[42] But as it incorporated that neo-Whig model of motivation, *In a Defiant Stance* transforms our picture of the reasonableness of Whig fears of conspiracy and corruption. What, after all, is the comparison to Ireland but a validation of the Whig analysis of the fragility of freedom? If the institutions of imperial control could do that there, they could do something very similar in Massachusetts Bay.

To us, the contrasts between the two societies of Ireland and Massachusetts are overwhelming: the relative wealth of the American colonists, the absolute deprivation of the Irish peasantry; the vibrancy of American institutional life, the centralization of imperial administration and the corruption of local government in Ireland; the century and a half of liberty that preceded the first systematic introduction of

---

[42] It was not a desire for local rule or American nationalism that persuaded lawminded whigs such as John Adams to suppress fear of the crowd's ultimate potential and cling to their whig principles. Rather it was the constitutional theory then current that power corrupted rulers no matter how well intentioned. If government were not restrained, tyranny was unavoidable and liberty doomed. In the end the dilemma could be resolved only by individual convictions as to what was the greater danger, which alternative more dreadful and which presented the larger menace. . . .

IN A DEFIANT STANCE, *supra* note 1, at 164 [footnote omitted]; see footnote and text accompanying *infra* note 45.

parliamentary regulations and controls in 1763, on the one hand, the history of an occupied and oppressed country, on the other hand, "condemned . . . to barrenness, and its inhabitants to misery and want."[43] And John Reid is at pains to point out the contrasts between the two societies. "The legal, social, and economic worlds in which the eighteenth-century American lived," he writes, "were beyond the comprehension of the average Irishman . . . Ireland had a tradition of violence because the Irish had more to be violent about."[44]

At the same time, we should not underestimate the contemporary significance of the "Irish comparison":

> The lessons of Ireland were important to prerevolutionary America for the Colonial whigs, perhaps more than any other American generation, were attuned to reading danger signals from current history. They feared that what had occurred to other people could occur to them unless they manned the barricades of freedom and fought for every threatened right. Otherwise they could end as "slaves" of the British parliament. . . . Surely from their perspective, the history of English and British rule in Ireland was the most dangerous signal of all.[45]

To us, these fears may seem obtuse. We are all, to one degree or another, materialists; we all believe that social and economic conditions are the preeminent determinants of the quality of political life. American Whigs read history differently, however. To them, England had become a great commercial state because of its free institutions. English power ensured and maintained the poverty, the ignorance, and the violence of Irish life.

If John Reid's picture of Massachusetts institutional life is generally correct, as I believe it is, then what was supposed to have been settled by the Glorious Revolution was not.

    [43]*Id.* at 13, quoting J. A. Froude, THE ENGLISH IN IRELAND IN THE EIGHTEENTH CENTURY (1881), 468.
    [44]*Id.* at 136.
    [45]*Id.* at 12.

Old Whig thought was not an archaic and mistaken vision of an imaginary world, but a more or less realistic analysis of what was constitutive of American society and of what most threatened that unwritten "constitution." The institutions of Massachusetts Bay belonged to the Whigs of Massachusetts in a way that we should find incomprehensible; no local public institution can ever be said to belong to us in anything but the most abstract and ultimate sense. But English parliamentary actions, the impositions of a centralized state, could destroy those institutions, could destroy the autonomy to which Americans had grown accustomed, could reduce the American colonies to another Ireland.

A sense of the reasonableness of Whig fears for their constitutional order emerges from Professor Reid's continuing emphasis throughout his book on English timidity and restraint. Tories were always on the defensive throughout the period from 1763 to 1775; they were always playing by rules made up and enforced by Whigs. The English allowed their parliamentary agents to be sued and indicted by Whig juries. They failed to suppress obviously illegal agreements and associations like the nonimportation associations of 1768 or the Stamp Act Congress of 1765.[46] They allowed the Whig Governor's Council to neutralize official action[47] and legitimate the actions of mobs.[48] English officials appeared innocuous and incompetent whenever they faced aroused Whigs.

Yet, the reader of *In a Defiant Stance* is always aware of the incongruity of English incompetence. The agents of the British empire showed restraint and timidity. But they need not have. They played by Whig rules. But they could have stopped the game whenever they wished. The imperial state could have sent in troops to close the courts and establish martial law; it could have followed the "Irish comparison." Whigs closed the courts when it suited their purposes, not the British. And one is constantly reminded that the suc-

[46]*Id.* at 132.
[47]*Id.* at 7–16.
[48]*Id.* at 90.

cessful exercise of Whig law depended not on English pow-
erlessness but on English tolerance and passivity.

Why England did so little to assert its rights, until the
very end of the crisis, is not a question Professor Reid deals
with. The important point from the perspective of Whig
motivation is that they might have,[49] and that point was
made by the Irish comparison. Whigs were not powerless;
their actions and their institutional roles were not play-act-
ing. But they knew they were defenseless against the power
of an active and aggressive modern state whose interests
were aroused. They attempted in an almost obsessive fashion to justify their actions by conventional standards of the
maintenance of public order and the preservation of private
property.[50] But ultimately a colonial political culture of
largely autonomous local institutions resistant to centralized
control could not be in the interests of a modern England
undergoing the first stages of an industrial revolution.[51] If
a perception of British-colonial community, of a common
culture and of common origins, were replaced by an insistence the colonies were only markets for the capitalist econ-

---

[49] Consider the following excerpt from a letter written by Francis Bernard to a
member of the British cabinet:

Ireland affords an Example of the Usefulness of this Work and the Manner
of doing it. It was owing to the wise Administration of S/ir/ Edward Poynings
in the Henry the 7/th's/ Time, that the Form of Government of that Island,
which is as perfect for a dependent, as that of Great Britain for a supreme
Power, has lasted now for 270 years, without wanting the least Amendment
of Fundamentals. . . .

Ireland also affords Instances of every Kind of Regulation which America
wants; . . . . 5. There should be a solemn Recognition of the Supremacy of
the Parliament of Great Britain over the American Governments, which
should be the first act of each Legislature after its new Establishment & be the
condition of its Activity. 6. There should be a general Revisal of the Laws of
America, that they may be reduced as near as possible to the Standard of
England & the Administration of Government & Law may be rendered as
similar thereto as well may be.

Id. at 15–16 [footnote omitted].

[50] *Id.* at 95.

[51] W. WILLIAMS, THE CONTOURS OF AMERICAN HISTORY 27–223 (1961); *see also*
P. DEANE, THE FIRST INDUSTRIAL REVOLUTION 202–19 (1965); P. MATHIAS, THE
FIRST INDUSTRIAL NATION (1969); H. PERKIN, THE ORIGINS OF MODERN ENGLISH
SOCIETY 1780–1880 123 *passim* (1969).

omy of the mother country, then tolerance of local autonomy and local freedom would quite probably be replaced by
attempted centralized control. And it was therefore not un-
reasonable for colonists to see in every minor administrative
regulation and in the insistence that the colonies ought to
be producers of tax revenue for England, the first tentacles
of an enveloping Leviathan.

"We are all Latent Tories." [52]

In a Defiant Stance might be read as a verbal equivalent of
an album of photographs, a series of frozen poses of colonists in revolt. There, on one page is a civil traverse jury
assigning liability and damages to a hapless customs official;
there, on the other side, are Francis Bernard and Thomas
Hutchinson apoplectic with rage at the frustration of their
hopes for a rationally administered and centrally controlled
colony. Throughout the album we can see a variety of mobs
in a variety of poses: sometimes as an ordained *posse comitatus* doing the sheriff's bidding, sometimes as an informal
"constitutional" institution righting the wrongs committed
by more formal political agencies, sometimes as a lesser
evil—the best available alternative to violence. One third of
the album is devoted to a series of contrasting images of
Irish resistance and revolt: of defiant speeches, random violence, local corruption, and English military power.

The effect of Professor Reid's book is then roughly like
the cumulative impact of a photo essay. His achievements
are the achievements of a photographer: of the brilliance of
composition, of the intensity and clarity of significant detail,
of the shock of contrasting images. What one may miss in
the book is a sense of the continuity and constancy of
change. In *In a Defiant Stance* there is change, but it is a
change of stark oppositions—of Whig against Tory or of
Massachusetts Bay against Ireland—rather than the
"change over time" which is the staple of most historical
writing.

[52] In a Defiant Stance, *supra* note 1, at 162.

All forms of representation produce their own characteristic distortions. Narrative histories for example may lull the
reader into a false commitment to the inevitable and incre-
mental nature of change. By contrast, John Reid's frozen
images may lead the reader to underestimate the amount of
change that was occurring in Massachusetts throughout the
prerevolutionary period. As compared to European societies, Massachusetts Bay and other colonies of North America may have remained singularly egalitarian and locally
controlled (even "democratic"). But when looked at from
the vantage point of its own recent past, Massachusetts was
changing rapidly. Land was growing scarce in the older, settled portions of the colony, forcing families to move away
from communities and weakening traditional commitments
to local institutions.[53] Recent studies by historians reveal
that Massachusetts society was becoming significantly more
stratified. The distribution of wealth was skewed in an increasingly unequal fashion (more wealth being held by a
smaller percentage of the population);[54] there was, moreover, a growing perception of class differences.[55] In the last
few years a flood of articles by social historians has demonstrated that the last half of the eighteenth century was a
time of great social change. America was developing a "mature" social structure, less unlike the "old world," and
whether we call those changes "anglicization,"[56] commer-

[53] Lockridge, *Land, Population, and the Evolution of New England Society,
1630–1790*, in COLONIAL AMERICA 466 (S. Katz, ed. 1971); Lockridge, *Afterthought*,
in *id.* at 485; P. GREVEN, FOUR GENERATIONS (1970).

[54] Kulikoff, *The Progress of Inequality in Revolutionary Boston*, 28 WM. & MARY Q
375 (1971); Jones, *The Strolling Poor, Transiency in 18th Century Massachusetts*, 8 J.
Soc. HIST. 28 (1975); J. Henretta, The Evolution of American Society, 1700–1815
83–117 (1973).

[55] Murrin, *The Legal Transformation: the Bench and Bar of Eighteenth-Century Massachusetts*, in COLONIAL AMERICA 415–50 (S. Katz ed. 1971); Murrin & Berthoff,
*Feudalism, Communalism, and the Yeoman Freeholder; the American Revolution Considered
as a Social Accident*, in ESSAYS ON THE AMERICAN REVOLUTION 256–288 (S. Kurtz
and J. Hutson eds. 1973).

[56] Murrin, *The Legal Transformation: the Bench and Bar of Eighteenth-Century Massachusetts*, in COLONIAL AMERICA 415–50 (S. Katz, ed. 1971).

cialization,[57] or modernization,[58] Massachusetts Bay was becoming increasingly unlike the world Whigs thought they were defending.[59]

There is at least scattered evidence that the growing geographical mobility of prerevolutionary society was leading to a breakdown of the local publics on which local legal institutions had always depended. Well before the Revolution some local courts were becoming increasingly bureaucratic and narrow in the business they would hear, leading to a decline in their local authority and autonomous significance.[60] Some historians, indeed, imply that the 1760s and 1770s were characterized by a general decline in all forms of traditional authority—public or private.[61] If they are correct we might better see the revolutionary Whigs as romantic conservatives of a sort, however accurate their analysis of how to make a revolution, trying, even as they asserted their traditional rights, to recreate a world fast disappearing from their lives.

In any case, in the years immediately after the Declaration of Independence the new state of Massachusetts moved quickly to assert its centralized authority over all local institutions. During the 1780s most all of the discretionary and rule making authority of local courts were assumed by the General Court, by the legislature of the new Commonwealth of Massachusetts.[62] Towns and counties became

---

[57] Appelby, *The Social Origins of the American Revolutionary Ideology*, 64 J. AM. HIST. 935 (1978).

[58] Smith AND Hindus, *Premarital Pregnancy in America, 1640–1966; an Overview and Interpretation*, 5 J. INTERDISCIPLINARY HIST. 537 (1975); Smith, *The Demographic History of Colonial New England*, 32 J. ECON. HIST. 165 (1972).

[59] Lockridge, *Social Change and the Meaning of the American Revolution*, 6 J. SOC. HIST. 403 (1973); J. HENRETTA, THE EVOLUTION OF AMERICAN SOCIETY, 1700–1815 119–157 (1973).

[60] Hartog, *The Public Law of a County Court; Judicial Government in Eighteenth Century Massachusetts*, 20 AM. J. LEG. HIST. 282 (1976).

[61] R. GROSS, THE MINUTEMEN AND THEIR WORLD (1975); Smith AND Hindus, *Premarital Pregnancy in America, 1640–1966: an Overview and Interpretation*, 5 INTERDISCIPLINARY HIST. 537 (1975).

[62] Hartog, *The Public Law of a County Court; Judicial Government in Eighteenth Century Massachusetts*, 20 AM. J. LEG. HIST. 324–25 (1976).

mere administrative agencies of the state.[63] After the Revolution there was no place for decentralized local problem solvers that were not tied to the sovereign people of the whole Commonwealth. The "public" for the actions of local institutions had become, in effect, the General Court. I have argued elsewhere that this centralization of authority was not so much a radical shift away from a pre-existing state of affairs as a rationalization of much that had occurred in an informal and piece-meal fashion prior to the Revolution.[64] The centralization of the new state of Massachusetts was perhaps only the political realization of the fundamental transformation occurring in the society generally. And others have argued that the Revolution is only an interlude of relatively minor significance in that transformation, a squiggle in the otherwise straight line on the graph of American modernization.[65]

What does this "narrative" approach tell us about the meanings and the truths of John Reid's photographs? It ought, in the first place, to confirm our suspicion that those reigning old Whig values of the American Revolution, the values which shaped the political behavior of American Whigs, were both premodern and increasingly anachronistic. The responses of the Whigs to the perceived threat to *their* institutions posed by an active British state were reasonable, but they were also doomed to failure. For the threat to a multi-centered, locally controlled polity came not just from the external forces of imperial centralization but also from within, from the changing nature of American society. How did they make a revolution? They made it by temporarily reasserting their control over institutions that were fast slipping beyond their grasp, that were changing even as they, the colonists of Massachusetts Bay, were changing.

The pictures Professor Reid has given us are pictures of

---

[63] O. AND M. HANDLIN, COMMONWEALTH 94–95 (rev. ed. 1969).

[64] Hartog, *The Public Law of a County Court; Judicial Government in Eighteenth Century Massachusetts,* 20 AM. J. LEG. HIST. 324–29 (1976).

[65] Greene, *The Social Origins of the American Revolution: an Evaluation and an Interpretation,* 88 POL. SCI. Q. 1 (1973).

a "world we have lost," of a world to which we cannot give even our philosophical loyalty.[66] It is a world which would be familiar to many anthropologists.[67] Like many modern "less-developed" countries, but unlike the legal orders of Western Europe and the United States since the early nineteenth century, eighteenth-century Massachusetts had a multiplicity of legal systems, responsive to differing but overlapping publics.[68] As in some new states of modern Africa, the instrumental and rationalistic orders of a centralized modern state could be negated at will by the resistance—the uncooperativeness—of a traditional local legal infrastructure.[69] The success of the Whigs in manipulating local legal institutions to destroy central planning and control need not be incomprehensible to the modern reader, but it is an unlikely point of origin for our American political and legal life.

Whatever our political values and commitments, we can no longer be eighteenth-century Whigs, much as we might wish to the contrary.[70] In revealing that to us, *In a Defiant Stance* does what all good history books do: it separates us from a spurious identification with an imaginary past. In the words of Lucien Febvre, books like this are "a way of organizing the past so that it does not weigh too heavily on the shoulders of men."[71] We have little more in common with the men and women who made "our" Revolution than we have with resistant traditional groups in the new states of the Third World. Indeed, if we have anything in common with anyone in John Reid's album, it is with the Tories

[66]*But see*, F. Michelman, *Political Markets and Community Self-Determination: Competing Judicial Models of Local Government Legitimacy*, 53 IND. L. J. 145, 148 (1978).

[67]*See* Henretta, *Families and Farms: Mentalite in Pre-Industrial America*, 35 WM. & MARY Q. (3d ser.) 3 (1978).

[68]*See* L. POSPISIL, THE ANTHROPOLOGY OF LAW: A COMPARATIVE THEORY 98–126 (1971); M. SMITH, CORPORATIONS AND SOCIETY (1974).

[69]Moore, *Law and Social Change: The Semi-Autonomous Social Field as an Appropriate Subject of Study*, 7 LAW AND SOC. REV. 710 (1973).

[70]*See* Morgan, Book Review, 25 NEW YORK REV. BOOKS 38 (Aug. 17, 1978) [reviewing G. WILLS, INVENTING AMERICA: JEFFERSON'S DECLARATION OF INDEPENDENCE (1978)].

[71]L. FEBVRE, A NEW KIND OF HISTORY 41 (1973).

Light in Ashes: The Problem of "Respect for the Rule of Law" in American Legal History*

⌐ Peter R. Teachout ⌐

The refinement of our historical sense chiefly means that we keep it properly complicated. History . . . involves abstraction: we abstract certain events from others and we make this particular abstraction with an end in view, we make it to serve some purpose of our will. Try as we may, we cannot, as we write history, escape our purposiveness. Nor, indeed, should we try to escape, for purpose and meaning are the same thing. But in pursuing our purpose, in making our abstractions, we must be aware of what we are doing; we ought to have it fully in mind that our abstraction is not . . . equivalent to the infinite complication of events from which we have abstracted.[1]

Introduction

IN RECENT years we have seen emerge two distinct views of law during the revolutionary period in American his-

---

*A review of John Reid, *In a Defiant Stance: The Conditions of Law in Massachusetts Bay, The Irish Comparison, and the Coming of the American Revolution* (University Park, Pa., 1977). This essay originally appeared in 53 N.Y.U.L. Rev. 241 (1978). It is reprinted by permission of the *New York University Law Review*.

[1] L. Trilling, The Liberal Imagination: Essays on Literature and Society 188–89 (Viking Press ed. 1950).

tory.[2] One view, representing a relatively new school of thought, posits a radical break between the way the revolutionary generation conceived of law and the way law came to be understood during the early nineteenth century.[3] Un-

[2] I use the term "revolutionary period" in this review, as does Professor Bailyn, to refer to the years between 1750 and 1776. It was during these years that the new intellectual and moral vision of society, which ultimately led to the break from England, emerged in comprehensive form. The pace of revolutionary thought and activity increased dramatically, of course, in the 1760s and 1770s. *See generally* B. BAILYN, 1 PAMPHLETS OF THE AMERICAN REVOLUTION 1750–1776 (1965) [hereinafter B. BAILYN, PAMPHLETS]. Other historians refer to the same period as the "prerevolutionary period." *See* W. NELSON, THE AMERICANIZATION OF THE COMMON LAW: THE IMPACT OF LEGAL CHANGE ON MASSACHUSETTS SOCIETY, 1760–1830 (1975).

[3] *See* M. HORWITZ, THE TRANSFORMATION OF AMERICAN LAW 1780–1860 (1977). The basic nature of the break between the eighteenth century and nineteenth century conceptions of law is described in the following passage:

> By 1820 the legal landscape in America bore only the faintest resemblance to what existed forty years earlier. While the words were often the same, the structure of thought had dramatically changed and with it the theory of law. Law was no longer conceived of as an eternal set of principles expressed in custom and derived from natural law. Nor was it regarded primarily as a body of rules designed to achieve justice only in the individual case. Instead, judges came to think of the common law as equally responsible with legislation for governing society and promoting socially desirable conduct. The emphasis on law as an instrument of policy encouraged innovation and allowed judges to formulate legal doctrine with the self-conscious goal of bringing about social change.

Id. at 30; *see id.* at 253–54.

The idea of a broad shift from a jurisprudence rooted in natural law to one in which positive law came to play an increasingly dominant role during this general period is not, of course, a new one. What is new about the new school of thought is its posited *radical* break between the earlier world and the later one; it is the denial that substantial continuities exist between eighteenth-century and nineteenth-century conceptions of law and the concomitant assertion that the notion of law as an instrument of social policy emerged *for the first time* in the nineteenth century.

When I refer to the "new school" of legal historical thought, I am referring primarily to the work of Professor Morton Horwitz and to the large ideological themes that are reflected in his various writings. *See* M. HORWITZ, *supra;* Horwitz, *The Conservative Tradition in the Writing of American Legal History,* 17 AM. J. LEGAL HIST. 275 (1973); Horwitz, *The Emergence of an Instrumental Conception of American Law, 1780–1820,* 5 PERSPECTIVES AM. HIST. 287 (1971), *reprinted in* LAW IN AMERICAN HISTORY 287 (D. Fleming and B. Bailyn eds. 1971) [hereinafter Horwitz, *Emergence*]; Horwitz, Book Review, 42 U. CHI. L. REV. 787 (1975); Horwitz, Book Review, 86 YALE L. J. 561 (1977) [hereinafter Horwitz, *The Rule of Law*]. I quite intentionally talk in terms of a "new school" rather than simply of Professor Horwitz, however, because the influence of Professor Horwitz's thought and writing upon the way others perceive the large patterns of American legal history has

til the end of the eighteenth century, according to this school, there was little or no sophisticated legal activity in America; law was essentially nothing more than rough communal justice.[4] The world of revolutionary America was both antilegal[5] and anticommercial.[6] The rise of law as a central force in human affairs coincided, rather, with the rise of the self-regulating market in the nineteenth century.[7] Americans of the earlier period conceived of the

---

been substantial. For example, it is possible to see the influence of Professor Horwitz's thought in the work of Professor William Nelson, *see* W. NELSON, *supra* note 2, and in that of Professor Sanford Levinson, *see* Levinson, *The Specious Morality of the Law*, in HARPER'S MAGAZINE, May, 1977, at 35. Yet there are many respects, it is important to recognize, in which the work of these two last-mentioned scholars does not fit neatly—or at all—within the definition of the "new school" as I develop it here. One does not find in Professor Nelson's work, for example, the same dark pessimism about "the rule of law" that one finds in the writings of Professor Horwitz.

The master theoretician of the new school appears to be Professor Roberto Unger. *See generally* R. UNGER, LAW IN MODERN SOCIETY (1976) [hereinafter R. UNGER, MODERN SOCIETY]; R. UNGER, KNOWLEDGE AND POLITICS (1975) [hereinafter R. UNGER, KNOWLEDGE]. The basic ideological dimensions of the vision of society to which both Professor Horwitz's historiography and Professor Unger's jurisprudence can be seen to respond are discussed in text accompanying notes 108–123 *infra*.

[4] In new school historiography, the legal worlds of the eighteenth century and the nineteenth century are portrayed as two polarized constellations of values. The world of the eighteenth century is seen as embodying the values of simple communal justice, uncomplicated by sophisticated legalisms; its central symbol is the colonial jury "met[ing] out rough and discretionary communal standards of justice." *See* M. HORWITZ, *supra* note 3, at 211; *but cf.* W. NELSON, *supra* note 2, at 30 (suggesting it would be a mistake to view the colonial jury as responding simply to local custom rather than to their understanding of the common law). It is a world in which the law is simply the expression of "substantive fairness" and the "moral sense of the community," *See* M. HORWITZ, *supra* note 3, at 253, and lawyers are nothing much more than "land conveyancers or debt collectors," *see id.* at 140. The world of the nineteenth century, by contrast, is marked by sophisticated legal activity, and is dominated by "the commercial lawyers." *See id.* at 140–41.

[5] For references to the "antilegalism" of the colonists, especially of the mercantile class, and to the "lower class hatred of lawyers," *see* M. HORWITZ, *supra* note 3, at 140, 145–46.

[6] The eighteenth-century legal world—both law and lawyers—is portrayed as "anticommercial" and as "hostile" to the interests of the mercantile class. *See id.* at 143, 146, 154.

[7] Professor Horwitz's historiography can be seen in many respects as an effort to embody the large themes of Karl Polanyi's classic with the content of American legal history. *See* K. POLANYI, THE GREAT TRANSFORMATION (1944); text accompanying notes 112–116 *infra*.

common law as "established" or "fixed";[8] they simply took the law as it had been inherited and applied it, almost without thinking.[9] Law was *not,* in other words, creatively employed as a medium for the expression of the new vision of society that was pressing itself into existence during this period. Only after the turn of the nineteenth century, according to the new school, did Americans begin to develop a creative—or   "instrumental"—relationship   to   law.[10] "[B]efore the nineteenth century," we are told, American lawyers and judges "almost never self-consciously employed the common law as a creative instrument for directing men's energies toward social change."[11]

In contrast to this view is the less idyllic, but more dynamic picture of the activity of law during the years leading up to the Revolution that emerges from the traditional humanistic scholarship on this period, represented best perhaps by the work of Professor Bernard Bailyn.[12] What strikes us most about the world of this period, as Professor Bailyn sees it, is the absolute centrality of law—the thought and activity of law—as a sustaining and creative force in the service of the Revolution. "To the colonists [the law] was a repository of experience in human dealings embodying the principles of justice, equity, and rights; above all, it was a form of history . . . and, as history, it helped explain the

[8] The implication is that the colonists did not look beyond the immediate case to the societal consequences of their decisions. *See* M. HORWITZ, *supra* note 3, at 1. *But see* text accompanying notes 55–65 & 89–97 *infra.*

[9] American lawyers and judges "conceived of their role as merely that of discovering and applying preexisting legal rules." M. HORWITZ, *supra* note 3, at 1. Professor Nelson similarly portrays the world of the revolutionary period as one in which lawyers and judges were expected "to be automatons who mechanically applied immutable rules of law to the facts of each case" and who adhered to precedent with a simple-minded rigor and consistency. The mere citation of precedent, in short, seemed to solve virtually every legal problem." W. NELSON, *supra* note 2, at 19. *But see* text accompanying notes 89–97 *infra.*

[10] *See* M. HORWITZ, *supra* note 3, at 1.

[11] *Id.*

[12] Professor Bailyn has written extensively on the revolutionary period. In this review, I limit my references to two of his major recent works: B. BAILYN, THE ORDEAL OF THOMAS HUTCHINSON (1974) [hereinafter B. BAILYN, ORDEAL]; B. BAILYN, PAMPHLETS, *supra* note 2.

movement of events and the meaning of the present."[13] "English law . . .," Bailyn goes on, "stood side by side with Enlightenment rationalism in the minds of the Revolutionary generation."[14] Nor did the colonists simply apply the common law as they had inherited it. One of the consuming activities of the colonists during this period, as Bailyn portrays it, was the creative adjustment by lawyers and nonlawyers alike of inherited legal thought and doctrine.[15] Time and again, it was the creative use of an essentially legal imagination that propelled and supported the movement of the Revolution, and that gave events and developments, otherwise beyond comprehension, their meaning, significance, and legitimacy.

These opposed perceptions of the activity of law during the Revolutionary period are only a surface manifestation of a much more fundamental difference that separates the "new school" of legal historians from the traditional humanistic school. What ultimately divides the two schools, it becomes clear, are radically different understandings of the role of law in society. The new school position is set forth succinctly by Professor Morton Horwitz in a recent essay:

> American legal historians . . . tend toward an excessively reverential and apologetic attitude towards law. . . . I do not see how [one] can describe the rule of law as "an unqualified human good"! . . . By promoting procedural justice [the rule of law] enables the shrewd, the calculating, and the wealthy to manipulate its forms to their own advantage. And it ratifies and legitimates an adversarial, competitive, and atomistic conception of human relations.[16]

As this passage suggests, the chief defining characteristic of the new school in legal historical thought is its radical antilegalism: its central preoccupation with law as a force for the destruction of those human values we hold most sacred in a civilization—of individual dignity, equality, and com-

---

[13] B. BAILYN, PAMPHLETS, *supra* note 2, at 26.
[14] *Id.* at 26–27 (footnote omitted).
[15] *See id.* at 99–103, 411–17.
[16] Horwitz, *The Rule of Law, supra* note 3, at 565–66.

munity. Thus, the world of the new school historian is one in which the law is seen primarily as a vehicle for the manipulation by the powerful in society of the powerless; in which one finds at every turn corruption and concealment; and in which individuals and groups are motivated by narrow self-interest, by lust for power and wealth, rather than by genuinely felt moral vision.[17] It is, as one reviewer has described Professor Horwitz's most recent work, a "[d]ark and Doestoyevskyan" universe.[18]

[17] In a recent review of Horwitz's book, Professor Stephen Presser describes the world created in that work:

Legal principles are subverted (p. 99), "class bias" prevails (p. 188), and "gross disparities of bargaining power" are brushed behind a facade of "neutral and formal rules" (p. 201). In sum, legal power is ruthlessly exercised to bring about economic redistributions, by powerful groups who carefully "disguise" their activities from the majority of Americans (p. 266).

Presser, Book Review, 52 N.Y.U.L. Rev. 700, 700 (1977) (citing M. Horwitz, *supra* note 3).

Generally Professor Presser's review is an excellent and discriminating summary of Horwitz's book. I think, however, that he overstates Professor Horwitz's contribution to legal history when he implies that Horwitz offers *new* wisdom in advancing the related ideas that "diverse forces—moral, political, and economic—go into making the law" and that "the law does *not* develop along strictly logical lines." *See id.* at 716 (emphasis in original). I confess I find it hard to imagine any student of law coming of age in the twentieth century believing that the law *does* develop "along strictly logical lines." And if there is any conventional wisdom in legal education, it is that "moral, political, and economic [forces] go into making the law." This "new" idea has been around at least since Holmes.

It is important to understand what is new and what is not new about the new school: The view that law should be seen in the broader perspective of the intellectual, moral, and cultural forces in which it evolves is not new. *See generally* P. Miller, The Life of the Mind in America (1965). Nor is the idea that law is not an objective science. *See, e.g.,* B. Cardozo, The Nature of the Judicial Process 98–141 (1921); O. Holmes, The Common Law 1–2 (2d ed. 1923). Nor is there anything new about the perception that common law doctrine was transformed during the nineteenth century to accommodate economic expansion and industrial growth. *See* L. Levy, The Law of the Commonwealth and Chief Justice Shaw 313, 331–32 (1957). These ideas are all part of the mainstream in contemporary legal thought. Thus, whatever is new about the new school must come from elsewhere: What it is, it seems to me, is what separates the writings of the new school from those of the humanistic school: a center of gravity in political theory or ideology, a certain cynicism about human motivation, and a dark view of the possibilities of the rule of law in society, *see* text accompanying notes 18–22 *infra*. In this respect, *compare* Professor Levy's Chief Justice Shaw in L. Levy, *supra*, with Professor Horwitz's Chief Justice Shaw in M. Horwitz, *supra* note 3.

[18] *See* Presser, *supra* note 17, at 700.

The view of the role of law in society, and in individual lives, that we find reflected in the work of the humanistic historian is more difficult to describe—and also to predict—precisely because it is more complex, measured, and subtle. By the same token, it is not what we would call simple-minded or uncritical. It is true, nevertheless, that the humanistic school *is* receptive to a positive vision of the rule of law in society in a way the new school historian is not. Thus, we would never find in the writings of the new school historian the kind of extended and, essentially, sympathetic treatment of "establishment" legal figures that we find, say, in Mark DeWolfe Howe's humanly perceptive biography of Holmes' early years,[19] in Leonard Levy's discriminating study of Chief Justice Shaw,[20] or in Bernard Bailyn's already classic portrait, *The Ordeal of Thomas Hutchinson.*[21] What distinguishes the work of the humanistic school is the presence of a mind that is constantly judging and discriminating, that is responding not to a single set of ideological coordinates, but to the whole of human experience. Even conservative legal figures are seen by the humanist school as rounded persons whose legal thought and activity have something to tell us not only about the period in which they lived but also about our own predicament. The humanistic historian has a more complex view of law, in other words, than does the new school historian. He recognizes its destructive potential in the hands of the stupid and the corrupt, but sees it also as a medium for the expression of important human values and ideals, and as a positive and powerful force for justice and good in the world.[22]

[19]*See* M. Howe, Justice Oliver Wendell Holmes, The Proving Years 1870–1882 (1963); M. Howe, Justice Oliver Wendell Holmes, The Shaping Years 1841–1870 (1957).

[20]*See* L. Levy, *supra* note 17.

[21]*See* B. Bailyn, Ordeal, *supra* note 12.

[22]This conception of law, which is implicit in the works of the humanistic school, *see* text accompanying notes 12 & 19–20 *supra*, is given explicit development in Professor James White's provocative and brilliant work, J. White, The Legal Imagination: Studies in the Nature of Legal Thought and Expression (1973). *See* text accompanying notes 132–142 *infra*.

Once we understand the fundamental difference between
the two schools' perceptions of the "rule of law" in history,
we can begin to understand why the new school posits a
radical break between the revolutionary period and the
early nineteenth century, and why it seeks to deny the existence of creative legal activity during the earlier period.
Since the revolutionary period represents a liberating and
visionary moment in our experience, and since, in the
moral universe of new school thought, creative law is a
"bad" and not a "good,"[23] it is critical for the new school
historian to separate by as much distance as possible the developments of the revolutionary period from the burst of
creative legal activity that occurred during the first few decades of the nineteenth century—the era that has come to
be known as "the golden age" of American law.[24] And it is
even more important, from the new school perspective, to
link this later creative period in American law to the rise of
the self-regulating market in the nineteenth century,[25] to
the development of the destructive contractarianism and individualism that ultimately results from an extreme adherence to market ideology,[26] and to a period in our national

[23] There seem to be two sources for this hostility to "creative" law. First, to allow
law even this role in society runs counter to the vision of a "world without law"
that drives the new school; and second, the new school historian sees "positive law"
(which is bad) as fundamentally incompatible with "natural law" (which is good),
and creative law falls within the broad category of positive law. *See* text accompanying notes 105–142 *infra*.

[24] *See* R. POUND, THE FORMATIVE ERA OF AMERICAN LAW (1938); THE GOLDEN
AGE OF AMERICAN LAW (C. Haar ed. 1965). *See generally* G. GILMORE, THE AGES OF
AMERICAN LAW (1977); K. LLEWELLYN, THE COMMON LAW TRADITION: DECIDING
APPEALS (1960). For a discussion of the essentially "mythological" character of this
"golden age" in our legal past, especially in G. GILMORE, *supra*, see Teachout, Book
Review, 2 VT. L. REV. 229, 239–49 (1977).

[25] *See* text accompanying note 7 *supra*.

[26] *See* Levinson, *supra* note 3. In this article, Levinson describes the transition
from the eighteenth-century legal world to the modern one in terms of the transformation from a "communitarian" to a "contractarian" conception of law:

[For John Adams and others in the eighteenth century] law was not only
timeless, but, more important, linked with moral norms. . . . Subordination
to law was . . . subordination only to that part of ourselves willing to recognize primary obligation to the community, a community in turn recognizing
obligations to adhere to fixed moral principles.

history during which the law in fact came to be employed by one class as a vehicle for repressing another[27]—in short, to everything that went wrong with the nineteenth century.

The historian of the humanistic school, by contrast, is not driven by the same deep antipathy to law, and thus is much more open to seeing the connections between the creative adjustment of common law institutions and doctrine during the revolutionary period and the burst of creative legalism that occurred in the early nineteenth century. He sees, as the new school historian cannot, the instrumentalism in the early nineteenth century, not as separate and distinct from what came before, but as the continuation—or, more accurately, redirection—of forces set loose and traditions begun during the revolutionary period.[28]

It is between these competing views of law in the revolutionary period, and of its relationship to developments in

---

These ideas have barely survived. We pride ourselves today on moral pluralism.

Id. at 36.

Under the contractarian conception of law, to which Levinson argues the eighteenth-century communitarian conception has given way, "[e]ach of us is perceived as an isolated being pursuing mutually exclusive, endlessly conflicting, personal visions." *Id.* at 38. Law, therefore, has become nothing more than "a bargaining process." *Id.* "The substantive [moral] content that underlay . . . Adams's concept of law has vanished, and the notion of law has decayed into pure proceduralism . . . ." *Id. See also* K. POLANYI, *supra* note 7.

For an example of the way in which extreme adherence to market ideology leads to a distortion in human response, see Posner, *Killing or Wounding to Protect a Property Interest*, 14 J. LAW & ECON. 201 (1971).

[27] This did not develop, however, until the end of the nineteenth century. The best work on this dimension of nineteenth-century legal experience is A. PAUL, THE CONSERVATIVE CRISES AND THE RULE OF LAW: ATTITUDES OF BAR AND BENCH 1887–1895 (1960).

[28] The nature of the redirection is exceedingly complex, but in rough terms, during the revolutionary period the law was creatively employed to serve the related goals of political independence and protection of local mercantile interests, and, at a higher level, to serve the emerging vision of a new, less corrupt, and more democratic society. After the Revolutionary War, the goal of political independence fell away, so to speak, and the creative energies of the law were increasingly turned to the other goal: domestic commercial development. This redirection was seen not as antagonistic to, but rather necessary for the achievement of, the larger vision of the new society. *See generally* J. HURST, LAW AND THE CONDITIONS OF FREEDOM IN THE NINETEENTH-CENTURY UNITED STATES (1956); L. LEVY, *supra* note 17.

the nineteenth century—and, at a higher plane, about how one should see the rule of law in history—that any new work in American legal history must make its way. This fact has particular significance, as we shall see, for Professor John Phillip Reid's interesting new book on law in the revolutionary period, *In a Defiant Stance*.[29] In this work, Professor Reid sets out to compare "the conditions of law"[30] in the American colonies during the years leading up to the Revolution with those in Ireland during roughly the same period. Although the American colonies and Ireland were, in a sense, both governed by the same common law and ultimately responsible to the same imperial administration, the conditions of law in these two British dominions could not have been more divergent. The critical difference, Reid suggests, is that in Ireland there was nothing that could properly be called the rule of law; the administration of law by imperial officials was arbitrary, brutal, and one-sided. Thus the revolutionary class in Ireland came to hate the "law," and to associate it with the arbitrary use of power by an imported English ruling class. In the American colonies, however, not only did the officials of the crown follow the law with scrupulous regard, but, perhaps more surprisingly,

[29] J. REID, IN A DEFIANT STANCE: THE CONDITIONS OF LAW IN MASSACHUSETTS BAY, THE IRISH COMPARISON, AND THE COMING OF THE AMERICAN REVOLUTION (1977). Many of the ideas and themes developed in this book can be found in Professor Reid's earlier articles on this period, but the comparison with the Irish experience is new. Related writings by Professor Reid include Reid, *In the First Line of Defense: The Colonial Charters, The Stamp Act Debate and the Coming of the American Revolution*, 51 N.Y.U.L. REV. 177 (1976); Reid, *In a Defensive Rage: The Uses of the Mob, The Justification in Law, and the Coming of the American Revolution*, 49 N.Y.U.L. REV. 1043 (1974); Reid, *In a Constitutional Void: The Enforcement of Imperial Law, the Role of the British Army, and the Coming of the American Revolution*, 22 WAYNE L. REV. 1 (1975); Reid, Book Review, 49 N.Y.U.L. REV. 593 (1974) (reviewing B. BAILYN, THE ORDEAL OF THOMAS HUTCHINSON).

[30] By the "conditions" of law is meant not merely substantive rules of law, but the certainty, the power, and the effectiveness of that law . . . .
It is important to stress the words "conditions of law." [The British authorities lamented] the conditions, not the substance of American law. It was, as they well knew, the same common law whose writs ran in Wales and Ireland as well as in the former kingdom of England. They were lamenting the conditions controlling that law, not its rules, its maxims, or its principles.
J. REID, *supra* note 29, at 2.

the revolutionary Whigs themselves had, throughout this period, a deep and genuine respect for the rule of law.[31] The reason for this radically different attitude towards the rule of law, Reid argues, is that the American colonists managed early on to gain and maintain effective control of the full range of legal processes in the colonies, especially in Massachusetts Bay. Thus, as events gathered momentum, the American revolutionaries sought to achieve their new vision of society through the creative employment of law rather than by rebellion against it. This difference, Professor Reid argues, had profound implications for the nature of the American revolutionary experience. Among other

[31] I use the term "rule of law" here to distinguish between the situation in which officials enforce the laws of a society in an arbitrary manner to protect established interests and the situation in which there is a principled commitment to the rule of law and to the fundamental values that underlie it. Therefore, the fact that there was a great deal of "law" in eighteenth-century Ireland, in the sense of writs, court decisions, statutory provisions, and so on, does not mean that Ireland was governed by the rule of law. Indeed, it was not. This distinction is basic to an understanding of what is meant by the rule of law. Another illustration is the world of Kafka's *The Trial*, in which we find a maze of legal forms and proceedings but the absence of anything that could be called the rule of law.

It is important to recognize, however, that the term "rule of law" is not always used in this way. One of the problems that plagues discussions about the rule of law is that the term is often used by different persons to mean different things. Thus, a review of recent legal literature will reveal at least five distinct conceptions of the rule of law:

(1) The Elemental Conception. The term "rule of law" is sometimes used to distinguish between a society governed in some significant part by formal rules and procedures and one in which the communal bond of shared value and purpose is so strong that there is no need for formal rules. Professor Unger seems to use the term in this sense in his LAW IN MODERN SOCIETY, *supra* note 3.

(2) The Established Order Conception. The term is sometimes used to refer to any use of law, no matter how manipulative or unprincipled, to maintain the established social order. Professor Horwitz seems to use the term in this way in *The Rule of Law, supra* note 3.

(3) The Procedural Regularity Conception. This conception differs in important respects from the first two in that it excludes from the meaning of the rule of law those impositions of legal sanctions that do not conform to minimal expectations of procedural regularity. Thus, a society that regularly sentenced offenders to death without opportunity for trial would not be governed by the rule of law. On the other hand, a society that made stealing bread a capital offense, and provided a full trial before imposing the death sentence, would be governed by a rule of law. What characterizes this conception of the "rule of law" is the radical refusal to concern itself with the substantive justice of legal decisions. It finds primary

things, it accounts for the remarkable lack of violence and bloodshed in the colonies in the years preceding the outbreak of war.

In the discussion that follows, my effort will be to place Professor Reid's *In a Defiant Stance* in the context of the large currents of contemporary legal historical thought, and in particular, of the competing conceptions of law in history represented by the new school hitorians on the one hand and those who write from the humanistic tradition on the other. Professor Reid's comparative approach to law in this period sheds important new light on the critical issues that divide these two schools. The evidence his study makes available tends generally to support the image of law in this period that we find in the work of Professor Bailyn and the humanistic school.[32] The revolutionary generation's relationship to law, Professor Reid's study shows, was in many

---

expression in the work of the classic, or Chicago, school of economics. *See* Posner, *supra* note 26.

(4) The Variable Content Conception. Some historians take the rule of law to be an open-ended concept capable of being infused with whatever values happen to prevail at a particular time. This seems to be the way the term is used in Levinson, *supra* note 3. *See* text accompanying note 26 *supra*.

(5) The Substantive Moral Vision Conception. This conception, in some respects the most sophisticated and difficult, is based on the notion that the rule of law embodies certain positive human values above and beyond those of procedural regularity: a respect for the integrity of the individual, for example, and a commitment to the ideals of equality, fairness, and justice. It is the conception we find reflected in the liberal, humanist tradition represented by Justice Brandeis' dissent in Olmstead v. United States, 277 U.S. 438, 471 (1928), in Justice Frankfurter's majority opinion in Watts v. Indiana, 338 U.S. 49 (1949), in Justice Harlan's concurring opinion in Griswold v. Connecticut, 381 U.S. 479, 501 (1965), and in Justice Harlan's dissent in United States v. White, 401 U.S. 745, 768 (1971). While this conception is given many different expressions, I would place in the same general tradition the recent works by Professor White, *see* J. WHITE, *supra* note 22, and by Professor Tribe, *see* L. TRIBE, AMERICAN CONSTITUTIONAL LAW (1978).

One of the weaknesses of Professor Reid's book is that he never makes clear exactly which conception of the rule of law he is using when he refers to "respect for the rule of law."

[32] By saying this, I do not mean to suggest that Professor Reid's work can be placed easily in one school or the other. There are some respects in which the image of law reflected in his book contrasts with that found in the writings of the humanistic school. *See* text accompanying notes 86–96 & 143–148 *infra*.

respects remarkably sophisticated and imaginative. More importantly, the colonists quite consciously employed law as an instrument for achieving the new vision of society that was beginning to take hold in America during this time. If this is true, then the currently accepted view of the development of instrumentalism in American law[33] will have to be substantially revised. Creative law in America, it becomes evident, did not have its origins in the early nineteenth century, but in the crucible of the years of crisis, from 1760 to 1776, almost fifty years earlier.

In the next section, I review the major observations and conclusions of Professor Reid's study. In the section following, I provide an assessment of the contribution *In a Defiant Stance* makes to our understanding of law in this period. Finally, I turn to a discussion of what is likely to be the book's most controversial aspect: its claims, implicit and explicit, for the importance in history of respect for the rule of law.

I. The Basic Thesis of *In a Defiant Stance*

In a Defiant Stance proceeds from an intriguing question: Why is it, Reid asks, that given a shared inheritance of English common law and British imperial rule, the independence movement in America took such a radically divergent path from the one in Ireland? The Irish activists were systematically arrested and tried for their activities, and not infrequently condemned to death. Yet this rarely happened in the American colonies. Why was it, for example, that Whig agitators in Massachusetts Bay Colony were not arrested and put on trial for seditious libel or acts of rebellion against the crown? The Irish struggle was characterized by violence and bloodshed on the part of both sides to the conflict, while in the American colonies, not only did mobs roam the streets without clashing with authorities, but their actions were remarkably restrained. The lord lieutenant of

[33] *See* Horwitz, *Emergence, supra* note 3.

Ireland (the administrative counterpart to the royal governor of an American colony) ruled with an iron hand, bending and manipulating the law as necessary to suppress rebellion at the earliest sign. The governor of Massachusetts, in contrast, followed the law with scrupulous regard and, as a consequence, often found himself paralyzed, unable to take effective action against the agitations of the rebellious colonists. How can these radical differences be explained?

The answer, Professor Reid suggests, lies in two critical factors: the differing traditions of law in the two dominions, and the relative degree of control exercised by the rebellious forces over local institutions and local law.[34]

The tradition of law in Ireland was defined in large part by the fact that the English considered Ireland a conquered land,[35] and regarded the native Irish as a wild and uncultivated people.[36] England's Irish policies were aimed in no

[34] J. REID, *supra* note 29, at 173. The claim that the difference was not in the substance of the law is one that Reid makes at several points. I understand his motivation in doing so: He wants to stress that *from the perspective of British administrators* the most problematic aspect of law in the American colonies was that the colonists had effectively taken over the local legal processes. And he seeks to bring this home by comparing the American experience with that in Ireland where, in sharp contrast, the native Catholic population was effectively excluded from participation in the legal process. Yet it seems to me he may tend to discount very real differences in the substantive law of the two realms. The distinction between "substance" and "tradition" of law is one that, in my view, Reid never fully works out.

[35] In *Calvin's Case,* 7 Eng. Rep. 11 (K.B. 1608), Lord Coke had held that English law was not automatically received in conquered lands (such as Ireland). The distinction was one the American colonists came to employ against repressive British measures, claiming such measures interfered with their natural-born rights as Englishmen. *See* B. BAILYN, PAMPHLETS, *supra* note 2, at 709–10 nn.25 & 26.

[36] This view of the Irish, which had existed from the earliest times, was cruelly reinforced by British measures designed to crush or to starve out the rebels, and to make desolate their lands. The poet Edmund Spenser, who served as Secretary to Deputy Lord Grey in Ireland in the late 1500s, was shocked by what he witnessed on his travels through Ireland: "the hanging of rebels, the pressing of men to death, the cutting off of the ears of rascally purveyors, the burning of crops in Munster, and the horrible desolation of that region, where those who had escaped the sword were barely able to drag themselves about, for famine." *Preface* to THE COMPLETE POETICAL WORKS OF EDMUND SPENSER at xvi (R. Dodge ed. 1908) [hereinafter SPENSER]. Spenser's depiction of the famine in Southern Ireland

small measure at keeping the native Catholic population a subject class.[37] Catholics were denied even the most elementary legal rights.[38] The tradition of law in the American colonies stands in marked contrast to that in Ireland, primarily because the colonists were not seen as pagan inhabitants of a conquered land. The American colonists were seen, rather, as Englishmen who carried with them to America the rights and duties of all English citizens. Thus, from the outset they shared with crown-appointed administrators a relationship not of conqueror and conquered, but of equal partnership in the colonial venture.[39]

The second factor, which Professor Reid regards as even more important, was the extent to which the indigenous population had effective control over the operation of the local legal processes. In Ireland the picture is uncomplicated: the lord lieutenant and his associates totally dominated the administration of Irish law, and they manipulated

---

starkly reflects this perception the English administrators had of the Irish peasants as being less than human.

> Out of every corner of the woodes and glinnes they came creeping foorthe upon theyr handes, for theyr legges could not beare them; they looked like anatomyses of death; they spake like ghosts crying out of theyr graves; they did eate of dead the carrions; happy were they yf they could finde them; yea, and one another soone after, insoemuch as the very carcasses they spared not to scrape out of theyr graves; and yf they founde a plotte of water-cresses or sham-rokes, there they flocked as to a feast for the time, yet not able long to continue therewithall; that in shorte space there were none allmost left, and a most populous and plentifull countrey suddaynly made voyde of man or beast.

Id. at xvi–xvii. *See also* text accompanying note 138 *infra*.

[37] "By the end of the eighteenth century the Catholics, who comprised three-fourths of the population, possessed one-fifteenth of the land." J. REID, *supra* note 29, at 13.

[38] The penal code of Ireland, a series of laws beginning in 1695 . . . was not . . . a criminal code, but a set of statutes placing civil disabilities on Catholics, forbidding such incidents of citizenship as education, land owning, and the practice of medicine or law. . . . A Catholic could lease property for only thirty-one years, at the end of which time he had to bid against others for a new lease and face eviction if someone offered the Protestant owner of the fee a higher rent.

Id. at 24; *see id.* at 22–26.

[39] The remoteness of the American colonies also played a role in the willingness of the British to let the colonists manage their own legal affairs.

it freely to effect the continued repression of the rebellious Irish population. But in the American colonies, Professor Reid shows us, the Whig forces gained almost complete control of local lawmaking and law-enforcing institutions. Thus, during the critical years of the 1760s and 1770s royal administrators and officials in the colonies found themselves without effective power to enforce repressive parliamentary legislation.

The way in which the Whigs gained control of the local legal machinery, and the resourcefulness with which they used it, form a major part of Professor Reid's study. Without attempting to review in detail the many interlocking steps involved, the linchpin developments can be briefly described. Our discussion will focus, as does Professor Reid's, on the experience in Massachusetts Bay, although to a certain extent this experience was repeated elsewhere in the colonies.[40] Of the many factors that contributed to effective Whig control of the operation of law in the Massachusetts Bay colony, four stand out as particularly critical: (1) the inability of the governor to act on crucial matters without the consent of the council; (2) the colonists' control over the selection of civil, criminal, and grand juries; (3) the broad powers of the colonial jury to rule on matters of law as well as fact; and (4) the creative employment by Whig lawyers of liability doctrine, under which, at that time, government officials were personally liable for injuries caused in the performance of official acts.

One major difference between law in the American colonies and in Ireland was the extent to which the executive and legislative processes were responsive to the popular will. At the executive level, in Massachusetts Bay at least, most of the important decisions of the governor were subject to the consent or veto of the council. The council in

[40] There were, however, some important differences among the colonies. For example, the governor's council in New York was much less responsive to the popular will, and so was much less likely to act as a curb on the exercise of power by the royal governor than was the governor's council in Massachusetts. *See* Katz, *New York Government and Anglo-American Politics, in* COLONIAL AMERICA: ESSAYS IN POLITICS AND SOCIAL DEVELOPMENT 268 (S. Katz ed. 1971).

turn was elected by the lower house in assembly, and the lower house was elected annually by the colonists in town meetings. Thus, on critical matters, such as the appointment or removal of judges and justices of the peace,[41] or decisions involving the stationing or mobilization of British troops,[42] the governor's powers could be exercised only to the extent they coincided with the popular will. The decisions of the lord lieutenant of Ireland, in contrast, were subject to review only by the British cabinet.

At the legislative level, the differences were even more pronounced. While the Massachusetts assembly was elected annually by the people in town meeting,[43] the Irish parliament, its legislative counterpart, was not popularly elected, but rather was constituted through a process similar in many respects to that used in England during this period. Two-thirds of the members were returned by individuals, and a majority of the borough representatives were elected by less than a hundred persons.[44] Moreover, the decisions of the Irish parliament lacked political integrity because of the practices of buying and selling votes and of creating new peers and pensions in reward for votes in support of crown policies.[45] Finally, the Irish parliament was not freshly constituted each year, but rather was summoned and dissolved by the king. The length of time a parliament

[41] *See* J. REID, *supra* note 29, at 18–19.
If it is asked why the Governor does not turn all the Justices of the Peace out of Commission, and put others in who will do their Duty? It is Answered, that the Governor can neither appoint Justices or [*sic*] turn them out, but by Consent of Council; and that the Council opposes everything proposed by the Governor for the Service of Government, that is unpopular.

Letter from General Thomas Gage to the earl of Hillsborough (Oct. 31, 1768), *quoted in id.* at 191 n.1.

For an interesting treatment of this subject, see B. Black, *Judicial Independence in Colonial Massachusetts* (paper presented to the American Society for Legal History, in Boston, Nov. 4, 1977).

[42] Under the charter of Massachusetts Bay Colony, the governor had full power to " 'use and exercise the Law Martiall,' " but his authority was limited to " 'time of actuall Warr Invasion or Rebellion.' " J. REID, *supra* note 29, at 114.

[43] *Id.* at 9.

[44] *Id.* at 10.

[45] *See id.*

might sit was thus indeterminate; one parliament, for example, sat for 33 years.[46]

In spite of the greater responsiveness to the people that these differences allowed, the key to Whig control of the legal process in the American colonies lay in the colonists' influence in jury selection, and in the broad powers of the colonial jury. In Massachusetts Bay, jurors were returned by selectmen who had been elected in town meeting. In Ireland, by comparison, the lord lieutenant appointed sheriffs, and the sheriffs handpicked jurors favorable to the administration.[47] Even more significant was the colonial jury's power to decide matters of law as well as fact. An American court had little authority to override the jury's decision on the law even when the decision clearly contravened established precedent.[48] Interestingly, courts in both Ireland *and* England during this period had much greater latitude to control and limit jury decisions.[49]

Reid does an excellent job in showing the way the three major types of jury in the American colonies—the grand jury, the criminal traverse jury, and the civil traverse jury—were resourcefully employed in service of the colonial effort. The grand jury served the colonists' cause through its refusal to indict Whig activists for seditious libel[50] and its concomitant readiness to indict royal officials for their attempted enforcement of hated parliamentary legislation.[51] On at least one occasion, a New York grand jury legitimized a mob's destruction of British troop barracks by declaring

[46]*Id.* at 9.

[47]*See id.* at 41.

[48]*See id.* at 29; W. NELSON, *supra* note 21, at 28–29. For a description of the shift in the jury's role in the period following the Revolution, see W. NELSON, *supra* note 2, at 169–71.

[49]"In Ireland there were grounds for overturning [jury verdicts] and civil courts had some authority to grant new trials." J. REID, *supra* note 29, at 42. The situation in England is described by Professor Nelson: "[T]he judges of England [during the Revolutionary period] had broad power to shape law by virtue of the fact that special pleas were often interposed and that they could grant new trials when juries failed to follow their instructions . . . ." W. NELSON, *supra* note 2, at 31.

[50]*See* J. REID, *supra* note 29, at 52–53. The Irish experience with seditious libel stands in stark contrast to the American experience. *See id.* at 47–48.

[51]*See id.* at 41–46.

the barracks to be a public nuisance.[52] In much the same way, the criminal traverse jury demonstrated its readiness to convict customs officials and others who showed sympathy for the loyalist cause whenever appropriate grounds could be found for doing so.[53]

Professor Reid's most helpful contribution to our understanding of this period, however, is his explanation of the critically important role played by the civil traverse jury in the colonial effort. The significance of the civil jury, Reid shows, lay in Whig lawyers' creative use of liability doctrine. During this period, officials at all levels of government were personally liable for harm caused in the performance of their official duties,[54] and it did not take long for the Whig lawyer to see the political potential in this body of liability doctrine. Almost every effort to enforce repressive parliamentary legislation could be transformed, it soon became evident, into an action for damages by the injured local merchant against the relevant official for illegal trespass or confiscation.

---

[52] *See id.* at 45.

[53] *See id.* at 55–64.

[54] Professor Nelson provides a succinct description:

[O]fficials were subject to common law actions for damages whenever in the exercise of their duties they committed a wrong. Such actions were frequently brought, for instance, against sheriffs for their own misconduct or that of their deputies, for whom they were liable. Most such suits alleged some misfeasance or neglect in performing a duty relating to civil litigation, such as failing to serve a writ of attachment, failing to take bail of a defendant, failing to keep attached goods in possession pending trial, or failing to levy execution or to levy it properly. Suits could be brought against constables for similar misfeasance or neglect, as well as against jailers who permitted prisoners to escape. All officials were also subject to damage actions for improper arrests and for wrongful invasions of a subject's property . . . . A fundamental rule was that on arrest, a search, or a seizure of goods following a search was an actionable wrong unless made pursuant to a lawful warrant; "Probable Cause [was] no Excuse to a[n] . . . officer making a Seizure," search, or arrest, "for it would be extremely bad to leave it to the discretion of the Court officer to assume w[ha]t[ever] power to search w[ha]t[ever] house he thinks fit." . . .

There was, in short, little that one acting on behalf of government could do without rendering himself liable to legal action in the event that he wronged another.

W. NELSON, *supra* note 2, at 17–18.

The case of *Erving v. Cradock*[55] provides a helpful illustration of the close interrelationship that existed between the creative employment of liability doctrine and the larger Whig political effort. The plaintiff, John Erving, was a local merchant and a member of the governor's council; George Cradock, the defendant, served as a customs collector at the port of Boston. The underlying facts and the basic stratagem of the Whig lawyer are described from a tory perspective by Governor Francis Bernard:

> Mr. *Cradock* . . . as collector, seized a Vessel of Mr. *Erving's* charged with contraband trade & libelled her in the Court of Admiralty. Mr. *Erving* appeared personally in Court & prayed leave to compound [i.e., to settle] which being agreed to by the Governor & Collector as well as the King's Advocate, was allowed by the Court at one half of the value, which upon appraisement was ascertained at above £500 sterling. This sum Mr. *Erving* paid into Court; & it was equally divided between the King, the Governor & the Collector. . . . And now Mr. *Erving* has brought this action against Mr. *Cradock* for damages accrued to him by means of this seizure.'[56]

"[A]fter compounding the seizure in open admiralty court and paying the compromise sum," Professor Reid goes on to explain:

> Councillor Erving turned to the common law courts to recoup his loss and, perhaps, to punish Collector Cradock for his official zeal. The writ was trespass, and as Bernard put it, "The pretence for this action is, that the seizure was illegal and a trespass, and that the payment of Mr. *Erving* was not voluntary, but extorted by violence and *duress.*" The governor . . . was alarmed. The common law suit was, he asserted, a plot to destroy the admiralty jurisdiction and the customs service. True it was a personal action, "But," he warned the lords of trade, "it is generally understood that Mr. *Erving's* is only a leading action to a great many others; and that if he meets with success, every one that has had goods condemned,

[55] 1 Quincy 553 (Mass. Bay Colony Superior Ct. of Judicature 1761) (S. Quincy ed. 1865), *discussed in* J. REID, *supra* note 29, at 30–35.

[56] Letter from Governor Francis Bernard to the Lords of Trade (Aug. 6, 1761), *quoted in* J. REID, *supra* note 29, at 30 (footnotes omitted).

or been allowed to compound for them at their own request, will bring actions against the officer who seized them. Your Lordships will perceive that these actions have an immediate tendency to destroy the Court of Admiralty and with it the Custom house, which cannot subsist without that Court."[57]

This passage reflects how the law was perceived—by both Whigs and Tories—during this period as an instrument of Whig policy.

A threshold problem for Erving's attorney was how to frame the case in such a way as to avoid having it dismissed by the court on a demurrer—how, in other words, to get it before a politically sympathetic jury. This is something Whig attorneys managed to do, as Reid shows us, with amazing resourcefulness and sophistication, and Erving's attorney was no exception. The lower court jury responded by granting Erving a verdict of " 'near 600 sterling damages,' " which was roughly a hundred pounds *more* than the amount for which he had settled in the vice-admiralty court.[58] At a trial *de novo* after appeal, a second jury awarded him almost the same amount.[59]

---

[57] J. REID, *supra* note 29, at 30 (footnotes omitted).

[58] *See id.* at 31.

[59] *Id.* This was not the end of the matter. As Professor Reid goes on to relate: Cradock was now in a serious position. He had been performing his duty and the upper court had ruled he was not liable, but the jury held otherwise and he faced the prospect of paying . . . or going to debtors' prison. The court could not enter judgment for him, no matter how valid the judges thought his defense. He might move for a new trial. : . . [But] a motion for a new trial could not be granted on ground that the jury had disregarded the court's instruction. In Massachusetts the civil jury's verdict was truly final. All that Collector Cradock could do was take an appeal outside the province, to the king in council. . . .

Cradock took his appeal and Erving withdrew. . . . [Erving, as John Hancock would do in a similar case,] knew that he had no more chance of winning before the king in council than the customs officials had of defending themselves before a Boston jury. . . . [I]f his purpose was to harass the revenue service, . . . Erving had done well enough. As these were personal actions the defendants had been put to expense out of their own pockets as well as to a good deal of trouble. . . .

Id. at 31–32 (footnotes omitted).

Another legal tactic employed by Whig lawyers was to ask the local jury for damages in an amount just one pound short of the statutory amount required for an

The *Erving* case illuminates our understanding of law in the period in several respects. First, it demonstrates the imaginative way in which Whig lawyers learned to circumvent and undermine the exercise of power by the only judicial institution in the colonies still in the effective control of the crown, the vice-admiralty court.[60] Second, it illustrates the willingness of colonial lawyers and juries to disregard legal precedent when it was perceived as inconsistent with the realization of the colonists' political goals. For example, the jury award to Erving was granted in the face of a clear judicial instruction to the contrary:

> [The superior court judges instructed] the jury according to precedent and precedent was clear: whether or not Cradock had been guilty of a trespass (a fact not proved, the court pointed out), he was purged of that trespass by [the settle-

---

appeal to London. *See id.* at 33. The same tactic, interestingly, was employed by New Yorkers against the holders of New Hampshire patents in a dispute over land rights in what is now Vermont. The New York patentees sued the New Hampshire claimants in New York courts, claiming that if the New Hampshire claimants were dissatisfied with the local judgments they could always appeal to the king in council:

> If the *New New-Hampshire* claimants imagined that they were aggrieved by the decisions of our judges, the means of redress were in their own power; and they ought to have sued their writs of error, and in the legal and ordinary mode, to have referred their cause to the final sentence of his majesty.

> 1 RECORDS OF THE COUNCIL OF SAFETY AND GOVERNOR AND COUNCIL OF THE STATE OF VERMONT 510 (1873) [hereinafter RECORDS OF GOVERNOR AND COUNCIL].

What the New Yorkers failed to point out, we are told by Ethan Allen, was that the local New York trials would be "decisive," since:

> in no case wherein the demand of the plaintiff is below the sum of five hundred pounds, a writ of error in favor of the defendent can issue. And the *New-York* attornies [sic] who compiled the *New-York* statings . . . well knew that every action brought against *New-Hampshire* claimants has been designedly laid below that sum.

[60] In response to the fact that Whig-dominated juries made it difficult to obtain convictions for violations of the Navigation and Revenue Acts, parliament "created vice-admiralty courts in all the North American provinces with judges appointed directly from London. As admiralty law was civil law, not common law, the court sat without a jury and factual issues were resolved by the judge." J. REID, *supra* note 29, at 67–68. The use of the civil traverse jury to overturn vice-admiralty proceedings was not the only method available for nullifying the effectiveness of this court. *See id.*

ment] in the vice-admiralty court. . . . Chief Justice Thomas Hutchinson was emphatic. There were no exceptions to the rule, he charged, "that the decree of the Court of Admiralty, where it had jurisdiction, could not be traversed and annulled in a court of common law." [61]

The jury's refusal to be bound by precedent is significant because it suggests that the "mystical regard" [62] the colonists had for the common law did not keep them from selectively applying or ignoring the law when it served their larger purposes to do so. They did not simply *follow* established law. Rather, they were keenly aware of the societal consequences of their legal decisions, and they shaped those decisions to achieve clearly understood social goals. The colonists' view of the world was informed by a deep respect for the tradition of the common law, but it was not an unduly deferential respect. Instead, it was a creative respect for what the inheritance of the past could contribute to their present struggle.

A third respect in which the *Erving* case aids our understanding of law in this period stems from the fact that the court did not enter a judgment over the verdict of the jury—even though the court found that Cradock's defense was valid *as a matter of law*. The primary reason it did not do so is that rules for controlling and limiting jury discretion had not yet been fully developed in the colonies. [63]

---

[61] *Id.* at 31 (footnotes omitted).

[62] *See* M. HORWITZ, *supra* note 3, at 5.

[63] One of the best descriptions of the jury's power to find law is found in W. NELSON, *supra* note 2:

[The jury's] power to find law was virtually unlimited. The frequent use of the general issue, which left to the jury the ultimate determination of the legal consequences of the facts of a case; the practice of counsel and judges giving the jury conflicting instructions on the law, which permitted the jury to select the rules for determining the legal consequences of facts; and the infrequency with which jury verdicts were set aside after trial tended to give the jury wide power to find the law. . . . In the words of John Adams, "a general Verdict, *given under the Direction of the Court* in Point of Law, . . . assuredly determined[d] . . . the Law." Even when a jury acted contrary to the direction of the court, Adams argued that its verdict determined the law, for it was "not only [every juror's] right but his Duty in that Case to find the Verdict accord-

Thus, a jury verdict, whether or not it was based on an "erroneous" interpretation of the law,[64] was final. In short, if a Whig lawyer could get his case before a jury—assuming, that is, the "politics" of the case were roughly those of the *Erving* case—he could be reasonably assured of success.

Finally, the *Erving* case exemplifies the important connections that existed in the Whig legal mind between the politics of independence and the support of local commercial activity. The jury could have gone either way in the *Erving*

---

ing to his own best Understanding, Judgment and Conscience, tho in Direct opposition to the Direction of the Court.'

Id. at 29.

The law-finding function of the jury served not only as a check against the arbitrary exercise of power by colonial judges, but also gave the jury "effective power to control the content of the province's substantive law." *Id.* Although this meant, as Professor Nelson notes, that "the legal system could not serve as an instrument for the enforcement of . . . social policies formulated by political authorities," *id.,* it meant at the same time that the legal system *could* serve as an instrument for the enforcement of local Whig policies—as Professor Reid shows us it did. This last point—that Whig lawyers and juries creatively employed law as an instrument of Whig policy—has been overlooked by Professors Nelson and Horwitz.

The role of the jury in shaping "the content of the province's substantive law" explains in large part why it is not until the nineteenth century that we begin to see the judicial transformation of common law doctrine in this country. As long as the jury could shape substantive law to implement social policy, legal doctrine *did not have to be reformed.* It was only after restrictions were placed on the power of the jury to find law, that judges found themselves with no choice but to alter the legal rules themselves. This observation is closely related to the question of why the development of rules for controlling jury discretion was delayed in this country long after their development in England and Ireland. *See* text accompanying note 49 *supra.* The reason for the delay seems to be that maintaining the jury's ability to decide questions of law was a political necessity until the struggle for independence from parliamentary domination had been won. Only after the Revolutionary War could rules be developed restricting the law-deciding power of the jury. Were it not for the political struggle in the colonies, in other words, it is conceivable that rules controlling the exercise of power by juries—and the judicial development of common law doctrine itself—might have occurred much earlier. The reasons such developments did not occur earlier is not that the colonial world was anticommercial, but that it was anti-imperial. But see M. HORWITZ, *supra* note 3, at 143.

[64] I place "erroneous" in quotations to underscore the fact that such a jury decision would be "erroneous" only from the standpoint of the expectation that a jury was bound to follow inherited precedent; the colonial jury did not see things that way, but quite consciously shaped legal doctrine to accommodate the pursuit of Whig political and economic policy much as common law judges, such as Chief Justice Shaw, would do a half-century later.

case (at least in theory). In voting as it did for the local merchant, Erving, it was casting a vote not simply for independence from English domination but also in support of local commerce. The jury had in its power the ability to place the loss of the seizure either on the local merchant or on the representative of the crown. By placing it on the crown, the jury in effect "subsidized" local commercial activity. To the revolutionary generation, the goals of independence and of local commercial development were *not* perceived as incompatible. Indeed, the colonists of this period would have been startled to learn that they were "anticommercial"—or, for that matter, "antilegal.'[65] It was only much later in our history, and under radically different economic conditions, that the view began to take hold that the interests of commercial development were not always compatible with those of individual liberty and dignity.

It is impossible in the context of this review to more than touch upon the surface of what Professor Reid shows us to have been the rich interplay of creative legalism and political action during this period. There are, however, two additional aspects of this experience that deserve mention: the extraordinarily innovative character of Whig political organization; and the precipitation in the American colonies, under the pressure of events, of two distinct legal cultures.

[65] Professor Horwitz maintains that the legal world of revolutionary America was "anticommercial." *See* text accompanying note 6 *supra*. While it would be absurd to suggest that the expansion of local commerce was the sole motivation for the rebellion against British rule in the colonies, it would be equally misleading to deny the important role played by such concerns in maintaining the momentum that led ultimately to the break from England. Many of the leading Whig activists were happily occupied with commercial dealings, and they perceived their commercial interests as inextricably tied to their political agitations.

With regard to Horwitz's description of the colonists as antilegal, *compare* text accompanying note 5 *supra* with General Gage's letter to the earl of Hillsborough about the legal imprecision of a cashiering provision in parliamentary legislation:

I would take the Liberty My Lord to represent, that the Clause in Question, is by no means calculated for the Circumstances of this Country, *where every Man Studys Law, and interprets the Law as suits his Purposes. And where the measures of Government are opposed by every Evasion and Chicane, that can be devised.*

Letter from General Thomas Gage to the earl of Hillsborough (Oct. 31, 1768), *quoted in* J. REID, *supra* note 29, at 110 (emphasis added); *see id.* at 65–66.

One of the most fascinating aspects of the colonial legal experience was the remarkably fluid—indeed, protean—character of institutional life. Those assembled at a town meeting might vote to adjourn and immediately thereafter to reconstitute themselves as members of a less politically constrained Committee of Merchants. Alternatively, the same group could transform itself, as the situation demanded, into a political mob; and the mob, in turn, could be transformed, by the utterance of a few magic words, into an official *posse comitatus*.[66] In such a world, whether certain activities were perceived as "lawful" or "unlawful" often depended upon one's particular political point of view.[67]

[66] *See* J. REID, *supra* note 29, at 77–78, 94–97.

[67] *See id.* at 92–99, 162. This phenomenon is also reflected in the literature pertaining to the struggle between New York and New Hampshire claimants over land grants in what is now Vermont, *discussed in* note 59 *supra*. The New Hampshire grantees, led by Ethan Allen, saw New York legislation in much the same light as the Boston Whigs saw parliamentary legislation, as is reflected in the following statement:

[I]f the *New-York* patentees will remove their patents . . . and suspend those criminal prosecutions against us for being rioters (as we are unjustly denominated) then will our settlers be orderly and submissive subjects to government; but, be it known to that despotic fraternity of law-makers . . . that we will not be fooled or frighted out of our property; they have broke over his majesty's express prohibitions . . . and when they act in conformity to the regal authority of *Great-Britain*, it will be soon enough to obey them. . . . [T]heir pretended zeal for good order and goverment, is fallacious, . . . they aim at the lands and labours of the grantees [and] they subvert the good and wholesome laws of the realm, to . . . bring about their vile and mercenary purposes. . . . [T]he first knowledge we had of said laws, was the completion of them; which informed us, that if we assembled, three or more of us together, to oppose (that which they call legal) authority, we shall be adjudged felons, and suffer the pains of death; and that some fraternity of plotters knew . . . that they have for a number of years last past, endeavored to exercise such a course of what they call law, that they had not been opposed by the people of these grants (called the MOB) in the executing the same, they would, before this time, have been in possession of that territory, for which the laws aforesaid are calculated.

RECORDS OF GOVERNOR AND COUNCIL, *supra* note 59, at 478–79. This statement reflects the extreme "relativeness" of conceptions of law in the colonies: Whether or not a particular activity was perceived as "lawless" depended, finally, upon one's ultimate allegiances and purposes.

The creation of local "committees of safety" in the New Hampshire grants to legitimize the settlers' repulsion of New York authorities sent to claim land grants for New York patentees, *id.* at 517, provides yet another example of colonial legal ingenuity.

The Whig invention of the Committee of Merchants is a perfect example of the enormous creativity of mind with which the colonists approached inherited institutions. The purposes and activities of these Committees are perceptively described in a letter by the British Commander, General Gage, in 1769:

> Committees of Merchants . . . contrive to exercise the Government they have set up, to prohibit the Importation of British Goods, appoint Inspectors, tender Oaths to the Masters of Vessels, and enforce their Prohibitions by coercive Measures. In Times less dissolute, and licentious, it would be matter of Astonishment, to hear that British Manufactures were prohibited in British Provinces, by an illegal Combination of People, who at the same Time, presume to trade under the Protection of the British Flagg in most Parts of the World; and surely wonderfull, that such an Imperium should be set up, and at length established without the least Shew of Opposition.[68]

The Committees of Merchants, Reid argues, represented an important early experiment in self-government. The critical role they played in legislating and enforcing "Whig law"[69] underscores again the important interrelationship between the political cause of independence and the advancement of local mercantile interests.

The same forces that explain the creation of the Committee of Merchants also help explain the curious phenomenon of the "lawful mob." The actions of colonial mobs during these years were characterized by "a singular self-restraint."[70] Why was it that the American colonies did not witness the indiscriminate violence and bloodshed that has

[68] Letter from General Thomas Gage to Lord Barrington (Dec. 2, 1769), *quoted in* J. REID, *supra* note 29, at 205 n.1.

[69] *See* text accompanying notes 75–78 *infra*.

[70] The role of violence and the threat of violence in the American Revolution is curiously complicated. For in that upheaval, unlike the French Revolution in which thousands were killed, directly or indirectly, as a result of mob action, there was "a singular self-restraint. . . . [T]he participants invariably stopped short of inflicting death."

B. BAILYN, PAMPHLETS, *supra* note 2, at 581 (quoting Schlesinger, *Political Mobs and the American Revolution, 1765–1776*, PROCEEDINGS OF THE AMERICAN PHILOSOPHICAL SOCIETY 99 (1955)), *quoted in* J. REID, *supra* note 29, at 167.

accompanied mob activity elsewhere? Professor Reid suggests that two critical factors were at work. First, from the outset, the mob was perceived by the Whigs not as an illegal group, but as something of an unofficial *posse comitatus* constituted on the spot to enforce Whig law.[71] This explains the remarkable discipline with which the mob generally proceeded about its business. There existed in the colonies, as Reid demonstrates, a keen sense of the line between legitimate and illegitimate mob activity. On the few occasions when the mob engaged in looting and destruction beyond that necessary to the achievement of Whig policy, the actions of the mob were condemned not only by Tories but by Whig leaders themselves.[72]

The second factor is that the mobs could do their political work at leisure without fear of arrest or harassment from the British military forces stationed in the colonies. Under existing law, the British troops could not be invoked to suppress rioting until the Riot Act was read. The official responsible for reading the Riot Act, however, was the local magistrate, or justice of the peace; and since, in Massachusetts Bay, justices of the peace were not appointed by the governor (nor could they be removed by him),[73] the Riot

[71] "Lawlessness" in the Whig sense implied that the act complained of—such as a riot—was not only in violation of constituted law but was performed either for an irrational purpose or for personal gain or had a negative or antisocial aim. "Lawful" or "semilawful" in the Whig sense was an act contrary to statutory or common law, but when Tory or imperial law was broken and the purpose was to defend Whig constitutional principles the act was not necessarily "lawless."

J. REID, *supra* note 29, at 163. The Boston Tea Party, for example, was perceived as "lawful" in this special sense. *See id.* at 94–99.

[72] The wanton destruction of Thomas Hutchinson's house, for instance, was generally condemned by leading Whigs. *Id.* at 76. As the tory Francis Bernard noted, "great pains [were] taken to separate" the riot that forced Andrew Oliver to resign as stamp agent (which was perceived as a show of resistance against submission to the Stamp Act) and the looting of Hutchinson's house (which was perceived as vandalism); "it has been publicly hinted that if a line is not drawn between the first riot and the last, the civil power will not be supported by the principle people of the town. . . ." Letter from Governor Francis Bernard to the earl of Halifax (Aug. 31, 1765), *quoted* in J. REID, *supra* note 29, at 89.

[73] *See* J. REID, *supra* note 29, at 81. In contrast, the magistrates in Ireland were considered "the shock troops of the Protestant occupation. Appointed by the lord

Act was almost never read. The mob, therefore, was left free to pursue its business without fear of clashing with authorities, and could pursue it with a deliberateness and discipline that in other circumstances would have been impossible.[74]

Cumulatively these institutional innovations had a profound effect on the nature of law in the colonies. What they led to ultimately, Professor Reid argues, was the precipitation of two distinct legal cultures: one centered around British imperial law, the other around "whig law."[75] To the royal administrators and the Loyalists, "law" meant "the command of parliament";[76] to the Whig it meant "Lord Coke's custom and right reason" creatively employed in service of the new political vision that had taken hold of the colonists' imagination.[77] In other words, there was *not* a uniform conception of law in the colonies during this period. As the colonial legal world became increasingly polarized, Professor Reid shows us, more than just economic and political interests were affected; the Tories' and Whigs' most basic perceptions of law also came to be fundamentally opposed.[78]

The way in which popular control over local legal insti-

---

lieutenant, they were, quite often, not men from the community, but military officers. . . . Whether army officers or landed gentry, the magistrates of eighteenth-century Ireland could be depended upon to support British rule." *Id.* (footnotes omitted).

[74] *See id.* at 171–72.

[75] As the prerevolutionary controversy intensified, two distinct legal theories began to emerge. On one side was the imperial law applied by the royal officials and endorsed by the judges of the provincial superior court. On the other was whig law, supported by most of the local institutions of government, including the inferior courts, the magistrates, and the grand and traverse juries, both civil and criminal.

It is important to note [that] whig law . . . was not merely constitutional, but positive law as well.

Id. at 66.

[76] *Id.* at 71.

[77] *Id.*

[78] The political perspective Reid brings to this period sheds helpful light on the question raised, but never fully answered, by Professor Nelson: "why a legal system that was structured to render officials so weak was acceptable to the dominant groups in society"? W. NELSON, *supra* note 2, at 31.

tutions shaped the colonial Whigs' perception of law is help-
fully summarized by Professor Reid:

> By their control of the council, the magistrates, and the grand
> and traverse juries, the Massachusetts whigs were assured
> that the agents of British imperialism would not impose ar-
> bitrary measures of the type so freely resorted to by their
> counterparts in Ireland. When challenging the constitution-
> ality of parliamentary legislation—the Stamp Act or the
> Townshend duties for example—the Americans had less
> need to act outside the substantive criminal or civil law, to be
> "lawless" to the degree of the Irish [rebels]. Control of the
> legislature, of the executive council, and of the town meet-
> ings, put the goal of opposition through legal methods almost
> within their grasp.[79]

The essence of the difference between the American and
Irish experience with law is symbolically expressed, Reid observes, by the fact that, when John Adams sat down to draft
a frame of government for the new political society in
America, his overriding instinct was to call for a government of laws and not of men.[80]

"In Ireland the law was governed by men. In North
America men were governed by law." [81] In the end it came
down to the fundamental humanity of the society itself. "It
is difficult to imagine Thomas Hutchinson [the governor of
Massachusetts Bay] even contemplating the repressive statutes that flowed from the pen of John Fitzgibbon [the lord
lieutenant of Ireland]." [82] Though "[b]oth were native sons
of British colonies," their approaches to the administration
of law could not have been more different.[83] Hutchinson's
administration may have been, at least from the vantage
point of imperial law, ineffectual—indeed, even tragic—but
it was not, as was Fitzgibbon's, destructive and brutal. "The
difference," Reid concludes, "may not be in the substance

---

[79] J. REID, *supra* note 29, at 162.
[80] *See id.* at 165 (quoting 4 THE WORKS OF JOHN ADAMS 230 (C. Adams ed.
1851)).
[81] *Id.* at 173.
[82] *Id.*
[83] *See id.*

of the law but how much those who govern respect the rule of law."[84]

II. The Significance of *In a Defiant Stance*

There are two principal ways to understand the significance of *In a Defiant Stance,* both deriving from Professor Reid's comparison of the experience with law in revolutionary America and Ireland during the same period. First, the Irish perspective casts the legal world of mid-eighteenth century America in a revealing new light. If we approach law in the colonial period solely from the perspective of nineteenth-century law in this country, it may appear to have been "precommercial" (because commercial activity in America had not yet developed to the extent it would in the nineteenth century); to have been applied largely in terms of rough communal justice (because of the relatively broad powers of the jury during this time); to have been lacking an appreciation of law as an instrument of political or social reform (because the major work of transforming common-law doctrine to accommodate the rise of the market did not occur until the nineteenth century); or to have been defined by a uniform and harmonious sense of purpose and of "law" (because it would be a century before the legal world would be split by class divisions and competing socialist and laissez-faire ideologies). Yet, when we approach this same mid-eighteenth-century legal world from the perspective of the Irish experience, it becomes apparent that our earlier view of law in this period may have been overly simplistic. Reid's comparison of the colonial legal world with that of eighteenth-century Ireland serves to complicate our sense of the past. It throws into relief certain salient aspects of the American colonial experience that pass unnoticed when we approach this period solely from the perspective of law in nineteenth-century America. It leads us to appreciate, for example, the extent to which the colonists perceived law, not simply as an inheritance "mystically regarded," but as a

[84] *Id.*

creative force in the struggle against a repressive established order; to realize that legal activity in the colonies, far from being crude and simple, was sophisticated, imaginative, and inspired by the same vision that everywhere was transforming American society; and to see clearly the extent to which law was employed by Whig lawyers and juries as a creative instrument for the achievement of this new vision.

The second way in which *In a Defiant Stance* contributes to our understanding of law in history is in some respects more difficult to appreciate, but by the same measure, even more significant. It is the way the radically different experiences with law in Ireland and America during this period illuminates the difficult problem of what to make of respect for the rule of law in history. The problem is an extremely controversial one in American legal history because the new school historians argue that "the rule of law" is nothing but a slogan used by the powerful and corrupt to legitimize the established order; to the new school an ideal world is a "world without law."[85] This is something to which we will turn our full attention in the final section of this review.

Let me begin my discussion of the contribution *In a Defiant Stance* makes to our understanding of law in the revolutionary period by first identifying what I found to be perhaps the most troublesome aspect of Professor Reid's treatment of this period: his failure to bring home more forcefully the connections between the creative institutionalism he described and the transforming developments in substantive legal thought that were occurring during this same period. Occasionally, Professor Reid hints at the existence of such connections,[86] but his development of them is

---

[85] *See* text accompanying notes 110–123 *infra.*

[86] *See, e.g.,* R. REID, *supra* note 29, at 66, 88–90. It seems to me that Professor Reid never fully works out the relationship between what he calls Whig law and the constitutional issues that were dividing the legal world of the colonies during this period. In insisting that the concept of Whig law is *distinct* from the constitutional arguments, Reid sometimes treats Whig law as *separate* from, rather than as *more embracing* than, the constitutional arguments. Thus, some of the important connections between these two interlocking spheres of thought and activity are never fully developed.

at best half-hearted. What fails to come through in this book is the sense of intellectual and moral excitement that pervaded legal thought and activity during the years of crisis, the intense drama of working out powerful tensions between the inheritance of the past and a gripping new vision of the future.[87] Yet Reid often seems to head in the other direction, to seek to separate developments in "the sub-

---

For example, I would like to have seen more emphasis given to the conceptual struggle over what was meant by "constitution." In Professor Bailyn's words:

> The word "constitution" and the concept behind it was of central importance to the colonists' political thought; their entire understanding of the crisis in Anglo-American relations rested upon it. So strategically located was this idea in the minds of both English and Americans, and so great was the pressure placed upon it in the course of a decade of pounding debate that in the end it was forced apart, along the seam of a basic ambiguity, to form the two contrasting concepts of constitutionalism that have remained characteristic of England and America ever since.

B. BAILYN, PAMPHLETS, *supra* note 2, at 45. The emerging conception of constitutionalism in the colonies has particular bearing on Professor Reid's thesis because, as suggested below, Reid's idea of Whig law stresses institutional over substantive developments. The evolution of the colonists' conception of constitutionalism was, if anything, however, *away from* an institutional conception and towards a substantive one. The colonists came increasingly to emphasize principles above institutions. *See id.* at 99–104. The colonists rejected the earlier conception of the English constitution as "a nice piece of machinery" in favor of one in which fundamental ideals and values, rights and principles, were central. *See id.* at 99. One problem with Professor Reid's approach to Whig law is that it seems to move in an opposite direction. *See* text accompanying notes 143–48 *infra.*

A similar objection exists, I think, with respect to Professor Reid's summary treatment of the concept of "sovereignty." *Compare* J. REID, *supra* note 29, at 72 & n.23 *with* B. BAILYN, PAMPHLETS, *supra* note 2, at 115–38. The colonists' understanding of law was powerfully influenced by competing conceptions of sovereignty, and the very *legitimacy* of their takeover of local legal institutions turned on how they resolved the sovereignty problem. Yet Reid does not discuss at all the crucial interrelationships involved.

[87] *See generally* B. BAILYN, PAMPHLETS, *supra* note 2, at 90–138. Developments in legal thought were central to the larger transformation of American political consciousness: The dramatic changes "in the view of what a constitution was and of the proper emphasis in the understanding of rights . . . were momentous; they would shape the entire future development of American constitutional thought and practice." *See id.* at 109. It is possible to argue, of course, that the enormous creative energies given expression in the constitutional area simply stopped at the boundaries of constitutional legal thought, while the rest of the American legal world lay sleeping until the dawn of the nineteenth century. This, or something like it, it seems to me, must necessarily be the view of the new school historians.

stance" of legal thought and doctrine during this period from the institutional creativity he describes. As a result, one comes away from this book with the disconcerting sense that something is missing, that something important has been left out.[88] To criticize a historian for leaving out what he perhaps never intended to include may seem unfair, but in my view it is absolutely impossible to understand the colonists' creative employment of legal institutions during these critical years without understanding the relationships of these institutional innovations to the dramatic currents of legal thought that were shaping the consciousness of the revolutionary generation.

Let me give just one example of what I mean. Professor Reid omits any discussion in this book of James Otis' argument in the famous "writs case"[89] of 1761. This is curious because, more than any other, this case set the tone of legal thought for the period.[90] Without elaborating in great detail, the basic dimensions of the case are worth developing here because they illustrate the vital interconnections that existed during this period between creative legal thought and the emerging ideology of independence. At one level, the case involved nothing more than a typical dispute between a local merchant and a customs official over the use of general search warrants, or "writs of assistance." The technical issue was whether the superior court was authorized to act as an exchequer court for purposes of issuing the writs. In the mind of presiding Chief Justice Hutchinson, informed as it was by the perspective of imperial law, the issue was not a difficult one: First, writs of assistance were valid in English law and commonly used by customs officials in that country; second, their use in the colonies

---

[88] *See* text accompanying notes 143–148 *infra*.

[89] 1 Quincy app. 1, at 471–76 (Mass. Bay Colony Superior Ct. of Judicature 1761) (S. Quincy ed. 1865) (John Adams' report of the first argument). For a full account of the issues involved, see 2 LEGAL PAPERS OF JOHN ADAMS, 111, 113 n.2 (L. Wroth and H. Zobel eds. 1965). The following discussion is based largely on Professor Bailyn's treatment of the case in B. BAILYN, ORDEAL, *supra* note 12, at 54–56; B. BAILYN, PAMPHLETS, *supra* note 2, at 99–103, 411–17.

[90] *See* B. BAILYN, PAMPHLETS, *supra* note 2, at 99–115.

was provided for in parliamentary legislation; and third, the superior court was authorized to act as an exchequer' court for the purpose of issuing the writs. "This was the law, and the only arguments that Hutchinson could conceive of as worthy of the court's consideration were queries directed to these points."[91] Yet it was particularly the mark of the Whig legal mind, epitomized in many respects by the highly successful lawyer James Otis,[92] to inquire beyond the legal technicalities to the large principles that lay behind them.

> The ultimate problem, Otis said, was not so much the writs as the laws of Parliament controlling the American economy that made such writs necessary. These navigation laws and the writs issued to enforce them invaded the invaluable "privilege of house" by which every subject of English laws was rendered "as secure in his house as a prince in his castle." Both nagivation laws and writs of assistance, therefore, violate "the fundamental principles of law"; both, therefore, run against the constitution, and they are, consequently, void. For "an act against the constitution is void: an act against natural equity is void: and . . . the executive courts must pass such acts into disuse," the common law having the power to control an act of Parliament.[93]

It was at this moment—when Otis first argued that the principles of common law superseded an act of parliament—that, as John Adams later noted, "the child Independence was born."[94]

Otis' appeal for elevating principle over precedent was based on much more than a simple plea for justice or eq-

[91] B. BAILYN, ORDEAL, *supra* note 12, at 55.

[92] Otis, son of a politically ambitious lawyer, attended Harvard College and later entered the practice of law. "By the mid-fifties he had settled in Boston, and enjoyed not only an increasingly successful practice at the bar but membership in [Boston's] literary and intellectual circle." B. BAILYN, PAMPHLETS, *supra* note 2, at 410. He served as advocate general of the vice-admiralty court for a few years, but resigned out of anger at the administration of then-governor Francis Bernard for passing over his father in favor of Thomas Hutchinson for a recently vacated post on the Superior Court. It was this incident that eventually led to Otis' early and famous attacks on the government's efforts to enforce the Navigation Acts. *See id.* at 411.

[93] *Id.* at 411–12 (footnote omitted).

[94] *See id.* at 100.

uity. It was based rather on a highly sophisticated interpretation of Lord Coke's celebrated *Bonham's Case*.[95] Otis' plea epitomized, in other words, the transforming imagination of the Whig lawyer; he took doctrine that Coke had developed in the private law context, and creatively applied it to the emerging political controversy taking shape between England and America. The historical implications of this subtle, but important, shift in legal thought was profound. The ideas that were first given expression in response to this concrete legal dispute later came to powerfully shape the course of the American Revolution.[96] Significantly, the currents of thought that were to inspire John Adams and others of his generation, and which ultimately found their way into the celebrated pamphlets of the Revolution, had their origins—as Adams himself recognized—in the creative reading of the law.

This is just one example of what I perceive to be the major shortcoming of *In a Defiant Stance:* Reid's failure to make more of the connections between the colonists' innovative institutionalism and the creative transformation of legal thought that was occurring during this period. This failure, however, should not overshadow the genuine and important contribution this book makes to our understanding of law during the revolutionary period. The most significant contribution in this respect, perhaps, is the *political perspective* that Reid's book supplies. In recent years, we have seen some interesting and excellent work on the legal world of this period,[97] but what has been missing is a sense of how divided the legal world had become in the colonies as the result of the policies of independence. Reid's notion of the polarization of the legal world in revolutionary America into two distinct legal cultures is particularly valuable in this respect, because it leads us to appreciate the complexity of this world.

[95] For an excellent discussion of Otis' argument and its political consequences, see *id.* at 413–17.

[96] *See id.* at 99–103, 413–17.

[97] *See generally* W. NELSON, *supra* note 2.

Let me illustrate the way that taking into account the political dimensions of legal experience helps us to "see more" about legal thought and activity in revolutionary America by comparing the view of this world we find in Reid's book with the one we find in Professor Horwitz's recent work, *The Transformation of American Law.*[98] In his *Transformation,* Horwitz makes the claim that "[t]he generation of Americans who made the American Revolution [conceived of] the common law as a known and determinate body of legal doctrine."[99] Because the colonists conceived of the common law as immutable, Professor Horwitz argues, they would have found alien the idea of shaping law to accord with "reason" or "will"—that is to say, with enlightened public policy. There is, of course, a certain *relative* validity of this claim; the job of adjusting common law doctrine to accommodate the emerging market economy did not get fully underway, everyone agrees, until after the turn of the nineteenth century. But that is not what Professor Horwitz is saying. His claim is that there was a uniform conception of common law throughout the colonies during the revolutionary period, and that it was uniformly hostile to the idea that the law can be creatively employed as an instrument of political or social policy.[100] What is relevant here, however, is that to support this assertion, Horwitz cites a 1767 statement *by Chief Justice Hutchinson* to the effect that "laws should be established, else Judges and Juries must go according to their reason, that is, their Will."[101] The implicit claim is that, in urging the importance of respecting "established" law, Chief Justice Hutchinson is advancing a conception of law uniformly accepted in the colonial world. What Professor Horwitz fails to recognize in making this claim, of course, is

[98] M. HORWITZ, *supra* note 3. It is particularly surprising that Professor Horwitz comes off the worse for this comparison, since he has long been an advocate of the importance of seeing law in its political context.

[99] *Id.* at 4.

[100] *See id.* at 1–9; *see* text accompanying notes 2–11 *supra.*

[101] M. HORWITZ, *supra* note 3, at 5. Horwitz also cites a similar statement by John Adams. But if anyone was impressed by Otis' daring innovations in legal thought, it was Adams. *See* B. BAILYN, ORDEAL, *supra* note 12, at 54–56.

that Chief Justice Hutchinson was a strong loyalist, and when he spoke, he spoke from the perspective of imperial law. In this and other statements to the grand jury, as Professor Reid demonstrates, Hutchinson was advancing a viewpoint with which "the generation of Americans who made the American Revolution" would have very sharply disagreed. His admonition against shaping the law to implement "Will" or policy was aimed, it is important to understand, at the refusal of whig grand juries to indict for seditious libel.[102] This is more fully revealed in a similar charge made by Hutchinson to the Suffolk County grand jury two years later, in 1769.

> We, who are to execute the Law, are not to enquire into the Reason and Policy of it . . . . I mention this, Gentlemen, because, from my own Observation, both in this and some other counties, I have found Juries taking upon them to judge of the Wholesomeness of the Laws, and thereby subverting the very End of their Institution.[103]

Hutchinson's concerns were not the concerns of the Whigs; and his conception of law was not their conception. This is something we cannot appreciate, however, until we know the political context of his remarks, and, at a more general level, until we understand the way the law was polarized along the Whig-imperial axis during this period. The ironic fact, of course, is that in stressing the importance of strict adherence to inherited law, Hutchinson was expressing an "imperial" reaction to the creative liberties Whig lawyers and juries had been taking with it. And, it is crucial to note, they had been taking liberties with inherited law not simply to do justice in individualized cases, but in conscious awareness of law as an instrument in the political struggle for independence from British domination.

This is just one example, moreover, of the way in which *In a Defiant Stance* serves to complicate our sense of law during this period in our past. By documenting the colonists' imaginative employment of law—of legal institutions, pro-

---

[102] *See* J. REID, *supra* note 29, at 46–47, 52–53.

[103] 1 Quincy 306–08 (Mass. Bay Colony Superior Ct. of Judicature 1769) (S. Quincy ed. 1865), *quoted in* J. REID, *supra* note 29, at 71.

cedure, and doctrine—in the service of an emerging new vision of American society, Reid's study suggests that the relationship of legal thought and activity during the latter half of the eighteenth century to the creative transformation of the common law in the early nineteenth century may be much more complex than we have been led to believe. If Reid's interpretation of law in the revolutionary period is right, it seems impossible not to conclude that—in at least one sense—creative instrumentalism in this country had its origins not in the early nineteenth century, but rather in the years of crisis leading up to the Revolutionary War, at least fifty years earlier.[104]

III. The Problem of "Respect for the Rule of Law" in History

(The communist looks forward to a day of order without law, bless his merciful heart.)[105]

Perhaps the most provocative aspect of Professor Reid's book is his conclusion that "the difference" between the

[104] There are remarkable similarities, for example, between Otis' approach to legal precedent in the "writs case" in 1761 and Chief Justice Shaw's general approach to precedent in the mid-nineteenth century (1830–1860). To both men, the essence of legal decision was extracting from the morass of inherited precedent "fundamental principles"; and to both, the law was something to be employed in the service of a larger vision of the public interest. *Compare* Professor Bailyn's description of Otis' approach to precedent, and John Adams' perception of it, in B. Bailyn, Ordeal, *supra* note 12, at 56, *with* Professor Levy's portrayal of Chief Justice Shaw's conception of law in L. Levy, *supra* note 17, at 23–24.

Shaw, like Otis, would not dispose of a case simply on the grounds that " 'so it was ruled in the Year Books.' " *See id.* " 'The question will still be put, [Shaw] declared, "upon what principle is it founded?" This question must be fairly met and answered.' " *Id.* Shaw described the activity of law in the following way, much of which—though admittedly not all—could as easily have been spoken by Otis:

> The ultimate object of all laws, and of all jurisprudence, is, to do justice between parties; and the judge who . . . can unravel a complicated case, seek out its governing principles with their just exceptions and qualifications, and, without violating the rules, or weakening the authority of positive law, can apply those principles in a manner consistent with the plain dictates of natural justice, may be considered as having accomplished the most important purpose of his office.

See id. at 23–24.

Of course there are differences between Otis' and Shaw's understandings of law, but there is also a direct line of inheritance from Otis through Adams to Shaw.

[105] R. Frost, *The Constant Symbol, in* Atlantic Monthly, Oct. 1946, at 51.

American and Irish experiences with law during this period
lay not in "the substance" of the law, but in the fact that in
the American colonies there existed genuine "respect for
the rule of law." [106] It was because of respect for the rule of
law, Reid argues, that Thomas Hutchinson would never
have considered the brutal and repressive measures imposed by the Irish lord lieutenant, John Fitzgibbon; and,
conversely, it was the lack of respect for the rule of law by
the Irish royal administrators that explains why the legal
world of Ireland during this period was characterized by
arbitrariness, exploitation, and bloodshed. What the comparison of the American and Irish experiences with law
suggests, in other words, is that it is a fundamental misconception to see the rule of law, as do the new school historians, as nothing more than an instrument of repression, or
as the embodiment of a destructive—"adversarial, competitive, and atomistic"—conception of human relations. [107] Underlying Reid's study is an opposite, and potentially radical,
conclusion: that the rule of law is a positive and powerful
force for human decency and justice in the world.

The problem of "respect for the rule of law" is an ancient
one, in many respects as old as civilization itself. [108] It is also,

---

[106] *See* J. REID, *supra* note 29, at 173.

[107] *See* Horwitz, *The Rule of Law*, *supra* note 3, at 565–66; text accompanying note
16 *supra*.

[108] The rule of law problem has its foundations in the same fertile tension that
has given rise to much of the world's great dramatic literature: the tension between the rule of law on the one hand, and equity, or justice on the other. Certainly Aeschylus' *The Oresteia* and Sophocles' *Antigone* build upon this tension, as
does much of Elizabethan drama. Indeed, one can trace Shakespeare's development as a dramatist in the way he returns to this theme in almost every play, from
his early *Comedy of Errors* to his late *The Winter's Tale*, working and reworking it at
increasing levels of subtlety and complexity. The same tension informs many other
literary classics, including such disparate works as Book Five of Spenser's THE
FAERIE QUEENE, Jonson's VOLPONE, and Melville's BILLY BUDD.
Without the rule of law "problem"—without the enduring tension between the
rule of law and equity—we would be without this rich body of literature. The
utopian fails to appreciate this; and his failure explains why, in the end, utopian
visions of the world are so deeply dissatisfying. For what utopians unwittingly create—by doing away with those powerful tensions that constitute the life of a culture, and of the mind—is a world without drama.
For a look at the way this tension has found literary expression at different

at the present time, a very controversial one in American legal history. The immediate controversy has its origins in the emergence in the early 1970s of the new school of legal historical thought; and it reflects, perhaps not unexpectedly, that school's deep hostility to law in any form—not just to "legalism" in the pejorative sense of that term,[109] but to the rule of law, to the activity of law and, finally, to law itself.

It is important to understand that the new school's despairing view of law is not simply negativism for negativism's sake, but rather is grounded in deep convictions about the nature of law and its potentially destructive impact on human relationships and on the possibilities for community. This conviction is reflected in the new school historian's association of law with the rise of the self-regulating market.[110] If the law is nothing more than an instrument of the market, then it must be rejected, since a world dominated by the market values of efficiency, competition, and greed is a world that fails to provide for the deep human needs for integrity of self, love, and community.[111]

---

points in American history, *compare* John Adams' description of the Otis argument in the "writs case" in B. BAILYN, ORDEAL, *supra* note 12, at 56 (eighteenth century) *with* James Fenimore Cooper's description of the confrontation between Natty Bumppo and Judge Marmaduke Temple in P. MILLER, *supra* note 17, at 99–101 (nineteenth century) *with* the confrontation between Moses Herzog and the law in S. BELLOW, HERZOG 235–40 (1964) (twentieth century).

[109] The new school attack on law is more than an attack on the kind of mindless legalism that any thinking person would find objectionable. If that were all that were involved, then there would be no controversy. Most of us would agree, I take it, that a healthy infusion of antilegalism—at least, *discriminating* antilegalism—into our understanding of American legal history would be for the good. Lawyers and law teachers, like everyone else, can lose sight of ultimate commitments and become mere technicians, grinding out something called "law" not because it advances the cause of justice but simply because that is what they have been trained—or, worse, hired—to do. Thus, anything that serves to restore to the legal mind a proper sense of humility, and inspire a renewed commitment to fundamental ideals and principles, ought to be welcomed with open arms. Yet this is *not*, I think it will become clear, the intent or purpose of the new school. What sets the new school apart is not that it is antilegalistic—we all are—but that it is antilaw.

[110] *See* text accompanying notes 25–27 *supra*.

[111] *See* R. UNGER, MODERN SOCIETY, *supra* note 3; R. UNGER, KNOWLEDGE, *supra* note 3; Levinson, *supra* note 3. It is possible, of course, to accept the importance

But the new school historian's association of law with the market is only a surface expression of a much deeper, more integrated mythology,[112] whose general outlines can only be roughly described here. The basic dimensions of new school mythology are set forth in Karl Polanyi's classic, *The Great Transformation.*[113] According to Polanyi, the major consequence of the industrial revolution was the disintegration of both the community and the human personality. The forces set loose by the industrial revolution drove the common "folk" off the land and into the cities, and created the conditions that gave rise to the self-regulating market and to the political ideology from which it derived its support, classic liberalism.[114] Men left the integrated experience of small, rural communities for the disintegrated, anonymous, exploitive experience of industrial life in the cities. With the rise of the market and of liberal ideology, our most basic

---

of community in human experience without adopting the full ideological baggage of the new school. *See, e.g.,* L. Tribe, *supra* note 31, at 979–90; Teachout, *Chains of Tradition, Instruments of Freedom: Contours of the Emerging Right to Community,* 7 Cap. U. L. Rev. 683 (1978).

[112] I use "mythology" here in the sense used by Malinowski when he defined "myth" as "a narrative resurrection of a primeval reality, told in satisfaction of deep religious wants." *See* B. Malinowski, Myth in Primitive Psychology 19 (1926).

[113] K. Polanyi, *supra* note 7. Polanyi's rich and often powerfully written The Great Transformation has sometimes been referred to as ideological melodrama. To appreciate this one has but to compare Polanyi's views of the impact of the industrial revolution with the view presented in P. Deane, The First Industrial Revolution (1965).

[114] It should be noted that liberalism has two distinct meanings in twentieth-century thought. The mainstream tradition of liberalism is expressed in the common notion of a liberal education. This tradition of liberalism—liberal humanism—is reflected in the work of Professor Lionel Trilling, for example, and involves an integrated conception of human experience. *See generally* L. Trilling, *supra* note 1. Perhaps the most coherent expression of legal thought and activity in this tradition is J. White, *supra* note 22.

There is, however, an extreme branch of "liberal" thought that has taken some of the basic tenets of liberalism and divorced them from their humanistic context. This radical branch finds expression in classical economic thought (in America, the Chicago school), and is closely associated with the self-regulating market. What is ultimately so dissatisfying about the radical interpretation of liberal thought is that it reduces all experience to the terms of cost-benefit analysis. *Compare* L. Trilling, *supra, and* J. White, *supra, with* Coase, *The Problem of Social Cost,* 3 J. Law & Econ. 1, 28–30 (1960) *and* Posner, *supra* note 26.

perceptions of the world were changed: Men became nothing more than labor, and land nothing more than a commodity. That part of experience that was "relevant" increasingly became the part that was relevant to the operation of the market. The central notion in Polanyi's writing is that the rise of the market led to the disintegration of human experience, the destruction of the wholeness, the naturalness—the meaningfulness—of the earlier world.

In Professor Horwitz's historiography, these themes find expression in what is an almost Wordsworthian conception of American legal history. Horwitz's view of history builds upon the notion that "back there" at one time there existed a happy, uncomplicated communal existence that has since become corrupted by the forces of modern life.[115] That is why we find in Professor Horwitz's *Transformation,* for example, the heavy emphasis on the role of the colonial jury in "meting out rough and communal standards of justice" during the eighteenth century.[116] It also explains why Horwitz perceives the nature of the transformation of law in the nineteenth century primarily in terms of a constellation of "separations": of law from justice, law from community, law from morality, procedure from substance, means from ends, and so on. The basic metaphor upon which Horwitz's conception of the nineteenth century proceeds is the Polanyian metaphor of "disintegration."

The same impulse that drives Professor Horwitz's historiography is given elaborate theoretical expression in the work of Professor Roberto Unger, the leading jurisprudent of the new school. It is in Unger's work that we begin to see clearly the basis for the new school's hostility to law.[117] In his *Law in Modern Society,* Professor Unger imagines for us a world in which the communal bond is so strong that the law as we know it simply falls away.[118] It is a world in which

---

[115]*See* M. HORWITZ, *supra* note 3, at 24–25.

[116]*See id.* at 28–30, 211.

[117]*See* R. UNGER, MODERN SOCIETY, *supra* note 3; R. UNGER, KNOWLEDGE, *supra* note 3.

[118]Professor Unger's thought, like Horwitz's, develops around two polarized constellations of values. In Unger's universe, a society centered on "communal

human relationships are no longer defined by the market-dominated values of competition and greed, but rather by an overriding sense of community and love. In polar opposition to a society governed by "liberal" principles, Unger sets up the model of "tribal life."[119] It is the model of a world in which, quite wonderfully, law in the sense of explicit rules would be unnecessary. "Only [in a liberal society] do explicit and formulated rules become possible and necessary." Professor Unger argues:

> Positive law remains superfluous as long as there is a closely held communion of reciprocal expectations, based on a shared view of right and wrong. In this setting the normative order will not surface as formulated rules; indeed, it may remain almost entirely below the threshold of explicit statement and conscious understanding.[120]

The new school's hostility to law and the rule of law is based, in other words, on the notion that as long as law *in*

solidarity" is set off against one centered on individualism and "unharnessed economic warfare." *See* R. UNGER, MODERN SOCIETY, *supra* note 3, at 142. While it is difficult to do justice to the elegant fabric of Professor Unger's thought by quoting an isolated passage, the following reflects the nature of his idealized world without law:

> The members of the group believe themselves tied together by a deep and lasting communal bond. Typically, this bond rests both on a natural fact and on a sharing of common beliefs or ideals. The natural fact is the fate of being born into a family, a territory, a religion, or a race. But this predetermined circumstance is important only insofar as it contributes to a mental experience, which is the very core of tribal community: the sense of having a view of the world and of the good in which others participate, a view whose hold over the group is so strong that it need never be spelled out. Communal solidarity is precisely the condition of extensive, coherent, concrete, and intense moral communion identified earlier as a foundation for custom.

Id. at 142–43.

[119] Professor Unger associates "the rule of law ideal" with "a form of social life, which may be called liberal society or group pluralism." *See id.* at 67–68. "In such a society, every individual belongs to a large number of significant groups, but each of these groups affects only a limited part of his life. Thus personality is carved up into a long list of separate or even conflicting specialized activities." *Id.* at 143. In contrast to Professor Unger's view that group pluralism destructively "carves up" the human personality, Professor White sees in the conflict of institutional claims over our lives a "surprising freedom," a transcendant opportunity for self-definition and self-expression. *See* J. WHITE, *supra* note 22, at 301.

[120] R. UNGER, MODERN SOCIETY, *supra* note 3, at 61–62.

any form is a conscious and visible aspect of social existence, the possibility of genuine community can never be realized.

There is one other strand of new school ideology that deserves mention here because it has a direct bearing on our discussion of the rule of law problem: the emphasis in both Horwitz's and Unger's work on the extreme importance of the integration of law and morality.[121] The internal dynamics of a liberal society are such, according to new school thought, that law is necessarily cut off from substantive moral vision.[122] Thus the entire liberal edifice must be torn down before the new vision of society can be achieved. And what will define the new order when it is established, and distinguish it more than anything else from the existing

[121] The new school seems to conceive of the integration of law and morality in the essentially utilitarian terms of "result-oriented jurisprudence." *See id.* at 234–42. Witness Professor Horwitz's comment: "[W]e should never forget that a 'legalist' consciousness that excludes 'result-oriented' jurisprudence as contrary to the rule of law also inevitably discourages the pursuit of substantive justice." Horwitz, *The Rule of Law, supra* note 3, at 566. The liberal humanist takes a different approach to the integration of law and morality, stressing the interrelationships between the implications of legal decision and the integrity of the decisionmaker. An illustration of the liberal humanist approach is Professor White's introductory comment to his materials on the death penalty:

> In what follows I want to suggest that the death penalty is not merely wrong in itself as a brutal practice, but that it is vicious as a literature, that it is a way of imagining and talking about experience that corrupts our minds and lives, and that it is perhaps representative of other literatures in the law and elsewhere.

J. WHITE, supra note 22, at 128.

[122] *But see* J. WHITE, *supra* note 22. The difference between the two schools of thought is not that one school advocates the integration of law and morality while the other does not. Both schools reflect a deep commitment to an integrated understanding of experience. The difference lies rather in the fact that the new school has an ideological center of gravity, and its literature is couched largely in terms of political theory, while the literature and approach of the humanist school is centered in the traditional humanities—literature, history, and philosophy. The integrating notion in the liberal humanist tradition is in some respects a remarkably simple one: One should bring to the activity of law, as one brings to any endeavor, not just that part of the mind that has been technically trained, but *the whole mind.*

Another significant difference between the two schools is that the new school seeks to discover unity or harmony by eliminating contradictions in experience, while the humanistic school sees in the tensions between the contradictory strands of our experience a source of life and energy.

one, is that it will be a world without law.[123]

The perspective the new school brings to legal thought and history is in many respects important and valuable.[124] Yet there is something about the literature of the new school that in the end is strangely disappointing. It purports to be a literature of enlightenment, to open up a more sensitive and sympathetic understanding of human affairs. Yet for all its claims to this effect, there runs through the writing of the new school, as others have noted, a curious streak of darkness and cynicism about human nature.[125] Moreover, Professor Unger's elegant abstractions of communal life exist, as it were, in the void; we wait for the connections to be made with concrete human experience, but they never are. Perhaps it is this tone of cynicism and duality of abstraction that gives us the sense when we read the literature of the new school that we are not moving toward a new vision of human possibility, but rather tunneling in-

---

[123]The expression of longing for a world without law is by no means confined to the writings of the new school, of course. One finds much the same impulse expressed, for example, at the end of Professor Grant Gilmore's recent *The Ages of American Law*—and there is no reason to think that Professor Gilmore is a particular friend of the new school. After reviewing the broad development of American law from its early bright beginnings to its despairing present, Gilmore concludes by summoning up directly the image of a world in which there is no law:

> Law reflects but in no sense determines the moral worth of a society. The values of a reasonably just society will reflect themselves in a reasonably just law. The better the society, the less law there will be. In Heaven there will be no law, and the lion will lie down with the lamb. The values of an unjust society will reflect themselves in an unjust law. The worse the society, the more law there will be. In Hell there will be nothing but law, and due process will be meticulously observed.

G. GILMORE, THE AGES OF AMERICAN LAW 110–11 (1977). It is difficult to know just how to take this concluding paragraph, since Gilmore seems to be a strong admirer of Justice Story—a lawyer's lawyer if there ever was one. It is perhaps not without significance in this regard that Professor Gilmore's "world without law" is located not on earth, but in the hereafter.

[124]This is so not only because it provides an important counterperspective to the view of law advanced by the classical school of economic thought, *see* Posner, *supra* note 26, but more importantly because of the kind of criticism it aims at humanistic liberalism. For it is only through such criticism that liberal thought keeps alive to its full possibilities. *See Preface* to L. TRILLING, *supra* note 1, at xi–xv.

[125]*See* text accompanying notes 16 *supra* & 141 *infra*.

ward in a trough of pessimism and sentimentality—pessimism about the possibilities of law, and sentimentality about the possibilities of a world without it.

But to respond to the writing and thought of the new school in this way is not to answer the central and difficult question raised by the new school's attack on the rule of law: Whether there *is* a positive—a "creative"—role for the activity of law and the rule of law in human affairs? The answer to this question, I am certain, is yes. But why it is yes is something I can begin to address in only the most tentative way in the context of this review.

We must begin, I would argue, by asking more specifically what it is that the new school's conception of law leaves out of our understanding of law in American history. And one place to look for an answer is the writing of other historians who have succeeded in discovering dimensions of legal experience that the new school historian is either unable, or refuses, to see. For example, if we compare Professor Horwitz's understanding of law in the revolutionary period with that of Professor Bailyn, what strikes us immediately is how much of the richness and complexity of law in this period Professor Horwitz fails to see because of his ideological preconceptions about the nature of law in society. Essentially, the new school historian has only two ways to understand law during the revolutionary, or any other, period: either as "nonlaw," that is, as simple communal justice; or as an instrument for maintaining an unjust social and political order. The problem is that neither of these alternatives begins to describe—to say nothing of do justice to—the colonists' experience. This is true in at least three respects. First, the colonists conceived of law—whether as inherited tradition, as fundamental principle, as mastery of legal technique, as sophisticated procedure, as hard substantive rules: law, in short, in the most comprehensive sense of the term—as a positive force for shaping and helping realize the profoundly humanistic vision of the American Revolution. As Professor Bailyn tells us:

Just as the colonists cited with enthusiasm the theorists of universal reason, so too did they associate themselves . . . with the tradition of the English common law. The great figures of England's legal history, especially the seventeenth century common lawyers, were referred to repeatedly—by the colonial lawyers above all, but by others as well. . . . The common law was manifestly influential in shaping the awareness of the Revolutionary generation.[126]

Yet we get no sense of this from Professor Horwitz's "rough communal justice" conception of law during this period. Second, the relationship of the colonists to law was an extremely complex one. Far from being simple or harmonious, their understanding of law and its relationship to Enlightenment theory on the one hand and to their Puritan inheritance on the other was rich with tensions and contradictions that constituted the life of the mind during this period.[127] Third, the colonists did more than simply respect— or "discover"—law. At bottom, their relationship to law was a deeply creative one. As Professor Bailyn observes, "[the common law] did not in itself determine the kinds of conclusions men would draw in the crisis of the time. Otis and Hutchinson both worshipped Coke, but . . . they read significantly different meanings into his opinion in *Bonham's Case*. The law was no science of what to do next."[128] In the end, it was what the colonists made of their legal inheritance that made all the difference.

In other words, the colonists did not see law in new school terms. They did not see it as an instrument for maintaining a corrupt established order, or as a force that divides men and makes community impossible. Rather they understood law in quite the opposite terms: as a "repository of experience in human dealings" and above all as the embodiment of "the principles of justice [and] equity."[129] And

---

[126] B. Bailyn, Pamphlets, *supra* note 2, at 25–26.

[127] *See id.* at 26–29.

[128] *Id.* at 26.

[129] *See id.*

it is this conception of law that informs the liberal humanist tradition.

The first ground of objection to new school historiography, then, is that it fails to do justice to the complexity of the past; it is "sentimental."[130] To deny the revolutionary period the rich complexity of law and politics, to ignore the hard creative work of lawyers and nonlawyers alike in shaping inherited institutions and doctrine to the needs of an emerging society, is to allow ideological blinders to prevent one from seeing honestly what happened in this period, and why.[131]

The second respect in which the new school approach fails us is that it simply misconceives the dynamics of the

---

[130] New school historians are not the first to use an oversimplified vision of the past as a way of attacking what is perceived to be the corrupt present. They fall into an age-old tradition of political historiography. The pamphlet writers of the Revolutionary period often did the same thing, and *they* were inspired by the model of Roman writers such as Cicero and Tacitus,

> writers who had lived either when the Republic was being fundamentally challenged or when its greatest days were already past. . . . They hated and feared the trends of their own time, and in their writing had contrasted the present with a better past, which they endowed with qualities absent from their own, corrupt era. The earlier age had been full of virtues: simplicity, patriotism, integrity, a love of justice and of liberty; the present was venal, cynical, and oppressive.

See B. BAILYN, PAMPHLETS, *supra* note 2, at 22 (footnote omitted).

[131] But why should this trouble us? Suppose Professor Horwitz *is* "using" history for ideological purposes. All historians, as Professor Trilling tells us, *see* text accompanying note 1 *supra*, have purposes, and so they should, for history without purpose is history without meaning. Yet what the new school historians are doing still *does* trouble us, though it is not easy to say exactly why. Perhaps it is because, in the final analysis, there are purposes, and there are *purposes*. And when ideological preoccupations prevent a historian from doing justice to the complexity of a period, when they lead him to ascribe to it a kind of simplicity and harmony that we know never existed, then it is important to recognize that what is involved is not history, but something else. One of the things we expect from a historian is a certain openness and honesty not simply about his purposes, but about the past itself. Professor Bailyn described the ideal mode of historical interpretation in his preface to ORDEAL, *supra* note 12:

> [One achieves the ultimate mode of interpretation when] the distance has become so great, the connections so finely attenuated, that all the earlier assumptions of relevance, partisan in their nature, seem crude, and fall away,

rule of law in society. Professor Reid's comparison of the Irish and American experiences with law during the eighteenth century goes a long way to demonstrating this, I think. It is a simple empirical truth that where there is genuine respect for the rule of law and the principles that underlie it, brutality and oppression cannot survive. Nor do we have to stay in the colonial period, or in the eighteenth century, to demonstrate this. We can see the rule of law operating in much the same way with respect to the American institution of slavery during the nineteenth century. As Professor James White has demonstrated in his brilliant treatment of slavery opinions and slavery statutes in *The Legal Imagination*,[132] slavery and the rule of law were fundamentally incompatible. And it is this basic incompatibility that explains why Southern judges—Judge Ruffin of North Carolina, for example—were so torn by slavery laws and decisions. It was not simply that the institution of slavery offended the judge's own personal morality, though that was important. More than that, in upholding the master's complete discretion over the life of the slave, as the institution of slavery required him to do, the judge was forced to betray the most fundamental principles underlying the rule of law.[133] The same truth emerges from a comparison of the

---

and in their place there comes a neutrality, a comprehensiveness, and a breadth of sympathy lacking in earlier interpretations.

> *Preface* to B. BAILYN, ORDEAL, *supra* note 12, at ix.

It is this "neutrality," "comprehensiveness," and "breadth of sympathy"—the passionate disinterest in coming to terms with the past—that we expect and need from historical writing. And it is precisely this quality that, because of its ideological preconceptions, new school historiography fails to provide.

[132] *See* J. WHITE, *supra* note 22, at 430–88.

[133] *See* State v. Mann, 13 N.C. (2 Dev.) 263 (1829), *reprinted in* J. WHITE, *supra* note 22, at 451–54. In *Mann*, Judge Ruffin asserted he had no choice but to uphold the master's total authority over the life of the slave, even though it offended his personal morality to do so. *See* 13 N.C. (2 Dev.) at 266. Significantly, Ruffin said the decision was forced upon him by the "actual condition of things," *id.*, and by "things inherent in our political state," *id.* at 264, *i.e.*, by politics, *not law*. He cited no statutes or precedents to support his decision. It was not, therefore, adherence to the rule of law that forced this awful choice upon him. In approaching the same dilemma ten years later in State v. Hoover, 20 N.C. (3 & 4 Dev. & Bat.) 500 (1839), *reprinted in part in* J. WHITE, *supra* note 22, at 448–50, Judge Ruffin was able to discover in the principles underlying the rule of law grounds for re-

slave statutes in the various Southern states. These statutes reflect a powerful tension between the conceptions of the slave as person and the slave as property, though the expression of this tension varies dramatically from state to state. More important however, is the large pattern that emerges when we compare the worlds reflected in the various state codes. What becomes clear is that it is precisely the extent to which the underlying relationships *are spelled out in the law,* that the world of the statute reflects a genuine recognition of the personhood and individuality of the slave.[134] In states with almost nothing in the state slave code that could be called "the rule of law," the world reflected is one of hypocrisy, brutality, and racism.[135] In the following

---

jecting—or at least qualifying—the master's claims of total discretion over the life of the slave. *See* 20 N.C. (3 & 4 Dev. & Bat.) at 500 (master's unjustified killing of slave held to be murder).

The affirmative use of the rule of law and the principles and traditions underlying it to confine and subvert the institution of slavery can also be found in State v. Jones, 2 Miss. (1 Walker) 83 (1820) (Clarke, J.), *reprinted in* J. WHITE, *supra* note 22, at 447–48.

[134]*See* J. WHITE, *supra* note 22, at 434–35 (the slavery provisions of the Louisiana Civil Code of 1838). The Louisiana statutes emphasized not penalties, but the rights of slaves, for example, to contract for their own freedom and, in some circumstances, to inherit property and to appear in court. In the Louisiana code one finds absolutely no nexus between the status of slavery and the fact of being a Negro.

[135]*See id.* at 437–38 (the slavery provisions of the Laws of Mississippi of 1840). The hypocritical nature of Mississippi law is reflected in the fact that, although cruel and unusual punishment of slaves was prohibited, the only sanction involved was a small fine payable to the "literary fund." Moreover, the cruel and unusual punishment provision is followed by provisions that "any negro or mullatto [*sic*] slave [convicted of a felony] shall be burnt in the hand by the sheriff, in open court" and any "negro or mulatto"—whether or not a slave—found guilty of perjury,

> shall, without further trial, be ordered by the said court, to have one ear nailed to the pillory, and there to stand for the space of one hour, and then the said ear to be cut off, and thereafter the other ear nailed in like manner, and cut off at the expiration of one other hour, and moreover to receive thirty-nine lashes on his or her bare back. . . .
>
> *Id.* at 437.

Freedmen, moreover, were told to quit the state, or to remain only at the peril of being returned into slavery by measures both arbitrary and summary, that is, by a process utterly lacking in the qualities of law. Finally, the Mississippi statute is blatantly racist in that "slaves" and "Negroes" were treated for the most part as interchangeable categories. *See id.* at 437–38.

passage, Professor White provides an important insight into the dynamics involved:

> A legal system of the kind we can recognize and work with has at its heart certain fundamental principles, ideals, and values which are utterly inconsistent with the premises of slavery. The law as we know it is not a neutral tool for the expression of the will of the powerful but an actual force for justice in the world. This is demonstrated by the fact that as a slave system is more fully expressed in the law, either it becomes less and less a slave system or the more obvious it is that the "legal" system bears little resemblance to any we know, that it is no system of law at all. Either the rights of slaves as people are recognized . . . or the hypocrisy of any claim to principle is exposed for what it is.[136]

"If slavery is to exist," Professor White continues, "it must be the sole concern of the society subordinating every other value and interest." "This institutional truth," he observes, "explains why the South became at last hysterical, why its intellectual, social, and moral order fell into chaos. It was a totalitarian system founded upon a principle that destroyed every other, including the fundamental principles of legality."[137]

---

[136]*Id.* at 169–70.

[137]*Id.* at 170. It can be argued, of course, that the slavery example leads to an opposite conclusion. Even in Louisiana, perhaps the most humane of the slave states, the fact remains that law was used to maintain and perpetuate an inhumane and oppressive institution. To argue this way, however, is to ignore the distinction between the use of law and "the rule of law." *See* text accompanying notes 29–31 *supra.* If we begin with the institution of slavery as a given during this period, the important observation to make is that to the extent the legal system of a slave state approached the ideal of a rule of law, the system reflected a level of humanity, decency, and trust not approached in the states in which slavery was governed largely by human discretion.

Slavery provides an illustration in an extreme situation of the underlying dynamics of the rule of law. It throws into bold relief the fact that the rule of law operates in *all* situations as a constant pressure for the realization of certain fundamental human values: for the recognition of dignity and personhood, for fairness and justice, and, indeed, even for community. As a society departs from commitment to the rule of law, as decisions affecting the lives of the members of the society come to be characterized by arbitrariness and unfairness, pressures are created for disintegration and corruption. If the rule of law is to be something "we can recognize and work with," it must reflect a substantive vision of humanity

The same forces, it is evident, were at work in eighteenth-century Ireland. In denying the native Catholic population the most fundamental legal rights, the English royal administrators created an institution of subjection similar in many respects to the American institution of slavery. While there were differences, the basic tradition of law in Ireland, like that in the antebellum South, was not that of the rule of law, but rather of the arbitrary discretion by a master class over a disenfranchised and exploited *Untermensch*. So incompatible was this arrangement with the fundamental ideals and values that underlie the rule of law that it ultimately corrupted and destroyed those who were sent to govern, even more than it destroyed those who were governed.[138]

---

and not simply a restraint on power. *See* note 26 *supra*. The critical problem, then, is not how to choose between the rule of law and no rule of law, but how to develop a refined sense of the possibilities and limits of the rule of law in human relationships. Although the rule of law can sometimes act as an inspiration, *see generally* United States v. Olmstead, 277 U.S. 438, 483–85 (1928) (Brandeis, J., dissenting), the rule of law cannot ensure happy relationships, *see* J. WHITE, *supra* note 22, at 555–66.

[138] *See* J. REID, *supra* note 29, at 143–49. The "legal mind" of royal administrators in Ireland reflected long established traditions. Two centuries earlier, Irish Deputy Lord Grey approached the problem of developing Ireland by stating that there could be no consideration of building up "before force have planed the ground for the foundation." *Preface* to SPENSER, *supra* note 36, at xvii. And Spenser himself "could conceive of no other beginning than the absolute and final putting down of rebellion by the sword and by famine. That done, there would be opportunity to reform with some effect, upon a settled and orderly plan." *See id.* Although Spenser was quite aware of the way the "present state of things" in Ireland of the 1580's could change a "gentell, affable, loving, and temperate" person into a harsh administrator, *id.*, he never understood the way in which the cruel use of law shaped his own perceptions of the world and, ultimately, corrupted his thought and writing. The extent to which it did so is apparent in his otherwise humane *The Faerie Queene*. In Book Five, "On Justice," the wonderful world Spenser has created begins to change into a darker reality. Instead of approaching more closely the moral essence of experience, as does so much of his writing in the earlier books, Spenser suddenly becomes abstract, evasive, and cruel. He creates for his hero, Artegall, who symbolizes Justice, a mechanical sword-wielding "yron man," Talus, who goes about the "Salvage Island" slaughtering the citizens and inflicting "grievous punishment." "True justice" is finally reduced to nothing more than the "busie paine" of colonial administration:

During which time that [Artegall] did there remaine
His studie was true justice how to deale,
And day and night employ'd his busie paine

Irish "law" was really not law at all; hence it carried with it the seeds of distrust, hatred, and violence—and those, as well, of its own ultimate destruction.

This fundamental insight, that the rule of law operates as a constant pressure for the realization of important human values, is one that Marxist thinkers have begun to accept. For example, the Marxist historian, E. P. Thompson, in his recent study of penal law in eighteenth-century England,[139] reaches the following conclusion:

> I am insisting only upon the obvious point, which some modern Marxists have overlooked, that there is a difference between arbitrary power and the rule of law. We ought to expose the shams and inequities which may be concealed beneath this law. But the rule of law itself, the imposing of effective inhibitions upon power and the defense of the citizen from power's all-intrusive claims, seems to me to be an unqualified human good. To deny or belittle this good is, in this dangerous century when the resources and pretensions of power continue to enlarge, a desperate error of intellectual abstraction.[140]

In this statement, one would like to think, lies the basis for reconciling the two competing schools of thought concerning respect for the rule of law.[141]

How to reforme that ragged common-weale:
And that same yron man, which could reveale
All hidden crimes, through all that realme he sent,
To search out those that used to rob and steale,
Or did rebell against lawfull government;
On whom he did inflict most grevious punishment.

SPENSER, *supra* note 36, Book V, Canto XII, Stanza XXVI, at 579–80. As one astute reader has remarked, "It is awful that our serene and wandering poet should have come to this." *See* R. SALE, READING SPENSER: AN INTRODUCTION TO *THE FAERIE QUEENE* 178 (1968).

[139] E. THOMPSON, WHIGS AND HUNTERS: THE ORIGINS OF THE BLACK ACT (1975).
[140] *Id.* at 266.

[141] But, unfortunately, not so. In his review of Thompson's book, Professor Horwitz responds to Thompson's conclusion by arguing that such a view of the rule of law can be justified only if we subscribe to "Hobbesian pessimism." *See* Horwitz, *The Rule of Law, supra* note 3, at 566. Whereupon Horwitz proceeds to denounce the rule of law in the most "Hobbesian" and "pessimistic" of terms, arguing that the law will be cynically used by "the shrewd" and "the calculating" for their own

In the end, what we may be dealing with in the dispute between the two schools are two different understandings of what is meant by "respect for the rule of law." The new school historian means by this phrase, I take it, a kind of mindless adherence to technical legal rules, regardless of their relation to the "fundamental principles of legality." The humanistic school on the other hand, represented by writers like Professors Bailyn and White, sees "the rule of law" as something distinct from—though not incompatible with—technical legal rules. Respect for the rule of law therefore means respect for the fundamental values and principles embodied in a rule of law, and for those values and principles that make the rule of law something we can recognize and work with.[142]

---

selfish ends. Yet one senses that Horwitz knows his argument is hollow, unconvincing, and deeply contradictory, because he becomes increasingly shrill, summoning up "Hitler, Stalin and all the other horrors of this century," as if by simply invoking these names, what Thompson (whom Horwitz recognizes as a "brilliant Marxist historian") has said about the rule of law will be refuted. But even this does not work; so Horwitz turns finally—in a way that is as uncharacteristic as it is revealing—to an unworthy *ad hominem:* Thompson said what he did about the rule of law, Horwitz finally tries to tell us, because Thompson has reached "50 years of age." *See id.*

[142] *See* J. WHITE, *supra* note 22, at 169. The word "respect" in the phrase "respect for the rule of law" also seems to mean different things to the two schools. One of the curious aspects of the intellectual universe of the new school is that it allows only two types of relationship to law (or to the world): One can either return to natural rights jurisprudence, and adopt a posture of respectful reverence for a "god-given" order, or one can adopt a Benthamite-rationalist-utilitarian-instrumentalist approach to experience. In the latter case, one stands in a *manipulative* relationship not only to law, but also to human relationships and to experience itself. *See* R. UNGER, KNOWLEDGE, *supra* note 3, at 25.

The liberal humanist, in contrast, does not share the same deep antagonism to the creative activity of law. Thus, to the humanistic historian, "respect" for law means much the same thing that we understand by the artist's "respect" for his medium and for the reality with which he must work. It is a relationship neither manipulative, nor passive, but something much more complex and creative—the way Rodin felt, for example, about a block of stone as he set about to carve from it the figure that it contained. To the humanistic writer, the essence of the common law experience is perfectly expressed by James Joyce when his poet-hero Stephen Daedalus says, "I go to encounter for the millionth time the reality of experience and to forge in the smithy of my soul the uncreated conscience of my race." J. JOYCE, A PORTRAIT OF THE ARTIST AS A YOUNG MAN 252–53 (Viking Press ed. 1964). It is this conception of "respect for the rule of law," with its emphasis

Yet for all their differences, the two schools share a critical commonality: the deep conviction that without a foundation in substantive moral vision, law is nothing but power, and respect for law a path to exploitation and despair.

This last observation brings us back to Professor Reid's *In a Defiant Stance,* and to what it is about this book that leaves us feeling curiously uneasy. It is, I think, Reid's failure to make the crucial connections between the colonists' respect for the rule of law and the substantive moral vision with which their conception of the rule of law was imbued. That is why we are made uneasy by Reid's concluding observation that "the difference" between law in Ireland and America was *"not . . . in the substance of the law"* but in respect for the rule of law itself.[143] We resist this conclusion—this dichotomy between "substance" and "rule"—partly because we know it does not faithfully reflect the colonists' own experience, but more importantly, because it runs against the grain of everything we know about the rule of law in history.

In making this objection, I do not think I am taking Professor Reid's concluding sentence out of context, moreover, because the problem runs like a thread through *In a Defiant Stance.* Indeed, the most puzzling thing about the book, which is in many respects deeply illuminating, is the way Professor Reid insists upon separating the substance of law from its institutional processes. We begin to sense that the colonists' experience with law involved nothing more than the clever manipulation of local legal machinery. Consider, for example, the sentence with which Professor Reid concludes his chapter on the criminal traverse jury: "In both cases the whigs of Boston, *by manipulating those instruments of the judicial process that they controlled, had rid themselves of a troublesome tory without a lynching."*[144] Another example is Reid's definition of the "essence" of Whig law as "whig con-

---

on "experience" and the creative dimensions of collective morality, that one finds in J. WHITE, *supra* note 22.

[143] J. REID, *supra* note 29, at 173 (emphasis added).

[144]*Id.* at 64 (emphasis added).

trol of certain institutions of legitimate judicial, legislative, and executive governmental machinery."[145] At another point, we are told: "The whigs thought more of *'legitimate'* force than of *'semilegal'*, but *in a discussion of attitudes about law the semantic difference is not important.*"[146] What kind of mind is it, we are led to ask, that does not care any more than this about the critical differences between what is "legitimate" and what is "legal"? A final example is Reid's explanation of why the American Whigs respected law while the Irish Catholics did not: "[T]he stress on legalism by the Massachusetts whigs is no more surprising than the disrespect for law in contemporary Ireland. Law was, more often than not, on the whigs' side. It was seldom on the side of the average Irishman."[147]

Is this all "respect for the rule of law" finally comes down to: whether or not law is "on one's side"? What Reid has done in this sentence, it seems to me, is to reduce the significance of respect for the rule of law—and of the American colonial experience itself—to the terms of a Saturday afternoon football contest, or worse, to an ideology that might makes right. Is the moral lesson we derive from the comparison of the American colonial experience with law to the Irish one simply that we respect the law if it is on our "side," no matter what its moral content, and conversely, if it is not on our side, we disrespect it no matter what important principles it embodies? At this point the world Professor Reid has constructed begins to crumble.

The objection I am making to the conception of the rule of law we find reflected in these statements, I want to insist, is not simply an academic one. It goes rather to our deepest understanding of the *legitimacy* of "Whig law." The question is one of profound importance. If all that was involved during this period was the manipulation by a local populace of legal institutions to achieve a highly partisan vision of society, then how can what the whigs did in Massachusetts in

[145]*Id.* at 72.
[146]*Id.* at 163.
[147]*Id.* at 161.

the 1760s and 1770s be distinguished from what the white racists in the American South did for the long, dark century following the Civil War? In each case an indigenous population took over the local legal processes and systematically employed the law to achieve local purposes, and in each case the takeover was inspired by the felt need to resist and subvert the law of a remote central government.[148] Yet we know that the two experiences were different—and different in ways that finally determine the moral essence of a civilization. But what *is* it that sets the two experiences apart?

The answer, it seems to me, brings us full circle, for it has to be "respect for the rule of law." What distinguishes the colonial experience is that it was inspired by those moral values that are embodied in the fundamental principles of legality, by a deep respect for the fundamental worth and dignity of all persons, and by a central commitment to the ideals of equality, fairness, justice, and freedom from arbitrary control. It is *this* that legitimized the Whigs' creative employment of local legal institutions in service of their vision of a new society. The white supremacists' manipulation of local legal institutions in the South, in contrast, had but one corrupting aim: the continued subjugation of the black race. There was no principled commitment to the rule of law, nor to the moral values that underlie it. And without such a commitment, all the creative legalism in the world could not save the Southern white legal order from ultimate collapse.

Professor Reid is wrong, I think, when he talks of Whig law during the revolutionary period as if it involved nothing more than control and clever employment of local legal machinery. And he is wrong in assuming that the rule of law can be understood separately from the substantive moral vision it embodies. But, in his final words, he is also cer-

---

[148] An article I wrote some years ago describes in both historical and contemporary terms the way the indigenous white population in the South used the local legal processes to enforce the Southern way of life. Teachout, *Louisiana Underlaw*, in L. FRIEDMAN, SOUTHERN JUSTICE 57 (1965).

tainly right: "the difference" *is* in "how much those who govern respect the rule of law."

Conclusion

[O]ur longest Sunne sets at right descencions, and makes but winter arches, and therefore it cannot be long before we lie down in dark-nesse, and have our light in ashes.[149]

In a Defiant Stance is, finally, a very curious and contradic-tory book. The insights it provides into law in the American colonies during the revolutionary period are potentially profound; and yet somehow the most important of these seem to be left pressing at the surface, never quite fully re-alized. Even more significant, perhaps, are the insights into the dynamics of the rule of law in society that Reid's com-parison of the Irish and American experiences makes avail-able. This comparison provides strong evidence that respect for the rule of law operates as an actual force in history for human dignity, equality, and justice. Yet here, too, one can-not help but sense that the insights that *could* have been made are often left only partially developed. Thus the light shed by this book on issues of the most pressing human importance is finally only an intermittent or flickering light, when one would have wanted something clearer, more de-finitive, more powerful. Yet the light is there, and it is im-portant. In the end, after all, it may be mistaken to think that history can provide us with much more than this. Per-haps in the modern world we must all proceed in "dark-ness," and the light we can expect from history can at most be only "light in ashes."

[149] Browne, *Hydrotaphia, Urne-Burial, in* 1 The Works of Sir Thomas Browne 167–68 (G. Keynes ed. 1964).

PART III

Conclusion

Distancing Oneself from the
Eighteenth Century:
A Commentary on Changing Pictures
of American Legal History

ༀ Hendrik Hartog ༁

RECENT commentary on work in American legal history has often focused on the ideological differences that divide legal historians. Sometimes these differences are phrased in terms of the relative centrality of consensus and conflict as fundamental characteristics of American life, rehearsing a debate which social and political historians had worked over a decade ago.[1] At other times, those differences focus on aspects of the role of law in society: the relative autonomy of law within a social order[2], the moral sta-

---

[1] Horwitz, *The Conservative Tradition in the Writing of American Legal History*, 17 Am. J. Leg. Hist. 275 (1973); Nelson, *Legal History*, 1973/74 Ann. Surv. Am. L. 625; Zainaldin, *The New Legal History: A Review Essay of "The Americanization of the Common Law: The Impact of Legal Change on Massachusetts Society,"* 73 Nw. U. L. Rev. 205 (1977); Reid, *A Plot too Doctrinaire* (review of Horwitz, *Transformation*), 55 Tex. L. Rev. 1307 (1977); J. Hurst, Law and Social Order in the United States (1977), 214–269; Hurst, *Old and New Dimensions of Research in United States Legal History*, 23 Am. J. Leg. Hist. 1 (1979).

[2] Tushnet, *Perspectives on the Development of American Law: A Critical Review of Friedman's "A History of American Law."* 1977 Wisc. L. Rev. 81 (1977); Tushnet, *A Marxist Analysis of American Law*, 1 Marxist Perspectives 96 (1978); Horwitz, 17 Am. J. Leg. Hist. 275 (1973).

tus of the rule of law[3], the unity and coherence—the class identity—of the legal profession.[4] Frequently, these discussions assume an explicitly presentist cast of argument, turning on the respective attitudes of reviewer and author toward the legitimacy and present utility of the American legal past.[5]

Peter Teachout's defense of the humanist tradition against Horwitz's cynical new school of antilegalist legal history represents a kind of apotheosis of this combative, polemical, explicitly ideological style of "law review" reviewing. American lawyers are asked to choose between a humanist-optimist perspective on their past, one represented by John Reid as Bernard Bailyn's surrogate, and a neo-marxist-pessimist perspective. All history is myth, and everyman is his own historian. The choice is not between truth and falsehood, or between more truth and less truth, but between competing functional organizations of the past. Would one prefer, Teachout might be seen as asking, to live and work as a lawyer while regarding the relevant past as defined and delimited by the way law came to be understood in the early nineteenth century? Or, would one rather incorporate the values of the Whig revolutionaries of the 1760s and 1770s into one's legal frame of reference? Can one retain any moral sensitivity as a lawyer once separated from the legal arguments of the lawyers who made our revolution, or is one bound to inhabit a legal world shaped solely by cynical calculation and an unerring ability to pauperize the poor and enrich the rich? According to Professor Teachout, the Whigs who made a revolution in Massachusetts in the 1760s

[3] Teachout, *Light in Ashes: The Problem of "Respect for the Rule of Law" in American Legal History*, 53 N.Y.U. L. Rev. 241 (1978), reprinted earlier in this volume; Presser, *Revising the Conservative Tradition: Towards a New American Legal History*, 52 N.Y.U. L. Rev. 700 (1977), reprinted earlier in this volume; Gilmore, Book Review (Horwitz, *Transformation*), 86 Yale L.J. 788 (1977); Horwitz, *The Rule of Law: An Unqualified Human Good?* 86 Yale L.J. 561 (1977).

[4] Horwitz, 17 Am. J. Leg. Hist. 275 (1973); Genovese, Book Review (Horwitz, *Transformation*), 91 Harv. L. Rev. 726 (1978).

[5] See for example, Presser, 52 N.Y.U. L. Rev. 700, Teachout, 53 N.Y.U. L. Rev. 241, and Levinson, *The Specious Morality of the Law*, Harper's Magazine 35 (May, 1977).

and 1770s provide a model of creative use of law, a demonstration of the vitality of the rule of law, and proof positive—should any be needed—of the fallacy inherent in any
simplistic equation between a legal order and the evils of
market capitalism.[6]

I believe that Teachout's heuristic use of the Massachusetts Whigs is historically inapt.[7] Given his jurisprudential
framework, though, I am not at all certain that my narrowly
historical arguments could—or indeed should—convince
him that the world of the Massachusetts Whigs is a world
beyond recapture or emulation. However, I am quite certain that Teachout has misunderstood *In a Defiant Stance* in
characterizing it as a work which does not posit "a radical
break between the way the revolutionary generation conceived of law and the way law came to be understood during the early nineteenth century."[8] Teachout is surely correct that Reid and other scholars of revolutionary political
thought are convinced of the "absolute centrality of law" to
Massachusetts Whigs.[9] And he is certainly right to argue
that "it was the creative use of an essentially legal imagination that propelled and supported the movement of the
Revolution."[10] But according to John Reid it was a very different kind of legal imagination that men like John Adams
were exercising, one formed out of a seventeenth-century
political tradition, one deeply opposed to the forms of legal
power represented by the Tories and by imperial rule in
Ireland, a form of consciousness almost directly antithetical
to the legal culture which would emerge at the end of the
eighteenth century in the newly independent states and
which would become dominant and pervasive in nineteenth-century America.

In the following pages I want to develop this point not
substantively but historiographically. My argument is that

[6] Teachout, 53 N.Y.U. L. Rev. 241.
[7] See Hartog, Book Review, 54 Ind. L. J. 65(1978), reprinted earlier in this volume.
[8] Teachout, 53 N.Y.U. L. Rev. 241, 241–2.
[9] *Id.* at 244.
[10] *Id.*

Reid, William Nelson, and Morton Horwitz all share a common set of organizing assumptions about the study of
American legal culture. Professor Teachout may be right
that there is a "new school" in American legal history, but,
if so, it is a school which joins Reid, Nelson, and Horwitz,
however uncomfortable they may be in sharing each other's
intellectual company. Of course, there are important differences between the three of them in their political and moral
orientations to our legal past, but in all of their works there
is a common picture of the history of American law: that
there is a division—a discontinuity if you will—between law
prior to the second half of the eighteenth century in the
American colonies and the law we understand as characteristic of nineteenth-century America. This new school is
formed not out of present politics but out of a theory of
periodization, out of a way of organizing and studying the
past. My task here is not to prove the truth of their picture
of the world, but to sketch out some of its most distinctive
features and to indicate its separation from the traditional
concerns of law school legal history. If in the process I succeed in suggesting something of its plausibility and significance as an interpretive scheme, so much the better.[11]

I. Shared Perceptions of Discontinuity.

This section constitutes a schematic and intentionally dogmatic presentation of perceptions drawn from the writings
of Reid, Nelson, and Horwitz. None of the three would
agree with the finished product. In some ways this essay
should be read as a deliberate and self-conscious misreading
of the works that are its ostensible subject matter. At best,
one might say that it is a reflection on their writings. John
Reid did not intend to make an argument about nineteenth-
or twentieth-century law in his *In a Defiant Stance,* yet his
book will be treated as if it reveals such an argument. Hor-

[11] Unlike Professor Teachout I do not believe that the notion of a "new school"
should be taken literally. Indeed, it may well be that everything that unites Reid,
Nelson, and Horwitz can be found in the earlier work of Willard Hurst.

witz nowhere talks about "Whig" law in his discussion of the precommercial substantive private law that existed prior to the "transformation" of American law; I will, however, treat his precommercial legal structures and "Whig" law as synonyms for one another. The arguments of William Nelson may also be used to serve purposes different than he had intended.

Indeed, the very act of treating their books as shaped by common perceptions of legal change and legal history may deserve more justification than I am willing to give it here.[12] *In a Defiant Stance, The Americanization of the Common Law,* and *The Transformation of American Law* are distinguished by more than their differing political orientations. They might be taken as prototypes of distinct forms of historical writing: as different from one another as the study of the intellectual origins of political rhetoric, the social history of law based on local records, and the history of elite legal ideas usually are from one another. Yet all three are obviously more than "mere" monographs: Theoretical presuppositions shape each of these works. And it is, as I hope to demonstate (and as vulgar marxists always say), *no coincidence* that all three rely on very similar assumptions. Whatever their differences, all share an overview of the course of American legal history from the middle of the eighteenth to the middle of the nineteenth centuries. For Horwitz, no less than for Reid or Nelson, an understanding of pre-nineteenth-century American law depends on a recognition of its archaic quality, its separation from the law of nineteenth-century America. His book is a study of "transformation" because there can be no easy transition or evolution from a colonial premodern, legal culture to the modern, capitalist legal culture of republican America. For both Reid and Horwitz there is an irreduceable conflict between the Whig law of colonial legal institutions and the "Tory" law of a capitalist republic. And even for Nelson, whose theme of "Americanization" is ostensibly more evolutionary than

---

[12] It is important to note, though, that both Reid and Horwitz do rely significantly on the previously published work of Nelson.

those of either Reid or Horwitz, the changes he narrates are ultimately beyond causal explanation. The origins of nine-teenth-century Massachusetts law cannot be found in the conditions of law we find in provincial Massachusetts in the 1760s. Those conditions inhabit another world, find their justification in a different basis of legitimacy, and model and reflect a different structure of values.

The central proposition, then, that characterizes the work of this "new school" is that the course of American legal history is defined by a discontinuity between the law of colo-nial America and the law of nineteenth-century America. This proposition hides an argument about stability and per-sistence as well as one about change. The "transformation" of Horwitz's title is not just *a* transformation; it is *the* trans-formation of American law. On either side of the line, law was shaped by a coherent and relatively stable legal culture. The assumptions of nineteenth-century law are "modern" not just because they are different than the assumptions of the "premodern" law of the seventeenth century, but, more importantly, because they are the assumptions which law-yers still today internalize in the course of their socialization as lawyers.[13] By the same token, the legal assumptions of the revolutionary Whigs of Massachusetts and of other col-onists were shaped by a legal culture defined as much by seventeenth-century conflicts and values as by the changing content of their legal world.[14]

The relationship between nineteenth-century American law and its past is then one of contrast and separation, rather than of evolution and development. It is the contrast between a world where property rights are definitive of cit-izenship and personality, indistinguishable from other civil rights, where a court or a city has a claim of ownership on its governmental authority and a mob on its right to riot

---

[13] These assumptions are also "modern" in a different sense, for as sketched out by Horwitz and Nelson they correspond closely to a sociological model of the transformation of consciousness generally attributable to modernization. See P. BERGER, B. BERGER, and H. KELLNER, THE HOMELESS MIND (1973) and P. BERGER and T. LUCKMANN, THE SOCIAL CONSTRUCTION OF REALITY (1967).

[14] See Reid, *The Irrelevance of the Declaration* in this volume.

against unresolved grievances, and a world where property is characterized by the relationship between a person and peculiarly economic resources, a world where land itself has been largely reduced to a commodity. Or, it is the disjuncture, on the one hand, between a locally controlled legal system in which juries determine both law and fact, justices of the peace derive their effective authority from local publics rather than from centralized institutions, and community standards determine the substantive outcomes of disputes, and, on the other hand, a tightly integrated legal system, defined by positive norms, in which a unitary sovereignty has been made operational, a system from which lay persons have been effectively excluded. In eighteenth-century America, to take a third example, the practice of government was functionally undifferentiated. Judicial, administrative, and legislative powers were blurred and diffuse and often converged in a single institution. By the second third of the nineteenth century, the practice of government in America everywhere reflected the functional, as well as the formal, acceptance of separation of powers theory. Reid, Nelson, and Horwitz teach us that in the eighteenth century perhaps the most important role of law was as a restraint on power—whether economic or political power. A generation of legal and economic historians have demonstrated that that vision of law was replaced soon after the Revolution by a legal and political theory which viewed law itself as an agency *for* the exercise of power. All of these examples indicate the irreduceable conflict between the legal worlds of the eighteenth and nineteenth centuries. There are no mediating principles. In every case, the assumption of modern, nineteenth-century values must ultimately involve the rejection of eighteenth-century values. The law we had becomes the law we forgot or reinterpreted.

To this perception of discontinuity it is easy to find counter-examples, easy to find instances of seeming doctrinal continuity or institutional longevity or attudinal persistence. Lawyers and legislators continued to apply values that they believed were drawn from an eighteenth-century context. Judges viewed themselves as the heirs of an immortal common law tradition, conservators of a methodology and of a continuing coherent point of view. None of them necessarily ever woke up one morning and said, "I am going to do things differently today than I did them yesterday." If change is to be viewed as radical and total, it must be so viewed from our vantage point—looking backwards— not from the viewpoint of those who lived through it.

To this, proponents of the new school might answer that law as a legal historian would understand it is not merely the cumulative total of so-called "legal" transactions or institutions, each of which may be more or less identical with previous "legal" transactions, but is a cultural artifact, an integrated body of norms and values which provide a context that makes individual doctrinal or institutional structures meaningful.[15] No one may ever have willed a transformation of law, even though our ordinary intuition would tell us that law is supremely an area of conscious calculation and choice. No one may ever have resolved to separate himself from his immediate past. But it is perfectly plausible to imagine someone—say Joseph Story or James Kent—waking up one morning to discover that, in doing the things he had always done, he had helped to create a world entirely different than the one he had always known.[16] John Marshall may have tried to utilize eighteenth-century consensual values and decisionmaking techniques as a way of mediating between competing political factions and values, as William Nelson has argued in a recent article.[17] One wonders if Nelson is right, but even if he is correct in locating the origins of John Marshall's jurisprudence in eighteenth-

[15] For example, the court structure of Massachusetts Bay was "modern" from 1692 on if we look at it as an arrangement of courts. It is only when the practices of the various courts as working institutions are observed, when the historian tries to place them in a social context, that their "premodern" qualities are revealed.

[16] See Note: *Justice Story's Doctrine of Judicial Supremacy and the Uncertain Search for a Neutral Principle in The Charles River Bridge Case*, 53 IND. L.J. 327 (1977–78).

[17] Nelson, *The Eighteenth-Century Background of John Marshall's Constitutional Jurisprudence*, 76 MICH. L. REV. 893 (1978).

century local government, that decisionmaking style was transformed in Marshall's nineteenth-century hands. Uprooted from its location in village communities and county courts where it had served as a conservator of local autonomy, it became the basis of legitimacy for a national judiciary, the symbol of a monolithic national sovereignty. Instead of undermining our perception of discontinuity, Nelson's interpretation of Marshall's jurisprudence can only serve to reinforce its plausibility.

Another type of criticism of a dichotomous history of American law would focus not only on the absence of change in selected areas but on the evolutionary, gradual quality of much legal change. One might argue that the research of Nelson and Horwitz reveals a much slower transition from old to new, reveals that there is a continuity of change in American legal history. It may be that this critical perspective is less critical of the idea of a break than of the particular timing attributed to it by some members of our new school. The limited proposition we set forth here is that in comparing the law of an American jurisdiction—say Massachusetts—in 1740 with the law of that same jurisdiction a century later there is an unmistakable contrast and dissimilarity, a statement which could not be made with equal definitiveness of the contrast between law in 1640 Massachusetts and 1740 Massachusetts or between 1940 and 1840 Massachusetts. It might well be, then, that change could be internally slow and evolutionary, yet, at the same time, dramatic and conclusive when viewed from the larger perspective of the whole course of American legal history.

Still, there is much in the work of our new school to suggest that even where evolutionary lines can be drawn, where there appears to be a continuity of change, the surface hides a much more tumultuous and discordant process. Consider the reform of common law pleading that Nelson details in *The Americanization of the Common Law.*[18] From one perspective the story he tells should be a model of gradual

[18] W. NELSON, THE AMERICANIZATION OF THE COMMON LAW 68–88 (1975).

Conclusion

change, for its novelty rests on the initiative taken by lawyers themselves in the early nineteenth century in reforming court procedures. Long before the Field Code, long before the development of legislatively drawn codes of civil procedure, lawyers had begun to simplify and to rationalize trial practice. Reform was not imposed externally on the old; it grew out of the internal control of the legal profession and reflected its changing perceptions of the functions of trial in the new republic. There was no "transformation," only the growing realization that the insane detail of the writ system was out of place in a republican society. And yet, that is not the only story Nelson tells. Change may have been internally controlled, but the reformers did not rationalize an ongoing system. If Nelson is correct, they "shattered the ethical unity of Massachusetts."[19] The system of pleading they worked on was not slowly coming to terms with the needs of a modernizing society. It was, from what we know, growing ever more rigid and cumbersome in revolutionary America.[20] And what the reformers accomplished was more a subversion than a rationalization of common law pleading. The results of their work were the separation of delimited spheres of substance and procedure, the destruction of "old formulary categories" and their replacement by "new substantive ones." The contrast between nineteenth-century Massachusetts procedure and its eighteenth-century past is heightened by the fact that the change could not, according to Nelson, have occurred through a simple process of refinement and reform. The reform of common law pleading as it actually occurred depended on the emergence of new substantive categories, depended on the emergence of a transformed legal culture. It could not, according to Nelson, have grown out of the writ

[19]*Id.* at 71.

[20]See John Murrin, *The Legal Transformation: The Bench and Bar of Eighteenth-Century Massachusetts,* in S. KATZ, COLONIAL AMERICA 415–449 (1971). See also R. Berthoff and J. Murrin, *Feudalism, Communalism, and the Yeoman Freeholder; The American Revolution Considered as a Social Accident,* in S. KURTZ and J. HUTSON, ESSAYS ON THE AMERICAN REVOLUTION, 256–288 (1973).

system as it existed at the time of the Revolution absent a radical change of context.[21]

The disjuncture between law in eighteenth- and nineteenth-century America bears a resemblance to the agrarian-commercial, precapitalist-capitalist, premodern-modern transitions familiar to American social historians. Yet the fit is not complete, for one postulate of recent legal history has been that American law was both more archaic than its social context in the eighteenth century and also more radically and quickly transformed in the early nineteenth century than social historians might have predicted. In the eighteenth century, according to Horwitz,[22] merchants relied on their own institutions for arbitrating and settling commercial disputes. Why they did not go to court is not clear from his account; but one may surmise—indeed, Horwitz asks us to surmise—that merchants thought courts and conventional legal doctrine unsuited to their specialized needs. The narrow purpose of Horwitz's book is to examine how an alliance of lawyers and merchants in the early nineteenth century worked to make a body of legal doctrine that would turn the courts into fit locations for commercial litigation. And the conclusion of his narrative is that well before the middle of the nineteenth century, at a time when many of the structures of market capitalism were still in formation and incomplete, American lawyers had created a fully formed body of capitalist law.

It would be incorrect to say, then, that the history of American law simply parallels the history of the rise to dominance of market capitalism in American society. However, as I have tried to suggest in my earlier essay,[23] it may be that the two "legal cultures" of our discontinuous history do in a rough way reflect different conceptions of the relationship between political power and economic organization. The Tories of the Revolution were more than mere officeholders and bureaucrats; they should be regarded as

---

[21] W. NELSON, *supra* note 18, at 87.

[22] M. HORWITZ, THE TRANSFORMATION OF AMERICAN LAW 140–149, 167 (1977).

[23] Hartog, 45 IND. L. J. 65, 72–77, also reprinted earlier in this volume.

the spokesmen for a nation undergoing an industrial revolution, a nation increasingly aware of its need for docile and uncompetitive foreign markets. Tory arguments articulated values of a capitalist state. Whigs, by contrast, reflected an earlier, largely agrarian tradition—even if only sentimentally. Their vision of decentralized, local institutions resistant to external authority would be antithetical to the expanding centrally controlled interdependency and the utilitarian calculation which we have learned characterizes the capitalist state.

For all three of the charter members of our new school, the source of the disjuncture, the source of the inception of deep change, is more easily reduceable to a transformation in political vision than to changes in social or economic organization. Consider Mr. Justice Johnson's statement, made in 1821, that "Government is the science of experimentation,"[24] and compare it with a line from one of the sacred texts of Whig theory, Recorder Treby's defense of the City of London against Charles II's writ of *quo warranto,* "All innovations . . . are dangerous."[25] The problem of law as viewed by the "new school" can at all times be equated with the problem of the legitimacy of public action. The provincials of eighteenth-century America followed Recorder Treby in their conviction that the function of law was the restraint of public action. By 1800, according to Horwitz, law had been reconceived as an agency—an instrument—of public policy, an experimental tool.

Reid, Nelson, and Horwitz share a perception that what is most radical and disruptive—transforming even—about modern law is the consciousness that legal institutions might be utilized by a state as instruments of social or economic change. It is, I would contend, less who the recipients of the legal redistribution of wealth are that is Horwitz's focus than the idea that law would become a self-conscious instrument of redistribution. The "transformation" of private law that he details is its transformation into a technology for

[24] Anderson v. Dunn, 6 Wheat. 204, 226 (1821).
[25] 8 Howell's State Trials 1039, 1143.

policy formation. By the same token, the assumption that the Tories intended, if they could, to use law as an instrument of directed change mobilized Reid's Whigs to defensive action. Indeed, it was change or "innovation" that captured much of the sense behind the Whig notion of "corruption."[26]

The argument is not that law was never an instrumentality of public policy before 1800 or that instrumental lawmaking as such was a novelty in Anglo-American law.[27] But in colonial America, such a conception of the exercise of public power would have had difficulty finding any support. The possibility of public action was always limited by the continuing authority of local legal institutions, by the forthright and pervasive defense of parochial interests and customary rights, by the fact that many central institutions were controlled by elites primarily responsive to local constituencies. Colonists defined law not as an instrument of state policy but as a bulwark against centralized authority, as a reflection and a defender of community, customary authority. And royal officials lacked mechanisms, as well as the authority, to call the colonists to account, to disprove their belief in law as nothing but a restraint on power. Royal officials were without process of appeal by which provincial judges could "correct" the decisions of local courts and justices of the peace, without a legitimated monopoly of the power to declare what was and what was not law, without a police force. Within the dominant legal culture there was, according to the hypothesis, no way of justifying instrumental public action. One could not define an autonomous public sphere. As of the time of the Revolution, American government lacked much of the moral and structural underpinnings of the positivist state.

The point is not that prerevolutionary America was some idyllic, communitarian, organic legal culture, although

---

[26] This notion of the dangers inherent in "change" is brilliantly captured in J. G. A. Pocock's, *Civic Humanism and its Role in Anglo-American Thought,* in POLITICS, LANGUAGE AND TIME (1973).

[27] See in particular, E. P. THOMPSON, WHIGS AND HUNTERS (1975).

all three of our "primary sources" do at times fall into that sentimental fallacy. But looking backwards from the legal universe created by the judges and legislators of the nineteenth century, America was, legally speaking, a very different place. The familiar world that Horwitz and Nelson show emerging in the early nineteenth century, in which law comes to be equated with the substantive doctrines of appellate courts, in which legal change becomes regular and systematic, would have been inconceivable in the early eighteenth century. The self-consciousness and self-confidence of a nineteenth-century judge that his decisions would inevitably and usefully impinge on the distribution of economic and political power in the country—more importantly, his acceptance of that role—cannot be connected to the concerns of an eighteenth-century equivalent. The notion that an appellate judge, a servant of the state, might, in a particular matter, discover and articulate "the public interest" on his own, directly contradicted several tenets of colonial legal ideology. To eighteenth-century Whigs such effrontery might have been seen as a paradigm of arbitrary government.[28]

It is possible to read in the writings of Reid, Nelson, and Horwitz a perception that the very possibility of thinking of law as a separated, bounded, distinctive sphere of activity and thought was a creation of the transformed political culture of the early republic.[29] For all three of our sources, a central element of prerevolutionary legal culture was the permeability of conceptual boundaries. For Reid, what was distinctive about Whig rhetoric was the indistinguishability of legal, moral, and political arguments within it; for Nelson, the significance of the jury in the prerevolutionary legal system of Massachusetts was its blending, its importation, of community standards into legal norms. For Horwitz

[28] J. REID, *In Legitimate Stirps: the Concept of "Arbitrary," the Supremacy of Parliament, and the Coming of the American Revolution*, 5 HOFSTRA L. REV. 459 (1977).

[29] See in general, G. WOOD, THE CREATION OF THE AMERICAN REPUBLIC (1969); indeed, a reductionist might want to argue that all American legal history is an extended footnote to the argument about political-constitutional change made in that book.

too it was the power of the community to enforce its own standards that was definitive of the political economy of eighteenth-century America. The doctrine of the just price, the equitable standards for contract enforceability, the concern with the ethical basis for negotiability, which he sees as shaping pre-nineteenth-century restrictions on the development of contract doctrine were also symbols of the inconceivability of autonomous legal standards for contract enforcement. The achievement of the makers of nineteenth-century legal order was the achievement of a conceptually autonomous legal sphere. And that autonomy, which of course implies among other things the possibility of a distinctively legal history of law, of the creation of a continuous legal past, is one measure of the discontinuous history of American law.

II. The Novelty of the New Legal History

Reid, Nelson, and Horwitz are not the first legal historians to argue that there is a disjuncture between American legal history before the Revolution and American legal history thereafter. In many ways it might seem that they are simply reviving the "formative era" thesis championed by Roscoe Pound at the beginning of the twentieth century. For Pound, as well as for our new school it is in the early republic that one locates the proper origin of our modern legal order; for all of them what is most significant about colonial law is its separation from our legal experience.

The purposes served by Pound's periodization were very different, however.[30] Two generations ago all American legal historians saw their function as the establishment and delineation of the linkages by which the law as modern

[30] At a session of the American Society of Legal History annual meeting of 1976 Stanley Katz argued that the then emerging work of Nelson and Horwitz was recreating the discredited periodization of Roscoe Pound. The origins of this paper may lie in both the plausibility of juxtaposing Pound with Nelson and Horwitz and my continuing conviction that such a juxtaposition is incorrect, that the differences far outweigh the similarities.

American lawyers know it was connected to the whole
length of the history of the English common law. Such a
definition of the role of legal history did not necessarily
deny the importance and utility of dividing American history into discrete periods. But the function of a periodization was to indicate the relationship between the legal practices extant at any particular time and the ongoing,
continuous (super-historical) history of the common law.
When Roscoe Pound argued that the period from the Revolution to the Civil War should be understood as the "formative era" in the history of American law, he did so on the
assumption that it was then that American judges, lawyers,
and treatise writers made the important connections between common law methodology—"the taught legal tradition"—and the particular content of American law. Periodization, for Pound, was a way of illuminating the continuity
of an Anglo-American legal tradition:

> One might tell the story of the formulating agencies of the
> law in our formative era with the emphasis on change rather
> than continuity. If we look only at the body of legal precepts
> which obtains in the United States today in comparison with
> those obtaining in seventeenth or even eighteenth century
> England, we might easily feel that the change has been radi-
> cal and complete. But change has been gradual, has been
> chiefly in details, and hence not to be understood without
> understanding what was changed, and has been guided by
> the received traditional technique, applied to received tradi-
> tional materials. Thus much that has been changed has con-
> tinued to furnish analogies and to serve as the basis of legal
> reasoning and even to affect the newer precepts in their
> interpretation and application.[31]

According to Pound, the achievements of the lawmen of his
"formative era" lay in their solutions to three problems in
the administration of justice: how to receive the English
common law, how to decentralize legal processes, how to
devise a criminal law and procedure sufficient to satisfy the
needs of a "vigorous pioneer race." "The [c]hief of these

[31] R. POUND, THE FORMATIVE ERA IN AMERICAN LAW 82 (1938)

problems," to Pound, "was the one first named, the problem of working out a system of rules and principles applicable to America," for English common law had not been the earliest source of authority in the colonies.[32]

Pound believed that what had passed as lawmaking in the American colonies could hardly be regarded as law at all. "When James Kent went upon the bench in New York in 1791, he could say with entire truth: 'There were no reports or state precedents. The opinions from the bench were delivered *ore tenus*. We had no law of our own and nobody knew what [the law] was.' "[33] One should note in the passage quoted in the previous paragraph how Pound conflated law itself with the reception of English common law. Without such a reception there could not be law. The significance of the 150 years of American legal history prior to the American Revolution lay, for Pound, in their insignificance. "For most practical purposes American judicial history begins after the Revolution."[34] As Zecharaiah Chaffee had written at the same time and in roughly the same spirit:

> . . . Almost the earliest task of the founders of a Colony was the regulation of the disputes which arise in a primitive civilization by a brief legislative code concerning crimes, torts, and the simplest contracts, in many ways like the dooms of the Anglo-Saxon kings. Gaps in these codes were not filled from the Common Law, as would be the case to-day, but by the discretion of the magistrate, or in some Colonies, in the early days, from the Bible. . . . Thus, instead of the English and modern American judge-made law, the Colonists received for the most part executive and legislative justice, and lived under a protoplasmic popular law, with the Common Law only one of its many ingredients.[35]

---

[32] R. POUND, THE SPIRIT OF THE COMMON LAW 115 (1921)
[33] *Id.* at 113.
[34] *Id.*
[35] Chafee, *The Law*, in CIVILIZATION IN THE UNITED STATES: AN INQUIRY BY THIRTY AMERICANS, 53, 54–5 (H. Stearns ed. 1922), quoted in Chaffee, *Colonial Courts and the Common Law*, in ESSAYS IN THE HISTORY OF EARLY AMERICAN LAW 68–69 (D. Flaherty ed. 1969) [hereinafter, ESSAYS]. In 1952 Chaffee would write that the "passage contains more sentences I now regret than anything else I have written." *Id.* at 68.

Such words probably constituted the most useful possible provocation to the study of colonial legal history,[36] and led by Julius Goebel, the first of the great "Pound-pounders," Pound's theory of a rude, crude, indigenous administration of justice in colonial America soon lay in ruins. Americans may not have adopted the structures of the royal courts, but they had transplanted the law they knew best, namely, the law of the county and local courts of rural England. Only adoption of a narrow and historically implausible definition of what was and what was not law would permit one to define colonial America as without it. Americans modified the legal culture they took from England to make it accord better with the conditions they found and with their religious beliefs. "[W]e are dealing not with an exact duplication of a definite model, but with the crude imitation of inaccurately remembered things."[37] But, wrote Goebel in 1931, "No one who has read the records of the local courts of seventeenth century England can fail to be struck with the remarkable resemblance between the English records and those of the Plymouth Colony."[38] The characteristics of colonial law were determined more by what colonists had experienced prior to when they came— by what they brought—than by what they found—by the frontier wilderness they entered.

A decade later, at the end of a monumental study of law enforcement in colonial New York, Goebel had grown more assertive.[39] The whole "formative era" thesis was absolutely fallacious. New Yorkers had "received" the common law not as a result of the labors of a Chancellor Kent, but through a long process in which colonial judges and lawyers slowly educated themselves and made themselves sophisticated in the legal ways of the Anglo-American world. At least in

[36] See in general the essays collected in ESSAYS, *supra* note 35.

[37] Goebel, *King's Law and Local Custom in Seventeenth Century New England* in ESSAYS, *supra* note 35, at 104.

[38] *Id.* at 105.

[39] J. GOEBEL AND R. NAUGHTON, LAW ENFORCEMENT IN COLONIAL NEW YORK: A STUDY IN CRIMINAL PROCEDURE (1944). The introduction was written by Goebel alone and is reprinted in ESSAYS, *supra* note 35, 367–391.

colonial New York City, "litigation was conducted as skill-fully as at York or Bristol, and . . . the picture of an oafish frontier jurisprudence is a mirage of writers who have never blown the dust from indictment, pleading or judg-ment roll."[40] Indeed, the myth of a formative era is a con-struct of an Anglophile jurisprudence. For the Americans who made the Revolution, "Their formative era was behind them, the years when the law of England had been molded to their needs, if not utterly to their desires. This they were committing to posterity, by good fortune unaware that scholars [meaning Pound] were to make of them and their knowledge figures as clownish as a Dogberry or a Justice Shallow."[41]

Pound's periodization was wrecked.[42] Yet, for our pur-poses, the completeness of the devastation is less important than the fact that Goebel's empirical critique was launched from motives not so different than Pound's own. For Goebel as for Pound the concern was how best to establish linkages to the Anglo-American legal tradition.[43] Goebel's conception of that tradition was more wide ranging than Pound's, who really restricted it to the authoritative state-ments of appellate judges and treatise writers. With Goebel we can begin to try to think of legal culture in ways that anthropologists would find interesting and legitimate—as the ways individuals in a society come to internalize and ap-ply a public normative structure—while for Pound a legal culture could only have been a high culture restricted to initiated elites. For both of them though, as well as for the legal historians who followed their example, the central ob-

---

[40] ESSAYS, *supra* note 35, at 377.

[41] *Id.* at 369.

[42] Pound's periodization may continue, however, to play a shadowy role in the place legal historians still give to the early republic as a golden age of American Law, a "creative outburst" in the history of law. See C. HAAR, THE GOLDEN AGE OF AMERICAN LAW (1965); HORWITZ, TRANSFORMATION OF AMERICAN LAW, 1; D. BOORSTIN, THE AMERICANS: THE NATIONAL EXPERIENCE, 35 (1958). But see foot-note 30 *supra*.

[43] This is perhaps best demonstrated by leafing through Julius Goebel's famous CASEBOOK IN LEGAL HISTORY, THE DEVELOPMENT OF LEGAL INSTITUTIONS (multiple editions).

ligation of a legal historian was less to comprehend the shape of an American legal history than to understand the place of American law in an Anglo-American tradition. The periodization of American legal history was shaped by questions about the divergence of colonial law and institutions from English models and about when (not whether) that divergence was overcome.[44] For all of them the proper subject matter of legal history (the rest is all journalism) "can be considered at an end when the records show judges and lawyers in an American court reasoning and using precedents like their contemporaries in an English court."[45]

By contrast, the disjuncture in American history that the new school posits is shaped not by the contrast between law and no law, but rather by the contrast between law at one time and law at another. Unlike Pound, the new school can easily survive Goebelian criticism of discontinuity because the aim of the new school is not to establish continuity with an English past. Unlike Pound, moreover, no new school legal historian ever claimed that prerevolutionary law was not law. Reid, Nelson, and Horwitz would all even concede that prerevolutionary law was in significant ways English law. The difference between the new and the old school lies in their conflicting conceptions of the enterprise of doing legal history. For Pound as for Goebel, legal history justified itself in the similarities it established; for our new school it is the differences that assume greater significance. And the central organizing difference is the difference between law in the early nineteenth century—modern law—and the law of colonial America.

The new school has in consequence lost interest in questions of the reception of the common law.[46] All members of the school might agree that there were important linkages between American law and the Anglo-American legal tra-

[44] Chaffee, *Colonial Courts and the Common Law*, in ESSAYS, *supra* note 35, at 55.
[45] *Id.* at 79.
[46] None of our three primary sources make any mention of the problem. However, the problem of the relationship between colonial law and its English antecedents has been explored in an innovative way by G. B. Warden in *Law Reform in England and New England, 1620–1660*, 35 WM. & MARY Q. 668 (1978).

dition, that one can usefully make comparisons between English and American law based on their common origins and common conceptual vocabulary. Yet the new school would still arrive at a picture of American legal history diametrically opposed to that suggested by Goebel in his polemic against Pound.

Indeed the assumption that at all times institutions are recognizably legal institutions, the assumption that elements of the formal vocabulary of law are continuous over time, lies at the heart of the picture of a discontinuous legal history presented in their work. It is only in the context of presumptive or facial continuity that hypotheses of disjuncture and "deep" change over time can be made subject to empirical confirmation. The point is obvious if one focuses on the time series of legal "subjects"—of court procedures, contract and property law, of the law of negotiable instruments—constructed by Nelson and Horwitz. Without the seeming persistence of language and structure, their arguments about change would be meaningless. However, the point is equally applicable to Reid's studies of the American Revolution as a legal conflict. Reid's writings constitute a critique—almost in a Goebelian mode—of historians' longstanding assumption that the Whig revolutionaries were never "really" making legal arguments, that Whigs drew from Enlightenment ideology, natural law, spurious history, anywhere but from a legal order which could only have justified the Tory case. Reid's achievement is in the first place critical, in demonstrating that historians have misread those arguments by refusing to understand the legal context of Whig rhetoric; yet, his achievement is also positive in the picture it provides of the substantive content of Whig ideology. Whig ideology was legal, but it was not a Tory legal ideology, and it was not the kind of legal theory that we or our nineteenth-century parents would have believed. In order to demonstrate the differences between Whig and Tory theories of law, Reid must first prove the legal nature of the conflict, that both sides were recognizably talking about English law. For Reid it was not the nonlaw of the revolutionaries against the law of imperial England. It was Whig law against Tory law. Just as for Nelson and Horwitz it was not the nonlaw of colonial America against the newly discovered common law of a formative era; it was the law of agrarian, non state-centered communities against the law of a capitalist state.

Reid, Nelson, and Horwitz share a common perception of the legal world of the eighteenth century as both a strange and unfamiliar place, yet also as the product of a demonstrably "legal" culture. Such a perception of colonial America is not unprecedented.[47] But until recently American legal history could not have been described as an enterprise devoted to studying the change and persistence over time of an American legal culture, rather than a study of the place of American law in the "Development of (Anglo-American) Legal Institutions." Credit for the formulation of that enterprise properly belongs to Willard Hurst.[48] But to that enterprise the members of the "new school" bring a renewed emphasis on a bifurcated legal past. And it is that picture of American legal history in the context of that enterprise that makes it possible to think of them as a new school.

III. Some Boundaries of Agreement

The fleeting perceptions presented in the first section of this essay should not be taken as a substantive description of the two halves of a bifurcated past. They are intended only as indications of the contrast between what law might have been in 1740 and what it probably was in 1840. But even to suggest the possibility of a common picture of the change between eighteenth- and nineteenth-century American law necessarily raises the most important questions that should be asked of any theory of periodization: When and

---

[47] G. Haskins, Law and Authority in Early Massachusetts (1960); Howe, *The Recording of Deeds in the Colony of Massachusetts Bay*, 28 B. U. L. Rev. 1 (1948).

[48] Gordon, *Introduction: J. Willard Hurst and the Common Law Tradition in American Legal Historiography*, 10 Law & Soc. Rev. 9 (1975).

how did change occur? The how is beyond the scope of this chapter, although, as I suggested earlier, all three of our "sources" imply a political transformation—a remolding of Whig into constitutional Tory, a transformation in the theory of public action—as the closest thing to a single cause of the disruption in the history of American law. The when, however, cannot be avoided. If contrast were all one was after, one might as well compare nineteenth-century American law with ancient Assyrian law. The burden of a theory of periodization is to demonstrate the particular significance of particular bounded periods. We know, we think, that change occurred. When did it occur?

Here the consensus we have constructed falls apart. For Horwitz the last decade of the eighteenth century seems to be an absolute starting point for his narratives of doctrinal development. Nelson suggests that it was the creation of state governments and state constitutions which ought to demarcate the inception of change. Reid, in contrast to both of them, seems to view the prerevolutionary period as a time when warring conceptions of the nature of law contended, that as a dispute over the legitimacy of central authority, the Revolution embodied a transformation in law which ended with our estrangement from Whig ideas.

Even narrowly empirical questions about the timing of change remain unanswered. It is clear, for instance, that the relative autonomy of local legal institutions is an important test of the kinds of changes described in this paper. Reid would say that it is in their local legal institutions that Whigs affirmed their continuing though fragile control over the colonial legal system. Nelson argues that local courts remained responsive to the particular wants of local publics throughout the revolutionary period, that they made decisions on the basis of moralistic standards that expressed the values of local constituencies. Yet, a systematic study of the business of at least one local sessions court in Massachusetts reveals that by the late 1750s that court was already well on its way to becoming a "modern" bureaucratic institution, that in its ordinary day-to-day business there was almost no

exercise of discretion, that even though its formal relationship to the provincial legislature and to the superior court
of judicature had not changed, its prior self-conception as
maintainer of the "peace" of the community was being
quickly replaced by a narrow commitment to providing a
limited number of public services.[49]

The truth is that the new school can tell us little about
when within the century, between 1740 and 1840, major
change began. The picture Nelson presents of a static consensual law in Massachusetts in the 1760s and 1770s,
though coherent, is easily the most controversial aspect of
his work. It directly contradicts the studies of numerous social historians that the second half of the eighteenth century
is peculiarly a time of intensive social change, conflict, and
disruption. Horwitz's model of pretransformation law in the
late eighteenth century is even less convincing, borrowed as
often from sociological theory as from relatively thin English and American sources. And Reid's research is really
limited to the political rhetoric of the revolutionary period.
It may be possible to invest their varying arguments with
greater degrees of plausibility. It may also be that our whole
period from the Great Awakening on constitutes a longer
transition toward a modern legal order, that 1740 is as
much an end point as a starting point for empirical investigation. One could argue, in contradistinction to Nelson and
Horwitz, that the basic structure of a modern legal culture
was in place—at least in states like Massachusetts and New
York—by the last decades of the eighteenth century. Horwitz's book might better then have been called, *After the
Transformation of American Law,* on the assumption that the
doctrinal developments he describes could not have occurred absent a prior transformed legal consciousness that
turned legal institutions into targets worth capturing by
prodevelopment capitalists and their lawyer minions.[50]

[49]*See* Hartog, *The Public Law of a County Court: Judicial Government in Eighteenth
Century Massachusetts,* 20 AM. J. LEG. HIST. 282 (1976).

[50]It might be, however, that the transition period could be extended until the
Civil War, that it is only the experience of a nation at war that conceptualizes the
positivistic authority and the unitary sovereignty implicit in our model of legal
change.

There are, moreover, basic problems with the comparisons that have been conducted between eighteenth and nineteenth century American law. The argument that a picture of a bifurcated legal past is revealed by the comparison of colonial and nineteenth-century legal cultures suffers from the fact that the methodology for conducting such a comparison remains underdeveloped, or at least underutilized.

Studies into the legal history of the prerevolutionary period customarily rely on a wide and eclectic range of sources: a variety of county court records—dockets, extended records, file papers, justice of the peace manuals, lawyers' papers, letters, newspapers, and autobiographies. Nineteenth-century legal historians may use similar sources, but almost always basic authority for propositions about the content of the law will depend on an analysis of published appellate opinions and contemporary legal treatises.[51] Those sources are simply not available for the legal historian who wishes to study American law prior to the end of the eighteenth century.

In some ways that difference in methodology might bolster our picture of the discontinuity of American legal history. After all, lacking appellate opinions there was no way for a centralized legal structure to control the decisions of local legal institutions. The absence of authoritative published statements of the law might stand as confirmation of our picture of a decentralized and partially autonomous local legal culture. But how can we be sure? The political rhetoric that John Reid has studied gives us a partial answer, but it is too distant from ordinary legal discourse. The time series of doctrinal change constructed by Horwitz are flawed by the incommensurability of the sources used to construct his picture of an untransformed eighteenth-century American law. The evidence used to construct a "before" is often unrelated to the proposition which it is said to support. Snippets of Blackstone, English cases, and so-called archaic nineteenth-century cases are made to stand

[51] On the development of legal literature in nineteenth-century America, see L. FRIEDMAN, A HISTORY OF AMERICAN LAW 282–92 (1973).

as proof of the substantive content of eighteenth-century American law. Without a body of eighteenth-century appellate cases and treatises to compare with their nineteenth-century equivalents, Horwitz seems at times forced to guess that the "before" is *a priori* the opposite of whatever law will become in the nineteenth century.[52]

William Nelson seems to avoid some of the hazards of trying to compare the incommensurable by relying in his analysis on a reading of all the cases in all of the county courts of Massachusetts between 1760 and 1830. Indeed, as Gordon notes in his review, whatever its failings as a work of interpretation, Nelson's book is the summation of an astonishing research project. But Nelson too seems to shift ground in his narrative as soon as appellate cases become available. Judges expected "to be automatons who mechanically applied immutable rules of law to the facts of each case,"[53] suddenly became utilitarian and calculating pseudo-legislators. Again, this may be based to some degree on Nelson's comparison of two bodies of local court records. But one wonders. In a paragraph in his chapter on the reform of common law pleading, Nelson argues that the various post-revolutionary departures from old-fashioned proper legal form were not attributable to simple carelessness on the parts of the various legal actors; rather they were "conscious attempts by skilled attorneys to compel the courts to focus on the substantive rather than the procedural aspects of their cases,"[54] a preference for substance over form which was shared by the Supreme Judicial Court. The cases which are used to justify this claim come in 13 instances from the published reports of the Supreme Judicial Court and in only eight instances from the manuscript records of the various local courts.[55] By contrast, his earlier discussion

[52] As others have noted, at times Horwitz's "before" seems to be little more than the opposite of whatever law will become in the nineteenth century: good when the nineteenth century is bad, equitable and subjective when the nineteenth century is rigid and objective, simple when the nineteenth century law is complex, and complex when nineteenth century law is simple.

[53] NELSON, AMERICANIZATION OF THE COMMON LAW 19.

[54] *Id.* at 79–80.

[55] *Id.* at 214–215.

of the automatic and rigid use of pleading rules relied almost entirely on the records of the colonial county courts.[56] It is hard to avoid concluding that Nelson's central contrast between a prerevolutionary legal system without central direction and motivated by the local concerns of local communities and a postrevolutionary calculating, utilitarian, self-conscious legal culture may be a product as much of problems inherent in Nelson's research strategy as an accurate description of the legal history of Massachusetts.

Indeed, the temporal discontinuity explored in this essay might be seen as founded on a legal version of the quantitative fallacy, the fallacy that something exists only when it can be counted.[57] Just as for years economic historians assumed that American economic growth began around 1840 because that was the first year when the census produced national economic statistics, so legal historians now believe that directed, policy-oriented legal decision-making began around the turn of the nineteenth century, when published reports of American appellate opinions first made a systematic appearance. The latter assumption might be just as wrong as the former assumption is now known to be.[58]

And yet I wonder. The history of statistics is only tangentially related to the history of economic growth. The appearance of GNP statistics cannot be correlated with the inception of economic growth. In contrast, the appearance of published reports, the dissemination of printed case records, might, one can hypothesize, be far more closely connected to the development of a state-centered, self-conscious legal culture. Printed case records gave American lawyers confirmation of their belief in the autonomous coherence of an American law. It became possible for appellate courts to disseminate standards of decision-making and

---

[56] *Id.* at 207–211.

[57] D. FISCHER, HISTORIANS' FALLACIES 90 (1970).

[58] See David, *The Growth of Real Product in the United States before 1840: New Evidence, Controlled Conjectures,* 27 J. ECON. HIST. 151 (1967); Gallman, *The Statistical Approach: Fundamental Concepts as Applied to History* in APPROACHES TO AMERICAN ECONOMIC HISTORY 63 (B. T. Taylor and Ellsworth eds. 1971); L. DAVIS, ET. AL., AMERICAN ECONOMIC GROWTH: AN ECONOMIST'S HISTORY OF THE UNITED STATES 17–32 (1972).

to enforce obedience through public reversals of dissident local courts. It was the foundation for a rationalized process of appeal. One might go farther and suggest that the shift in our legal history from a dominant oral culture to a print culture characterized by printed appellate records is definitive of our picture of a discontinuous history of American law. The role of print in the formation of a distinctively modern consciousness is a subject of great interest to many scholars, some of whom have argued that print is the most important determinant of centralized political structures and of a modern conception of public action.[59] A common-sense understanding of some of the distinctive characteristics of lawyer's craft in the nineteenth century might suggest that that craft (and particularly the rise of office practice) was closely connected to the development of an image of language as a commodity and of lawyers as individuals who "traded" in that commodity.[60] Until the statements of courts can be regarded as objectively given, can be regarded as truly authoritative, it is hard to imagine how lawyers might "plan" for their clients' welfare. It may be, therefore, that the identification of the timing of change in law with the appearance of published case records and treatises is less implausible than it at first appears to be.

Still, the model of discontinuity presented in this essay remains a largely empty construct; it lacks a useable description of the process of disruption, dissolution, and reconstitution that one imagines underlies a model of cultural transformation. Yet this failure may be evocative of the potential power of the model. The discontinuity that the "new school" posits between law in 1740 and law in 1840 is reduceable to the discontinuity between the absolutely unfamiliar and the relatively familiar. What all three of our sources share is a sense of the strangeness of the eighteenth-century legal world, its pervasive differentness from

---

[59] M. MCLUHAN, THE GUTENBERG GALAXY 235 and *passim* (1962); L. FEBVRE & H. J. MARTIN, the COMING OF THE BOOK (1976); E. EISENSTEIN, THE PRINTING PRESS AS AN AGENT OF CHANGE (1979).

[60] MCLUHAN, THE GUTENBERG GALAXY, 161; D. CALHOUN, PROFESSIONAL LIVES IN AMERICA; STRUCTURE AND ASPIRATION 1750–1850, 59–87 (1965).

the legal world we know and have internalized. We cannot with any expectation of success pretend to be a judge in a court in provincial America; but a modern legal scholar like Karl Llewelyn could rather successfully enter into the decision-making process of a judge like Esek Cowen of the New York Supreme Court in the 1830s and 1840s.[61] The culture of eighteenth-century American law may not be unknowable, but it cannot be apprehended through the ordinary tools of legal training. And that remains a measure of our separation from the legal world of eighteenth-century America.

[61] KARL LLEWELYN, THE COMMON LAW TRADITION: DECIDING APPEALS 64–68, 423–26 (1960).

Contributors

ROBERT W. GORDON is Associate Professor of Law at the University of Wisconsin Law School. He is a graduate of Harvard Law School. He has published articles on contract law and American legal history and is now working on a book on the ideology of American metropolitan lawyers in the late nineteenth century.

HENDRIK HARTOG is Assistant Professor of Law at Indiana University School of Law (Bloomington). A graduate of New York University School of Law, he has done graduate work in the History of American Civilization Program at Brandeis University where he held a Crown Fellowship. He has published articles in American legal history and is at work on a study of the development of a modern theory of public law using the municipal history of New York City as a case study.

BRUCE H. MANN is Associate Professor of Law at University of Connecticut School of Law. A graduate of Yale Law School, he also received a doctorate in history from Yale University, where he was a Whiting Fellow in the Humanities. He has written on rationality and legal change in eighteenth-century Connecticut.

STEPHEN B. PRESSER is Professor of Law at Northwestern University School of Law, and a member of the bars of the District of Columbia and Commonwealth of Massachusetts. He is a graduate of the Harvard Law School and has published several articles and book reviews on state and federal legal history. He is joint author of the first law-school casebook devoted principally to the treatment of American legal history and is currently at work on a book about the legal history of the federal courts of the third circuit.

JOHN PHILLIP REID is Professor of Law at New York University School of Law and a member of the New Hampshire bar. A graduate of Harvard Law School, he also has two advanced law degrees from New York University and an M.A. from the University of New Hampshire. Mr. Reid has published two biographies of nineteenth-century American judges, two studies of primitive Cherokee law, and two books on the legal history of the American Revolution. He is now working on the constitutional history of the Revolution.

PETER R. TEACHOUT is Professor of Law at Vermont Law School and a member of the Vermont, Massachusetts, and Washington, D.C. bars. A graduate of Harvard Law School, he also has a masters degree in English and American studies from the University of Sussex, England. The 1974–75 academic year, he was a Harvard Fellow in Law and Humanities. Mr. Teachout has published articles in American legal history and constitutional law and has recently co-authored a book on consumer credit law.

Index